INTERNATIONAL EFFORTS
TO COMBAT
MONEY LAUNDERING

D1522945

This volume may be cited as:

Gilmore (ed.),
International Efforts to Combat Money Laundering (1992)

RESEARCH CENTRE FOR INTERNATIONAL LAW
UNIVERSITY OF CAMBRIDGE

CAMBRIDGE INTERNATIONAL DOCUMENTS SERIES, VOLUME 4

Consulting editor: E. Lauterpacht CBE, QC

INTERNATIONAL EFFORTS TO COMBAT MONEY LAUNDERING

edited by
Dr. W. C. Gilmore
Head, Commercial Crime Unit, Assistant Director, Legal Division,
Commonwealth Secretariat

———————

In association with
THE COMMONWEALTH SECRETARIAT, LONDON

CAMBRIDGE
GROTIUS PUBLICATIONS LIMITED
1992

SALES &	GROTIUS PUBLICATIONS LTD.
ADMINISTRATION	PO BOX 115, CAMBRIDGE CB3 9BP,
	ENGLAND
FAX	0223 311032 (from abroad: 44 + 223 + 311032)

British Library Cataloguing in Publication Data

International Efforts to Combat Money
   Laundering. – (Cambridge International
Documents Series)
    I. Gilmore, William C. II. Series
   341.77

ISBN 1-85701-000-0

Printed by The Burlington Press (Cambridge) Limited, Foxton, Cambridge

FOREWORD

International measures to inhibit money laundering and associated activities are both new and important. Here, as already most notably in connection with the environment and the control and reduction of armaments, the boundaries of international law are being extended and novel techniques are being developed that advance far beyond previous levels of international cooperation.

Such progress has come about none too early. If it is to be fully effective, it is essential that it should be widely known and understood in the international community. The Research Centre for International Law has, therefore, warmly welcomed the idea that it should include in its Document Series – and thus give wider circulation to – the admirable collection of material originally prepared by Dr Gilmore for use in connection with the activities of the Commonwealth Secretariat. We are most grateful to the Secretary-General of the Commonwealth, H.E. Chief Emeka Anyaoku, for his consent to the publication of this expanded version of the collection; as we are also to Dr Gilmore for the additional work that he has undertaken.

E. Lauterpacht
Director

Research Centre for International Law
Cambridge
April 1992

FOREWORD

CONTENTS

CHAPTER V: Other Initiatives and Developments

INTRODUCTION

In recent years those involved in the criminal justice area have become increasingly aware of the nature and scope of the challenges posed by the growth of transnational criminal activity. As Lord Griffiths has stated in a recent judgment of the Judicial Committee of the Privy Council: "Unfortunately in this century crime has ceased to be largely local in origin and effect. Crime is now established on an international scale and the common law must face this new reality".[1] It is evident, however, that in seeking to confront this challenge effectively reliance on traditional unilateral domestic measures is no longer sufficient. As Peter Wilkitzki of the Federal Ministry of Justice in Bonn has remarked: "Modern criminal policy is no longer conceivable if it does not also include an international element. At a time when the mobility of the individual is increasing and the separation function of national borders is constantly decreasing, no domestic criminal legislator can afford to treat crime merely as a national phenomenon".[2]

Increasingly the members of the international community have demonstrated their acceptance of the need significantly to intensify criminal co-operation across national boundaries. At one level this has manifested itself in a willingness both to strengthen and to extend the mechanisms of international co-operation. Thus, to the longstanding but limited process of extradition a growing number of states have come to add mutual assistance in the investigation and prosecution of criminal offences and co-operation in the confiscation of the proceeds derived from criminal activity.[3] Similarly, one can point to the proliferation of crime-specific agreements in relation to forms of criminal activity of particular international concern, ranging from terrorism to insider trading.

These two strands of international activity, which are intended to be mutually reinforcing in character, often overlap in practice. This has been very much the case with the treatment of the problem of money laundering – the subject matter of this volume.

I. THE BACKGROUND

Sustained international interest in money laundering, and the closely related issue of the confiscation of the proceeds of crime, arose in the 1980s primarily within a drug trafficking context. Not only was there growing concern at the escalating nature of the drug abuse problem, there was also an increasing awareness of the vast profits generated by this form of criminal activity. By way of illustration, the Financial Action Task Force (FATF), created on the recommendation of the seven major industrialised nations (United States, Japan, Germany, France, United Kingdom, Italy and Canada) and the President of the Commission of the European Communities at the July 1989 Paris Economic Summit,[4] estimated that "sales of cocaine, heroin and cannabis amount to approximately $122 billion per year in the United States and Europe; of which 50 to 70% or as much as *$85 billion per year could be available for laundering and investment*. One Task Force member estimated global profits at the main dealer level, which might be most subject to international laundering, to be about $30 billion per year".[5]

It is easy to understand why domestic and transnational law enforcement strategies have increasingly emphasised the need to focus on the financial aspects of this trade with the object of more effectively disrupting major trafficking networks. As Nadelmann has pointed out in a US context, a number of rationales support the view that "going after the money" is the best way to tackle organised criminal activity of this kind:

> The most basic of these is that insofar as criminals ... act as they do for the money, the best deterrent and punishment is to confiscate their incentive. A second rationale is that, while the higher level and more powerful criminals rarely come into contact with the illicit goods, such as drugs, from which they derive their profits, they do come into contact with the proceeds from the sale of those goods. That contact often provides a "paper trail" or other evidence, which constitutes

---

[1] *Liangsiriprasert* v *U.S. Government* [1990] 2 All ER 866, at 878.
[2] P. Wilkitzki, "Development of an Effective International Crime and Justice Programme – a European View" (Paper delivered at the International Workshop on Principles and Procedures for a New Transnational Criminal Law, May 21-25, 1991, Freiburg, Federal Republic of Germany: typescript), p. 7.
[3] *See, e.g.,* R. Geiger, "Legal Assistance Between States in Criminal Matters" 9 *Encyclopedia of Public International Law* (1986), p. 248; D. McClean, "Mutual Assistance in Criminal Matters: The Commonwealth Initiative" (1988) 37 *ICLQ* p. 177; and D. McClean, "Seizing the Proceeds of Crime: The State of the Art" (1989) 38 *ICLQ* p. 334.
[4] *See*, Chapter I, document A.
[5] Chapter I, document B, at p. 6.

the only connection with a violation of the law. A third rationale is that confiscating the proceeds of criminal activities is a good way to make law enforcement pay for itself.[6]

A further impetus for action has come from the increasing recognition of the negative impact that such vast flows of "dirty money" can have on the financial sector. As the Basle Committee on Banking Regulations and Supervisory Practices[7] stated in December 1988: "Public confidence in banks, and hence their stability, can be undermined by adverse publicity as a result of inadvertent association by banks with criminals. In addition, banks may lay themselves open to direct losses from fraud, either through negligence in screening undesirable customers or where the integrity of their own officers has been undermined through association with criminals".[8]

Out of the above a twin track solution to the problem has gradually emerged. On the one hand it calls for the strengthening of the criminal law since it is widely acknowledged that the principal burden must be carried by invoking penal means. On the other hand, it is now recognised that the financial system can and must play an effective preventative role. In relation to each, however, it is accepted that national initiatives on their own would be insufficient. As has recently been stated:

> The laundering of proceeds of crime is truly an international phenomenon. No longer are operations limited to the country in which the illicit money is generated. On the contrary, the transborder movement of money is now a prominent feature of laundering operations.[9]

II. THE STRATEGY

a) Strengthening International Criminal Co-operation

Drug trafficking, like many other forms of criminal activity, is highly cash intensive. Indeed, "in the case of heroin and cocaine, the physical volume of notes received from street dealing is much larger than the volume of the drugs themselves". [10] Reliance on cash as the central medium of exchange in turn gives rise to at least three common factors:

– drug dealers need to *conceal* the true ownership and origin of the money;

– they need to *control* the money; and

– they need to *change* the form of the money.[11]

This is what gives the money laundering process its crucial role. It can be summarised as "the *conversion* of illicit cash to another asset, the *concealment* of the true source or ownership of the illegally acquired proceeds, and the *creation* of the perception of legitimacy of source and ownership".[12]

In their efforts to achieve these goals money launderers make use of a wide variety of techniques. Those most frequently mentioned in ICPO-Interpol circles[13] include: currency smuggling; the conversion of cash into negotiable instruments; the creative use of the facilities offered by tax and financial havens; the establishment and use of front or shell companies; the use of currency exchanges and brokerage houses; the creation of false or inflated invoices; the use of casinos and other gambling enterprises; the use of credit cards obtained from tax haven banks; the use of facilities provided by underground or parallel banking systems; and resort to cash purchases. As has been pointed out elsewhere: "The techniques of money laundering are innumerable, diverse, complex, subtle and secret".[14] What can be said with a degree of

---

[6] E. Nadelmann, "Unlaundering Dirty Money Abroad: US Foreign Policy and Financial Secrecy Jurisdictions" (1986) 18 *Inter-American Law Review*, p. 33, at p. 34.

[7] Membership of the Committee is drawn from the central banks and supervisory authorities of Belgium, Canada, France, Germany, Italy, Japan, The Netherlands, Sweden, Switzerland, the UK, the USA and Luxembourg. For an insight into the wider work of this body *see, e.g.*, Hayward, "Prospects for International Cooperation by Bank Supervisors" (1990) 24 *The International Lawyer* p. 787.

[8] Chapter V, document B, at p. 274.

[9] M.E. Beare *et al, Tracing of Illicit Funds: Money Laundering in Canada* (1990: Ministry of the Solicitor General of Canada, Ottawa), p. 304.

[10] Chapter I, document B, at p. 7. *See also*, P.O'Brien, "Tracking Narco-Dollars: The Evolution of a Potent Weapon in the Drug War" (1990) 21 *Inter-American Law Review*, p. 637, at p. 643.

[11] *Money Laundering: Guidance Notes for Banks and Building Societies*, (1990), p. 2.

[12] *Supra*, note 9, p. x., note 1.

[13] For an insight into the nature and extent of ICPO-Interpol activities in this area *see*, Chapter V, document C. For a recent analysis of this organisation *see generally*, M. Anderson, *Policing the World: Interpol and the Politics of International Police Co-operation* (1989).

[14] *International Narcotics Control Strategy Report: March 1, 1988* (US Department of State, Washington, D.C.), p. 46.

certainty, however, is that the transnational movement of funds often plays a role in these transactions. For example, a recent official analysis of Canadian money laundering police files revealed that over 80 per cent had an international dimension.[15] As the Commission of the European Communities noted: "Internationalisation of economies and financial services are opportunities which are seized by money launderers to carry out their criminal activities, since the origin of funds can be better disguised in an international context".[16]

The practical problems confronted by law enforcement officials charged with the investigation of such flows are thus enormous and the possibilities of success depend in a critical fashion on the range, scope and quality of the mechanisms of international co-operation which are available to them. Major problems have been and continue to be encountered in this regard. In the words of the Financial Action Task Force: "Many of the current difficulties in international cooperation in drug money laundering cases are directly or indirectly linked with a strict application of bank secrecy rules, with the fact that, in many countries, money laundering is not today an offense, and with insufficiencies in multilateral cooperation and mutual legal assistance".[17]

i) The 1988 UN Convention

The first major breakthrough in the effort to address these and related concerns came with the conclusion in Vienna in December 1988 of the UN Convention Against Illicit Traffic in Narcotic Drugs and Psychotropic Substances.[18] This instrument has, in turn, had a major influence on subsequent initiatives.

Central to any attempt to provide, in treaty form, an effective regime to counter the illicit traffic in drugs was the need to define with care the specific elements which that notion should encompass. The outcome of the detailed deliberations of the Vienna Conference on this point are reflected in Article 3(1) of the final text. This provision, frequently described as the cornerstone of the Convention, "requires Parties to legislate as necessary to establish a modern code of criminal offences relating to illicit trafficking in all its different aspects".[19]

To that end Article 3(1)(a) requires that each state party shall "establish as criminal offences under its domestic law, when committed intentionally"[20] a fairly comprehensive list of activities which have a major international impact. This includes such matters as the production, manufacture, distribution or sale of illicit drugs and the organisation, management or financing of illicit trafficking activities.

Article 3(1)(b) advances the process further by requiring the criminalisation of drug related money laundering by each state party. They are required to establish as criminal offences:

(i) The conversion or transfer of property, knowing that such property is derived from any offence or offences established in accordance with subparagraph (a) of this paragraph, or from an act of participation in such offence or offences, for the purpose of concealing or disguising the illicit origin of the property or of assisting any person who is involved in the commission of such offence or offences to evade the legal consequences of his actions;

(ii) The concealment or disguise of the true nature, source, location, disposition, movement, rights with respect to, or ownership of property, knowing that such property is derived from an offence or offences established in accordance with subparagraph (a) of this paragraph or from an act of participation in such an offence or offences.

Also of relevance in this context is Article 3(1)(c)(i) which requires Parties to take measures to render criminal: "The acquisition, possession or use of property, knowing, at the time of receipt, that such property was derived from an offence or offences established in accordance with subparagraph (a) of this paragraph or from an act of participation in such offence or offences." It is important to note that, unlike the conduct covered in subparagraphs (a) and (b), this obligation is qualified by the limiting wording "subject to its constitutional principles and the basic concepts of its legal system." As Sproule and St-Denis have explained: "Concern by many delegations ... that the establishment of certain offences would conflict with basic

---

[15] *See, supra.*, note 9, p. 304.
[16] Chapter IV(ii), document E, Explanatory Memorandum, I(1), p. 243.
[17] Chapter I, document B, at p. 14.
[18] For the full text of this Convention *see*, Chapter II, document B, p. 75. On the nature and extent of this initiative *see generally*, W. Gilmore, *Combating International Drugs Trafficking: the 1988 United Nations Convention Against Illicit Traffic in Narcotic Drugs and Psychotropic Substances* (1991).
[19] *Criminal Justice (International Co-operation) Bill: Explanatory Memorandum on the Proposals to Implement the Vienna Convention Against Illicit Traffic in Narcotic Drugs and Psychotropic Substances* (1989), at p. 28.
[20] *See also*, Art 3(3) which reads "Knowledge, intent or purpose required as an element of an offence set forth in paragraph 1 of this article may be inferred from objective factual circumstances."

concepts of their legal system led to some offences being placed in a separate subparagraph, thereby making parties' obligations to adopt them" subject to a constitutional safeguard clause.[21]

The significance of the approach adopted in Article 3 of the UN C drug related money laundering for future international co-operation should not be underestimated. By requiring its criminalisation and treating it as a serious offence the drafters have ensured that co-operation in respect of confiscation, mutual legal assistance and extradition will be forthcoming. For example, the US delegation has hailed the achievement of the Convention in relation to extradition, a subject addressed in detail in Article 6 of the Convention, in these words:

> Because all Parties are obligated to establish Article 3, paragraph 1 offences as criminal offences in their domestic law, any requirements of dual criminality, that is that the offence is criminal in both jurisdictions, in a Party's extradition law should be met. Although there has been almost universal recognition that illicit drug trafficking offences are extraditable offences, narcotics related money laundering is a new criminal offence for many states and has not been traditionally recognised as an extraditable offence. The universal recognition of narcotics related money laundering as an extraditable offence is one of the most important aspects of this article.[22]

The mandatory wording of Article 3(1) also means, at a practical level, that many states wishing to become bound by this significant international instrument will be faced with the need to enact complex implementing legislation in order to ensure that they can act in full compliance with its terms.[23]

A second and critical part of any enforcement strategy designed to impact on the financial aspects of drug trafficking is the provision for the confiscation of the profits derived from this form of criminal activity. In recent years a significant number of states have enacted legislation towards this end.[24] A number of considerations of both principle and expediency favour such an approach. As the Scottish Law Commission has stated: "Stripping the criminal of the profits made from criminal activities is increasingly being seen as an effective way to combat crime as well as a means of doing justice by restoring the criminal to the position he was in prior to carrying out those crimes.[25]

The need for substantial international co-operative activity in this sphere was clear to those charged with drafting the 1988 Vienna Convention. It was therefore decided that Article 5 would address both the measures to be taken at the national level and the necessary mechanisms to give effect to international co-operation in this area.

The approach adopted by the Convention in this regard was summarised by the US Department of Justice as follows:

> ... Article V requires each member nation to enact domestic forfeiture legislation enabling the nation in question to identify, trace, seize, freeze and forfeit all manner of property derived from or used in drug trafficking and drug money laundering. As importantly, Article V requires each member nation, upon the request of another member nation, to identify, trace, seize, freeze, or forfeit property or proceeds located in the requested nation, which were derived from, or used in drug trafficking and drug money laundering in violation of the laws of the requesting country.[26]

Of relevance in this context is the importance for those involved in moving drugs money through the international financial system of provisions for customer confidentiality or bank secrecy in the laws of some countries. Similarly, it has come to be recognised that "existing bank secrecy laws are being used in many instances to obstruct co-operation and the provision of information needed for the investigation of allegations of drug-related offences".[27]

The solution which commended itself to the drafters of the UN Convention, now reflected in Article 5(3), was to require that each state party empower its courts or other relevant

---

[21] D.W. Sproule and P. St-Denis, "The UN Drug Trafficking Convention: An Ambitious Step" (1989) *Canadian Yearbook of International Law*, p. 263, at p. 270. Here the concern was to afford protection to a *bona fide* purchaser. *See*, Chapter II, document C, at p. 104.
[22] Chapter II, document C, at p. 120.
[23] This may be so even for jurisdictions, such as England and Wales, where legislation of recent date was already in force. Thus s.24 of the Drug Trafficking Offences Act 1986, c.32 had to be supplemented by s.14 of the Criminal Justice (International Co-operation) Act, 1990, c.5 in order to meet Convention requirements in this regard. For a recent analysis of some of the complex issues which arise in this area *see generally*, M. Levi, *Customer Confidentiality, Money-Laundering, and Police-Bank Relationships: English Law and Practice in a Global Environment* (1991).
[24] *See, e.g.*, D. McClean, "Seizing the Proceeds of Crime: The State of the Art", *supra.*, note 3. For the position in England and Wales *see*, D. Feldman, *Criminal Confiscation Orders: The New Law* (1988). *See also*, M. Zander, *Confiscation and Forfeiture Law: English and American Comparisons* (1989). *See also*, The Home Office Working Group on Confiscation, *Report on the Drug Trafficking Offences Act 1986* (1991).
[25] Scottish Law Commission, *Forfeiture and Confiscation*, Discussion Paper No 82, June 1989, p. 1.
[26] M.B. Troland and J.C. Marrero, *An Introduction to International Forfeiture* (1991: US Dept of Justice, Washington, D.C.), p. 18.
[27] Chapter II, document A, at p. 69.

authorities to order that bank, financial or commercial records be made available. Most importantly it is specifically provided that: "A Party shall not decline to act under the provisions of this paragraph on the ground of bank secrecy." The inclusion of this affirmative obligation has been widely characterised as a major breakthrough. In the words of Sproule and St-Denis:

> The exclusion of bank secrecy as a justification for declining to act may prove to be one of the most important measures in combating drug money laundering operations.[28]

A number of other provisions relating to confiscation should also be mentioned. For example, Parties are encouraged to enter into detailed bilateral and multilateral confiscation agreements in order to "enhance the effectiveness of international co-operation pursuant to this article".[29] However, in the absence of any such international instrument Article 5(4) (f) stipulates, somewhat unusually, that where a Party requires a treaty nexus with the requesting state in order to provide such assistance "that Party shall consider this Convention as the necessary and sufficient treaty basis."

Furthermore, Article 5(6) addresses the need to "ensure that proceeds derived from and instrumentalities used in illegal trafficking could not escape forfeiture simply because their form had been changed or they had been comingled with other property".[30] Here again the Convention uses mandatory language — a decision of great practical importance, given "the skill and speed with which large-scale traffickers are able to launder their profits".[31] At the same time, it was felt necessary to provide that Article 5 "shall not be construed as prejudicing the rights of bona fide third parties".[32]

Finally, it should be noted that, pursuant to paragraph 7, each party may give consideration to reversing the burden of proof in regard to the lawful origin of the alleged proceeds of trafficking. It is, however, clear from both the wording of this provision and from its drafting history that there is absolutely no requirement to so act. In the words of the Chairman of Conference Committee I: "The provision constituted merely an invitation to States Parties to examine the possibility of doing so".[33]

The final aspect of the 1988 UN Convention which requires special mention is contained in Article 7 and relates to the provision of mutual legal assistance in relation to serious drug trafficking offences. To that end, Article 7(1) provides that: "The Parties shall afford one another, pursuant to this article, the widest measure of mutual legal assistance in investigations, prosecutions and judicial proceedings in relation to criminal offences established in accordance with Article 3, paragraph 1." The assistance which may be requested in this "mini" Mutual Legal Assistance Treaty (MLAT) includes: the taking of evidence or statements; effecting service of judicial documents; executing searches and seizures; examining objects and sites; providing information and evidentiary items; providing relevant documents and records including bank, financial, corporate or business records; and, identifying or tracing proceeds and instrumentalities for evidentiary purposes.[34] That the above is a non-exhaustive list is made clear by Article 7(3) which states that: "The Parties may afford to one another any other forms of mutual legal assistance allowed by the domestic law of the requested Party."

In the course of the Conference at Vienna a number of delegations pressed for the specific inclusion of a statement that requests for assistance could not be refused on the grounds of bank secrecy. Such concerns find reflection in the clear wording of Article 7(5) of the final text. The extent of the obligation so imposed was described by the then US Attorney-General as follows:

> First, it is an obligation to enact implementing legislation, if necessary, to modify domestic bank secrecy laws to permit execution of requests for bank records under the Convention. Second, with respect to an individual request for bank records under the Convention, it obliges a requested Party to grant the request, if the only basis for refusing would be bank secrecy laws.[35]

---

[28] D.W. Sproule and P. St-Denis, *supra*, note 21, at pp. 281-282.
[29] 1988 UN Convention, Article 5(4)(g). Reproduced in Chapter II, document B, p. 81. *See also*, W. Gilmore, "International Action Against Drug Trafficking: Trends in United Kingdom Law and Practice" (1990) 24 *The International Lawyer* p. 365, at pp. 388-390. To date the UK has concluded 24 Agreements the latest being with Uruguay. *See*, Foreign and Commonwelath Office, Press Release No. 19, 24 January, 1992. For the text of the UK Model Agreement in this respect *see*, Chapter V, document G, at p. 296.
[30] Chapter II, document C, at p. 118.
[31] D.W. Sproule and P. St-Denis, *supra*, note 21, at p. 284.
[32] 1988 UN Convention, Article 5(8). Reproduced in Chapter II, document B, at p. 82.
[33] UN Doc, E/CONF.82/C.1. SR.11, at p. 2.
[34] 1988 UN Convention, Article 7(2). Reproduced in Chapter II, document B, at p. 83.
[35] *See, United Nations Convention Against Illicit Traffic in Narcotic Drugs and Psychotropic Substances* 101st Congress, 1st Session, Senate, Exec. Rept. 101-15, at p. 185.

In spite of the great detail contained in these and other substantive and procedural provisions in this Article, an examination of which lies beyond the scope of this introductory overview, it was clearly recognised that the complexity of this subject is such that states might well wish to conclude further agreements of a bilateral or multilateral nature in order more adequately to address issues of importance. Account also had to be taken of the fact that a substantial number of such agreements already exist. The solution adopted has been summarised by the UK Home Office in the following way: "By paragraph 20, the Parties are to consider the possibilities of bilateral or multilateral agreements to give effect to or enhance the provisions of the article, and if such an agreement is in force the procedures specified therein shall prevail over the normative procedures specified in Article 7".[36]

There can be no doubt that, from an enforcement perspective, the conclusion of the 1988 UN Convention was a major achievement. As Stewart has noted: "The Convention is one of the most detailed and far-reaching instruments ever adopted in the field of international criminal law and, if widely adopted and effectively implemented, will be a major force in harmonizing national laws and enforcement actions around the world".[37] Reflecting this fact, the very first of the forty recommendations contained in the February 1990 FATF Report was that "each country should, without further delay, take steps to fully implement the Vienna Convention, and proceed to ratify it".[38] Unlike a number of global Conventions concluded in the past under United Nations auspices this instrument attracted swiftly the necessary 20 ratifications and it entered into force towards the end of 1990.

ii) The 1990 Council of Europe Convention

Significant though the achievements of the 1988 UN Convention were, it was not the intention or the expectation that efforts to combat the financial aspects of drug trafficking, let alone those related to other forms of criminal activity, would rest exclusively on that instrument. Indeed, since 1988 relevant initiatives have been launched or continued in a wide variety of fora.

One development of particular significance took place in September 1990 when the Committee of Ministers of the Council of Europe adopted a new Convention on laundering, search, seizure and confiscation of the proceeds from crime. The Convention was opened for signature in Strasbourg in November of the same year.

This new Convention represents the final product of an initiative taken by European Ministers of Justice in 1986 in order to combat the problems in the financial area posed by drug trafficking. The matter was, thereafter, transmitted to the European Committee on Crime Problems for appropriate action. It, in turn, established a Select Committee of Experts with fairly wide terms of reference. In particular, it was not obliged to restrict its focus to the proceeds derived from drug trafficking alone. It should also be noted that the Committee had the benefit of the direct participation of three non-members, namely, the United States, Canada and Australia. Furthermore, the European Commission was afforded observer status during these negotiations.[39]

In undertaking its study the Committee of Experts paid attention not only to the various existing Council of Europe Conventions dealing with penal matters but also to the 1988 UN Convention. As its members have pointed out:

> The relevant provisions of the United Nations Convention were constantly taken into consideration: on the one hand, the experts tried as far as possible to use the terminology and the systematic approach of that convention unless changes were felt necessary for improving different solutions; on the other hand, the experts also explored the possibilities of introducing in the Council of Europe instrument stricter obligations than those of the United Nations Convention on the understanding that the new Convention — in spite of the fact that it is open to other States than the member States of the Council of Europe — will operate in the context of a smaller community of like-minded states.[40]

Perhaps the clearest indication of the willingness of the Council of Europe to go beyond that which was agreed in the UN context is to be found in its much broader scope. As has been pointed out elsewhere: "One of the purposes of the Convention is to facilitate international co-operation as regards investigative assistance, search, seizure and confiscation of the proceeds from all types of criminality, especially serious crimes, and in particular drug offences, arms dealing, terrorist

---

[36] *Supra*, note 19, p. 29.
[37] D.P. Stewart, "Internationalizing The War on Drugs: The UN Convention Against Illicit Traffic in Narcotic Drugs and Psychotropic Substances" (1990) 18 *Denver Journal of International Law and Policy* p. 387, at p. 388.
[38] Chapter I, document B, at p. 14.
[39] *See*, House of Lords, Select Committee on the European Communities, *Money Laundering*, H L Paper 6, 1990-91, p. 7.
[40] Chapter IV (i), document C, at p. 197.

offences, trafficking in children and young women ... and other offences which generate large profits".[41]

The nature of and limits to this ambition can, in turn, be revealed by an overview of Article 2 of the 1990 Convention which addresses confiscation measures to be taken at the national level. In essence Article 2(1) obliges states to enact legislation to permit the confiscation of the proceeds of crime. It also contains an implicit invitation for such legislation to be as broad in scope as possible. It was not felt, however, that the time had been reached when it would be possible to impose an obligation to require confiscation in relation to all forms of criminal conduct. For this reason it was thought necessary to permit the formulation of reservations as to scope and this is the function of paragraph 2. The Committee of Experts agreed, however, "that such states should review their legislation periodically and expand the applicability of confiscation measures, in order to be able to restrict the reservations subsequently as much as possible. They also agreed that such measures should at least be made applicable to serious criminality and to offences which generate huge profits".[42] The decision positively to encourage states to extend procedures for the confiscation of proceeds beyond drug trafficking, though unique at the level of formal international agreements, does find support in the existing legislative arrangements of certain participating states.[43]

As with the UN Convention, this Council of Europe instrument also imposes (in Chapter III, Section 4) a number of specific obligations concerning international co-operation in the confiscation area. It is important to note in this context, however, that: "The mere fact that a Party may enter a reservation as regards a specific offence does not necessarily mean that it must refuse a request made by a Party which had not made a similar reservation. Article 18 of the Convention states only optional grounds for refusal".[44]

A further indication of the willingness of the Council of Europe to go beyond the 1988 UN precedent is provided by the treatment, in Article 6, of money laundering. The basic approach adopted has been summarised by the House of Lords Select Committee on the European Communities as follows:

> Article 6 of the Convention requires State Parties to establish an offence of intentional money laundering. The property involved in any conversion or transfer could be proceeds not only of drug trafficking or terrorism but of any criminal offence (described as the "predicate offence") and the State Party prosecuting need not have criminal jurisdiction over the predicate offence. Although this constitutes a very wide definition of money laundering, it is open to States on signature or ratification to limit the definition for themselves to more limited categories of predicate offences.[45]

The decision to thus expand the definition of money laundering beyond its traditional association with drug trafficking was not entirely unexpected. For example, it finds support in the existing legislative practice of certain states.[46] It is, in addition, a development in money laundering strategy which has the positive backing of the influential Financial Action Task Force. In its 1990 Report the FATF recommended that countries should consider extending the scope of the offence of money laundering to reach any other crime for which there is a link to narcotics, or to all serious offences.[47] The same Report also urged states to "encourage international conventions such as the draft convention of the Council of Europe on confiscation of the proceeds from offences".[48] It is of value to note that this trend mirrors the awareness of many experts of the disadvantages associated with drug-specific definitions of money laundering. As Levi has pointed out in the context of the UK Drug Trafficking Offences Act of 1986: "Sometimes — particularly in the laundering sphere and in the case of organised crime groups — the same people are involved in drug trafficking, fraud and terrorism".[49]

Extending the scope of the offence of money laundering beyond drug trafficking is not, however, the sole innovation contained in Article 6 of the 1990 Convention. For example, paragraph 3 anticipates the possible criminalisation of a series of acts, including negligent money laundering, which are not covered in the UN text.

---

[41] *Id.*, at p. 193.
[42] Id., at p. 204.
[43] This is so in the United Kingdom. *See, e.g.*, the Criminal Justice Act 1988 and the Prevention of Terrorism (Temporary Provisions) Act 1989.
[44] Chapter IV(i), document C, at p. 204.
[45] *Supra*, note 39, p. 7.
[46] *See, e.g.*, Article 305 (bis) of the Swiss Penal Code which came into effect on 1 August 1990 and renders money laundering in respect of all forms of crime a criminal offence.
[47] Chapter I, document B, at p. 15.
[48] *Id.*, at p. 23.
[49] M. Levi, "Regulating Money Laundering: The Death Mark of Bank Secrecy in the UK" (1991) 31 *British Journal of Criminology*, p. 109, at p. 115.

The European Convention, though signed by a significant number of states, has not yet entered into force.[50] Given the nature of the Convention and the likelihood that complex implementing legislation will need to be passed by most intending participants it may be some time before the full benefits of this landmark agreement are reflected in the practice of European co-operation.

b) *Prevention*

It is generally accepted that in the efforts to combat the financial aspects of drug trafficking and other forms of serious criminal activity particular reliance will have to be placed on the use of penal measures. It is, nonetheless, recognised that preventative strategies can play a significant and positive role. Indeed, it was this conception which lay at the heart of the Recommendation by the Committee of Ministers of the Council of Europe of 27 June 1980 on measures against the transfer and the safekeeping of funds of criminal origin.[51] This initiative, prompted in the main by concern over the growing number of acts of criminal violence such as kidnapping, failed at the time to find a receptive audience and the "recommendations were not generally implemented" ...[52]

Far more influential at the practical level has been the Statement of Principles for the guidance of bank supervisors issued on 12 December 1988 by the Basle Committee on Banking Regulations and Supervisory Practices. Its basic purpose is to encourage the banking sector to adopt a common position in order to ensure that banks are not used to hide or launder funds acquired through criminal activities and, in particular, through drug trafficking. As the preamble to the text makes clear, the document constitutes "a general statement of ethical principles which encourages banks' management to put in place effective procedures to ensure that all persons conducting business with their institutions are properly identified; that transactions that do not appear legitimate are discouraged; and that co-operation with law enforcement agencies is achieved." In an effort to maximise the impact of these principles the Committee took the step of commending the statement "to supervisory authorities in other countries".[53]

It is important to note that the Basle Statement of Principles is not a treaty in terms of public international law. Similarly it has no direct legal effect in the domestic law of any country. An exclusive concentration on the formal status of the text would, however, be extremely misleading. As has been pointed out elsewhere: "Although it is not itself a legally binding document, various formulas [sic] have been used to make its principles an obligation, notably a formal agreement among banks that commits them explicitly (Austria, Italy, Switzerland), a formal indication by bank regulators that failure to comply with these principles could lead to administrative sanctions (France, United Kingdom), or legally binding texts with a reference to these principles (Luxembourg)".[54] In spite of its relatively recent nature the Financial Action Task Force was able to report in February 1990 that practical measures towards implementation "have already been taken in many countries"...[55]

The philosophy of prevention is also central to the recently finalised plans of the European Communities in the area of money laundering. This takes the form of a Council Directive on Prevention of Use of the Financial System for the Purpose of Money Laundering of June 1991 which obliges member states to bring it fully into force by 1 January 1993.[56]

Community action in this area has been prompted by the perceived need to ensure "the integrity and cleanliness of the financial system"[57] in the light of moves towards the creation of a single financial market. As a House of Lords Select Committee noted, the free movement of capital and of financial services "offers great scope for organised crime as well as for legitimate enterprise".[58] Similarly, it is felt that "lack of Community action against money laundering could lead Member States, for the purpose of protecting their financial systems, to adopt measures which could be inconsistent with completion of the single market".[59]

---

[50] For a recent statement of the position *see*, (1991) 7 *International Enforcement Law Reporter* at p. 293.
[51] *See*, Chapter IV(i), document A, at p. 169.
[52] *Supra*, note 39, p. 7.
[53] Reproduced below, Chapter V, document B, at p. 275.
[54] Chapter I, document B, at p. 11.
[55] *Id.*, at p. 11. For the position in the U.K. *see, e.g.*, CM 1164 (1990), at p. 9; and, *supra*, note 11, at p. 5.
[56] *See generally*, Chapter IV(ii), document F, at p. 250.
[57] Chapter IV(ii) document E, Explanatory Memorandum II(2), at p. 244.
[58] *Supra*, note 39, p. 5.
[59] Chapter IV(ii) document F, Preamble, at p. 251.

In elaborating the Directive care was taken to ensure that it in no way undermined the achievements recorded in other fora. It is, for example, designed to complement rather than to replace the 1990 Council of Europe Convention mentioned above.

Like the 1990 text, the EC initiative recognises the fact that "since money laundering occurs not only in relation to the proceeds of drug-related offences but also in relation to the proceeds of other criminal activities (such as organised crime and terrorism), the Member States should, within the meaning of their legislation, extend the effects of the Directive to include the proceeds of such activities, to the extent that they are likely to result in laundering operations justifying sanctions on that basis".[60] Thus, whilst the definition of laundering contained in Article 1 is derived from that used in the 1988 UN Convention, it relates to "criminal activity" rather than merely serious drug trafficking offences. The term "criminal activity" is in turn defined to mean "a crime specified in Article 3(1) (a) of the Vienna Convention and any other criminal activity designated as such for the purposes of this Directive by each Member State".[61] In this regard Article 2 requires all Member States to ensure that laundering, as so defined, "is prohibited".

It is important to note that the decision has been taken to ensure that the Directive applies to the whole financial system including the insurance industry. This reflects the feeling that "partial coverage ... could provoke a shift in money laundering from one to another kind of financial institutions" ...[62] Furthermore, since laundering can also be carried out "through other types of professions and categories of undertakings, Member States must extend the provisions of this Directive in whole or in part, to include those professions and undertakings whose activities are particularly likely to be used for money laundering purposes".[63] In this regard it should be noted that Article 13 of the Directive establishes a Contact Committee the major function of which is to facilitate the co-ordination and harmonisation of implementing measures between Member States, including action taken regarding the extension of obligations to such additional professions and undertakings.

The Directive goes on to impose, in some detail, a number of specific obligations. Firstly, it requires the identification of customers and beneficial owners when entering into business relations "particularly when opening an account or savings accounts, or when offering safe custody facilities".[64] This identification requirement also applies when transacting business at or above an ECU 15,000 threshold "whether the transaction is carried out in a single operation or in several operations which seem to be linked".[65] Special derogation provisions have, however, been agreed in respect of the identification requirement in certain categories of insurance policy transactions.[66] However, it is specified in Article 3(6) that: "Credit and financial institutions shall carry out such identification even where the amount of the transaction is lower than the thresholds laid down, wherever there is suspicion of money laundering." Closely allied to the requirements concerning identification is the obligation to retain certain records for specified periods of time "for use as evidence in any investigation into money laundering".[67]

Secondly, provision is made to ensure the due diligence of credit and financial institutions.[68] Thirdly, obligations are imposed to ensure co-operation between relevant institutions and the authorities responsible for combating laundering activities. In particular, they must "on their own initiative" inform such authorities "of any fact which might be an indication of money laundering". Furthermore, they must, upon request, furnish those authorities with all necessary information.[69] The fact that such information has been transmitted must not be brought to the attention of the customer concerned or to other third parties.[70] In respect of such disclosures the institutions concerned are provided with a much needed form of legal immunity.[71] The information itself is subject to a limited form of speciality in terms of its future use by the authorities.[72] Finally, it should be noted that the Directive requires the establishment

---

[60] *Id.*

[61] *Id.*, Article 1. It should be noted that, like the new provisions in the Swiss Penal Code, the Directive's definition of laundering has an extraterritorial reach. Article 1 reads in part: "Money laundering shall be regarded as such even where the activities which generated the property to be laundered were perpetrated in the territory of another Member State or in that of a third country".

[62] Chapter IV(ii), document E, Explanatory Memorandum III(1), at p. 244.

[63] Chapter IV(ii), document F, Preamble, at p. 254. *See also*, Articles 12 and 13(1)(d).

[64] *Id.*, Article 3(1). *See also*, Article 3(5).

[65] *Id.*, Article 3(2).

[66] *See*, *id.*, Article 3(3) and 3(4).

[67] *Id.*, Article 4.

[68] *See, e.g., id.*, Article 5.

[69] *See, e.g., id.*, Articles 6 and 10.

[70] *See, id.*, Article 8.

[71] *See, id.*, Article 9.

[72] *See, id.*, Article 6.

of procedures of internal control by credit and financial institutions and the creation by them of appropriate training programmes.[73]

It will be apparent that the thrust of the EC Directive is radically different from that of both the 1988 and 1990 Conventions. Like the Basle Statement of Principles, though on a much wider scale, "its primary objective is one of preventing abuse of the financial system and detecting laundering, rather than increasing international co-operation in regard to punishment of offenders and confiscation of the proceeds of their crimes".[74] It also meets the goal of compatibility with other international initiatives as well as implementing no less than 15 of the 40 recommendations of the Financial Action Task Force.[75]

III. THE FINANCIAL ACTION TASK FORCE

On a number of occasions mention has been made of the work of the Financial Action Task Force on Money Laundering (FATF). Unlike the other initiatives mentioned thus far, the work of this important grouping is on-going and its future impact on government action is likely to continue to be profound.

The FATF was established by the Heads of State or Government of the seven major industrial nations (Group of Seven), joined by the President of the Commission of the European Communities, at their Summit Meeting in Paris in July 1989. The resulting Economic Declaration stressed the importance of tackling the financial aspects of drug trafficking and, towards that end, announced the decision to create the Task Force. Its mandate was: "to assess the results of co-operation already undertaken in order to prevent the utilisation of the banking system and financial institutions for the purpose of money laundering, and to consider additional preventative efforts in this field, including the adaptation of the legal and regulatory systems so as to enhance multilateral judicial assistance".[76]

In addition to the Summit participants eight other countries (Sweden, Netherlands, Belgium, Luxembourg, Switzerland, Austria, Spain and Australia) were invited to take part in this initiative. In February 1990 the FATF completed its first report which contained forty separate recommendations for action. Although viewed as constituting "a minimal standard in the fight against money laundering",[77] sight should not be lost of the fact that some of the recommendations failed to attract unanimous support. As the report itself admitted "the minimal standard we recommend can be viewed as rather ambitious".[78]

These so-called "action steps", a detailed examination of which lies beyond the scope of this introduction, focused on three central areas: i) improvements to national legal systems; ii) the enhancement of the role of the financial system; and iii) the strengthening of international co-operation. It is pertinent in this context to note that the report identified three measures which were unanimously regarded as constituting the overall general framework for its many specific proposals. These were:

1. Each country should, without further delay, take steps to fully implement the Vienna Convention, and proceed to ratify it;
2. Financial institutions secrecy laws should be conceived so as not to inhibit implementation of the recommendations of this group;
3. An effective money laundering enforcement program should include increased multilateral co-operation and mutual legal assistance in money laundering investigations and prosecutions and extradition in money laundering cases, where possible.[79]

At the Houston Summit in July 1990 it was agreed that the FATF process should be continued in order to "assess and facilitate the implementation of the forty recommendations, and to complement them where appropriate. It was agreed that all OECD and financial centre

---

[73] *See, id.*, Article 11.
[74] *Supra.*, note 39, p. 15.
[75] Chapter I, document D, at p. 38.
[76] Chapter I, document A, at p. 3.
[77] Chapter I, document B, at p. 15.
[78] *Id.*, at p. 15.
[79] *Id.*, at p. 14.

countries that would subscribe to the recommendations of the Task Force should be invited to participate in this exercise".[80]

With its membership again somewhat enlarged a series of meetings were held in Paris and a second Report was published during 1991. It was able to record that significant progress had been achieved in the implementation of the original recommendations particularly in the area of specified improvements to national legal systems and in securing the geographical extension of the FATF programme against money laundering. More importantly, it was agreed to continue the FATF process for a further five years. During this period the work of the Task Force will be serviced by a small Secretariat within the OECD.[81]

This decision will permit full advantage to be taken of what was perhaps the major accomplishment of FATF-2; namely, the agreement reached to move from self-reporting of progress towards implementation, to a system in which mutual assessment or evaluation plays a major role. As the 1991 Report states: "Individual members would be chosen for examination by the FATF with the examination carried out by selected other members of the FATF, according to an agreed protocol for examination and agreed selection criteria. The objective would be to examine every FATF member by the end of 1996".[82] Although this unprecedented move will, at least initially, not result in the publication of the country reports, agreement to allow "executive summaries" to see the light of day has been secured.

In addition to the above the Task Force will conduct three major tasks: i) co-ordination and oversight of efforts to encourage compliance by non-members; ii) facilitating further international co-operation; and iii) consideration, in the light of changing circumstances, of the need for additional recommendations and measures. In regard to the last of those, for example, it is anticipated that renewed attention will be devoted to a number of important issues ranging from changes in corporate criminal liability to the measures required to deal with the problem of "regulatory havens" and non co-operative countries.

IV. CONCLUSIONS

It will be apparent that substantial progress has been achieved in a relatively short period of time to facilitate co-ordinated international action against those who seek to launder the profits derived from transnational criminal activity. Particularly in the area of international drug trafficking, agreement has been reached on the imposition of obligations and the creation of formal mechanisms which together permit enforcement and prosecution officials to target the financial power of organised criminality more effectively than ever before. It is no exaggeration to say that in the area of drug-related money laundering the landscape of international co-operation has been radically and positively transformed.

Furthermore, new initiatives designed to increase the efficiency of international action against money laundering continue to be mounted. For example, in an effort to give effect to the Declaration and Program of Action of Ixtapa of April 1990,[83] the Inter-American Drug Abuse Control Commission has established a group of experts to prepare model regulations on the laundering of property and proceeds related to drug trafficking.[84] Actions of this kind and the on-going work of the FATF hold out the promise of further progress in improving the level, scope and effectiveness of international co-operation in the administration of justice in this now central area of concern.

William C. Gilmore

Marlborough House
London
January 1992

---

[80] Chapter I, document D, at p. 33. The original 40 recommendations have been considered in a number of different fora. *See, e.g.,* Chapter I, document C, at p. 25.
[81] *See,* Chapter I, document D, at p. 53.
[82] *Id.,* at p. 51.
[83] Extracts reproduced below, Chapter V, document F. This was, in turn, influenced by the 1986 Inter-American Program of Action of Rio de Janeiro, Chapter V, document A, p. 271, the 1990 Declaration of Cartagena, Chapter V, document D, p. 281, and the 1990 Declaration of the World Ministerial Summit, Chapter V, document E, p. 285. *See, e.g.,* Organisation of American States, Inter-American Drug Abuse Control Commission, Fourth Meeting of the Group of Experts to Prepare Model Regulations on the Laundering of Property and Proceeds Related to Drug Trafficking, 9-13 December, 1991, Final Report (Provisional Version), Chapter V, document I, p. 322.
[84] For a recent draft of the Model Legislation being developed *see* Chapter V, document I at p. 327.

ACKNOWLEDGEMENTS

This collection could not have been assembled without the willingness of both individuals and institutions. To those who kindly provided the various documents or offered expert advice I would like to express my appreciation. Thanks are also due to Ms Sarah Lubandi of the Commercial Crime Unit of the Commonwealth Secretariat, whose typing skills were relied upon throughout and to Mr J. G. Turner for his efforts in assembling many of the documents for the printers. Finally, I would like to express my gratitude to Mr Eli Lauterpacht, C.B.E., Q.C., and Dr Vaughan Lowe of the Research Centre for International Law and Mr Robin Pirrie for their kindness, understanding and co-operation.

CHAPTER I

THE FINANCIAL ACTION
TASK FORCE

DOCUMENT A

Group of 7 Economic Declaration of 16 July 1989
(extracts)
Source: Department of State Bulletin, September 1989

1)   We, the Heads of State or Government of seven major industrial nations and the President of the Commission of the European Communities, have met in Paris for the fifteenth annual Economic Summit.

Drug Issues

52) The drug problem has reached devastating proportions. We stress the urgent need for decisive action, both on a national and an international basis. We urge all countries, especially those where drug production, trading and consumption are large, to join our efforts to counter drug production, to reduce demand and to carry forward the fight against drug trafficking itself and the laundering of its proceeds.

53) Accordingly, we resolve the following measures within relevant fora:

●   Conclude further bilateral or multilateral agreements and support initiatives and cooperation, where appropriate, which include measures to facilitate the identification, tracing, freezing, seizure and forfeiture of drug crime proceeds.

●   Convene a financial action task force from Summit Participants and other countries interested in these problems. Its mandate is to assess the results of cooperation already undertaken in order to prevent the utilization of the banking system and financial institutions for the purpose of money laundering, and to consider additional preventive efforts in this field, including the adaptation of the legal and regulatory systems so as to enhance multilateral judicial assistance. The first meeting of this task force will be called by France and its report will be completed by April 1990.

DOCUMENT B

Financial Action Task Force on Money Laundering
Report of 6 February, 1990
Source: Foreign & Commonwealth Office, London

INTRODUCTION

The Heads of State or Government of seven major industrial nations and the President of the Commission of the European Communities met in Paris in July 1989 for the fifteenth annual Economic Summit. They stated that the drug problem has reached devastating proportions, and stressed the urgent need for decisive actions, both on a national and international basis. Among other resolutions on drug issues, they convened a Financial Action Task Force (FATF) from Summit Participants and other countries interested in these problems, to assess the results of the cooperation already undertaken to prevent the utilization of the banking system and financial institutions for the purpose of money laundering, and to consider additional preventive efforts in this field, including the adaptation of the statutory and regulatory systems to enhance multilateral legal assistance. They decided that the first meeting of this Task Force would be called by France, and that its report would be completed by April 1990.

In addition to Summit Participants (United States, Japan, Germany, France, United Kingdom, Italy, Canada, and the Commission of the European Communities), eight countries (Sweden, Netherlands, Belgium, Luxemburg, Switzerland, Austria, Spain and Australia), were invited to join the Task Force, in order to enlarge its expertise and also to reflect the views of other countries particularly concerned by, or having particular experience in the fight against money laundering, at the national or international level.

France held the presidency of the Task Force. Several meetings were held in Paris and one meeting in Washington. More than one hundred and thirty experts from various ministries, law enforcement authorities, and bank supervisory and regulatory agencies, met and worked together. The work of the Task Force, in itself, has improved the international cooperation in the fight against money laundering : contacts were established between experts and law enforcement authorities of member countries, and a comprehensive documentation on money laundering techniques, and national programs to combat them has been compiled. As a result, Task Force countries have already improved their readiness and ability to fight against money laundering, and to cooperate to this end .

To facilitate the work of the Task Force, and to take advantage of the expertise of its participants, three working groups were created, which focused respectively on money laundering statistics and methods (working - group 1, presidency : United Kingdom), on legal questions (working - group 2, presidency : United States), and on administrative and financial cooperation (working - group 3, presidency : Italy). Their comprehensive experts constitute part of the background material of this report, and of possible future work.

Building upon this substantial preparation, the Task Force report begins with a thorough analysis of the money laundering process, its extent and methods (part I) ; then, it presents the international instruments and national programs already in place to combat money laundering (part II) ; and it devotes its most extensive and detailed developments to the formulation of action recommendations, on how to improve the national legal systems, enhance the role of the financial system, and strengthen international cooperation against money laundering (part III).

I - EXTENT AND NATURE OF THE MONEY LAUNDERING PROCESS

A - EXTENT

The financial flows arising from drug trafficking might theoretically be estimated directly or indirectly.

A <u>direct estimation</u> would consist of measuring these flows from the international banking statistics and capital account statistics for the balance of payments. This could be done through an analysis of errors and omissions and other discrepancies. The task force asked the IMF and the BIS to conduct this work.Their conclusion was that although deposits covered by international banking statistics may include a substantial amount of drug money, there is no way in which this aspect can be singled out and it probably accounts for only a small percentage of the totals. The data for banks' liabilities suffers from insufficient coverage of offshore financial centers.

<u>Indirect methods</u> estimate the value of production or sales of narcotics, based on the fact that financial flows arising from drug trafficking are initially the counterparts of flows of drugs themselves. The parties involved in illegal narcotics trrransactions inevitably come to hold cash or balances in financial institutions whose connections with illicit activity they will wish to conceal. There is currently insufficient information to evaluate, on the basis of estimates of the value of drug sales, the level of these balances resulting from money laundering.

<u>Three indirect methods of estimation were used to assess the scale of financial flows arising from drug traffic.</u>They are based on estimations of drug production or consumption, valued using the retail price of drugs. Only a part of the calculated amounts are profits available to be laundered : production estimates must be modified by estimates of local consumption and losses in the production and distribution chain.

1 - The first method is based on <u>estimations of world drug production</u>. The United Nations estimated drug trafficking proceeds[1] worldwide at $ 300 billion in 1987. This estimation remains very uncertain.

The role of each kind of drug in the generation of proceeds available for money laundering is also difficult to assess. Estimates of US street yield are in the range of $29 billion for cocaine, $10 billion for heroin, and $67 billion for cannabis. Some drugs generate huge profits for the organisations controlling the traffic, making money laundering of large amounts, through complicated financial channels, a necessity, while some others generate profits mainly for the retailers, who may facilitate the laundering of these profits through very simple financial operations, as for instance by bartering drugs for stolen goods, and selling these goods for cash.

----

(1) For purposes of estimating the scale of money laundering as discussed above, "proceeds" means the value of the final sale of illegal drugs, without deduction of costs and without respect to whether payment is made with money or things of value.

For purposes of estimating the scale of money laundering as discussed above, "profits" means the value of drug sales less costs incurred by the traffickers (e.g, the cost of acquiring the drugs themselves, the cost of any precursor or essential chemicals, packaging materials, costs of transportation, costs of corruption, legal fees paid to defense lawyers, etc...).

Opium and its derivatives (e.g. heroin) originate mainly from South-East Asia (Golden Triangle) and South-West Asia (Golden Crescent) and Mexico. Proceeds from the sale of this multi-source drug are partly laundered through a sophisticated network of underground financial channels. Retail distribution networks are nonetheless largely controlled by persons located within Task Force countries.

Coca shrubs are cultivated in the Andean countries of South America (e.g. Bolivia, Colombia, Peru), and is converted into the most marketable form, cocaine hydrochloride, predominantly in Colombia. Several cartels are known to control the processing of cocaine hydrochloride in Colombia. Colombian nationals are also known to be involved in organising and controlling distribution networks in other countries. This means that there is a flow of funds destined to Colombia originating in Task Force countries.

The total global crop of cannabis is extremely difficult to estimate, as it grows uncultivated in many of the producing areas. Nevertheless, in many countries, major cannabis import, wholesale, and retail distribution organisations provide a structure which may also be used for distribution of heroin and cocaine. Large canabis seizures from offshore supply vessels, and bulk consignments of cannabis packed with heroin or cocaine are becoming more common in Europe. There is a rapid and troublesome growth in the size, power, and money laundering capability of some cannabis distribution organisations, raising the spectre of cartels developing in this area. Hence, in law enforcement and money laundering terms, cannabis trafficking constitutes a very serious problem requiring urgent attention.

Although a large part of heroin, cocain and cannabis production is consumed in industrialized countries, important quantities are also consumed in producing countries, especially heroin, where they also generate profits.

Finally, psychotropic substances such as amphetamines/methamphetamines and LSD are produced in clandestine laboratories, including some within Task Force countries. Large amounts of cash are derived, although not on the same scale as for cocaine and heroin.

However, the production-based method of estimation does not provide for an identification of financial flows within individual countries. Accordingly, all that can be said for certain is that the bulk of proceeds arises at the retail level within the Task Force area.

2 - A second method of estimating laundered drug proceeds is based on the consumption needs of drug abusers. But the information regarding drug use obtained through surveys is frequently of doubtful reliability since the activity is illegal : sample populations surveyed for example in homes or schools may miss a significant proportion of drugs users.

3 - A third method of estimating uses data concerning actual seizures of illicit drugs, and projects the total amounts of drugs available for sale by the application of a multiplier to recorded seizures, which is estimated on the basis of a law enforcement seizure rate varying between 5 % and 20 % according to the type of drug considered, and which, on a weighted average, could be approximately of 10 %. This approach, too, raises significant methodological problems.

Using these methods, the group estimated that sales of cocaine, heroin and cannabis amount to approximately $ 122 billions per year in the United States and Europe, of which 50 to 70 % or as much as $ 85 billion per year could be available for laundering and investment. One Task Force member estimated global profits at the main dealer level, which might be most subject to international laundering, to be about $ 30 billion per year.

B - METHODS

It would be impossible to list the entire range of methods used to launder money. Nevertheless, the Task Force reviewed a number of practical cases of money laundering. It stated that all of them share common factors, regarding the role of cash domestically, of various kinds of financial institutions, of international cash transfers, and of corporate techniques. These common factors indicate clearly where the efforts of the fight against money laundering should focus.

1 - Cash intensiveness

The form of the money obtained through drug trafficking must be changed in order to shrink the huge volumes of cash generated : unlike the proceeds of some other forms of criminal activity, drug cash usually comes in the form of large volumes of mixed denomination notes, and at least in the case of heroin and cocaine, the physical volume of notes received from street dealing is much larger than the volume of the drugs themselves ;

Drugs criminals are faced with major difficulties when in possession of large amounts of cash, and when large transactions cannot be performed in cash without arousing suspicion. A completely cashless economy where all transactions were registered would create enormous problems for the money launderers. Similarly, a rule that cash transactions were illegal above a certain amount for all but certain types of business regularly operating in cash would also create problems for launderers.

This is not to say that the cash intensiveness in one country is by itself correlated with the importance of money laundering. The cash intensiveness of Task Force economies varies greatly between countries. In countries like Switzerland, Germany, the Netherlands, Japan, Belgium and Austria, the cash/GDP ratio lies in the range 6,9 - 8,9 %, whereas at the other extreme are economies such as the UK and France with cash/GDP ratios at about 3 - 4 %. Important cash transactions are increasingly monitored in some countries, such as the United-States and Australia, and were recently prohibited in France over 150.000 francs per operation.

Another observation is that it is easier for the launderer if the cash in which he operates can be directly accepted abroad as a means of exchange. The US dollar in cash is acceptable as a means of exchange in large amounts in many parts of the world : Federal Reserve Board staff have estimated that adult residents of the US held only 11 - 12 % of issued U.S. notes and coins in 1984. The remainder were held by legitimate and illegitimate business enterprises, residents of foreign countries, and persons less than 18 years old.

2 - Role of formal and informal financial institutions.

a) Role of formal financial institutions

Banks and other deposit-taking financial institutions are the main transmitters of money both within the Task Force area and internationally. Clearly the stage of depositing money in institutions is a key one for money launderers. Whether a currency reporting system is in place, or whether the laws in the country only allow or require the reporting of suspicious transactions, many of the Task Force countries have measures in place which would make large cash deposits likely to be brought to the attention of the authorities. Therefore, deposits have to be disguised. In countries where there is cash transaction reporting, deposits have to be broken up into sizes which are lower than the threshold for that reporting ("smurfing"), in order to escape this reporting.

For criminals to avoid suspicion, the reduction of deposit size below reporting requirements is not enough. Deposits may be made in the name of a company whose beneficial owners do not have to be disclosed in the country in which it is headquartered. Those with signing authority for the company in a Task Force country -or receiving payments- do not necessarily know who the beneficial owners are. In some countries, bank accounts can also be opened in the name of trustees, and the beneficiaries under the trust may be kept secret. Deposits may be made by the legal profession in the name of clients to whom the rules of attorney confidentiality may apply.

Even if identity requirements were comprehensive and uniform, it is possible that officials of banks may become corrupt and accept deposits from persons with false identities. Most reputable banks do not open accounts without knowing their customer. But they may be less careful about cash transactions in foreign exchange over the counter, or in providing cashier's cheques or wiring money for non-depositors. It is not believed that automatic teller machines (ATMs) operated by banks at present cause any particular difficulty. But automatic foreign exchange changing machines - already in use in Europe - can provide anonymity during the laundering process. Similarly, any future ATMs which automatically and anonymously converted low value notes into high value ones would also facilitate money laundering.

b) Role of informal financial institutions

It is of course not necessary for criminals to use licensed deposit-taking financial institutions or to establish companies to help deal with their problems. Informal and largely unregulated financial institutions, which can not legally accept deposits, can also be used. The first category of these are Bureaux de Change, which accept money in one currency and convert it into another. This still leaves the cash problem open, but a first transformation has taken place which makes it more difficult to detect the origin of the funds. If informal financial institutions provide this service, they may not record the identity of transactors. Cheque cashers who provide a service mainly after bank hours, if unscrupulous, can work in reverse : selling cheques at a premium for cash.

Informal bankers, including "Hawalla" bankers exist mainly in countries with direct connections with Asia. They are often involved in the gold bullion, gold jewelry or currency exchange business, and may be a member of a family with similar businesses in several countries, or, at the other end of the scale, a street corner confectionery shop. Bona fide employees of foreign banks may operate such systems outside banking hours.

3 - Cash shipments abroad

Drugs proceeds can be deposited abroad in jurisdictions where the banking system is insufficiently regulated and where the establishment of "letter box" companies is permitted. Such jurisdictions may include, for instance, small countries who wish to establish a financial services industry as a supplementary source of income -the sale of banking licenses can constitute a major source of revenue to the authorities- and employement for the population. Such jurisdictions are sometimes also tax havens.

These jurisdictions are part of the world payments system without any restriction. So long as this is the case, cash exports will tend to go to these countries for integration into the financial system there and return by means of wire transfers. This means that detection of the outflow of cash becomes especially important when internal avenues have been blocked.

4 - Corporate techniques

Drug dealers must conceal the true ownership and origin of the money while simultaneously controlling it. To this end, they can use various corporate techniques.

Offshore companies can be used by launderers in ways other than simply as depositories for cash. Launderers can set up or buy corporations, perhaps in a tax haven using a local lawyer or other person as a nominee owner, with an account at a local bank. They can then finance the purchase of a similar business at home through a loan from their corporation abroad (or the bank), in effect borrowing their own money and paying it back as if it were a legitimate loan.

The technique of "double invoicing" can be used whereby goods are purchased at inflated prices by domestic companies owned by money launderers from offshore corporations which they also own. The difference between the price and the true value is then deposited offshore and paid to the offshore company and repatriated at will. Variants of the "double invoicing" technique abound.

*

All these techniques, however, involve going through stages where detection is possible. Either cash has to be exported over a territorial frontier and then deposited in a foreign financial institution, or it requires the knowing or unknowing complicity of someone at home not connected with the drug trade, or it requires convincing a domestic financial institution that a large cash deposit or purchase of a cashier's cheque is legitimate. Once these hurdles have been cleared, the way is much easier inside the legitimate financial system.

Hence, key stages for the detection of money laundering operations are those where cash enters into the domestic financial system, either formally or informally, where it is sent abroad to be integrated into the financial systems of regulatory havens, and where it is repatriated in the form of transfers of legitimate appearance.

II - PROGRAMS ALREADY IN PLACE TO COMBAT MONEY LAUNDERING

A - INTERNATIONAL INSTRUMENTS

Various international organisations or groups, including the Council of Europe (1), INTERPOL, among EEC members, the Mutual Assistance Group between customs administrations and the TREVI group between ministers in charge of security, as well as the Customs Cooperation Council, have already devoted much attention to the money laundering problem. Besides, two international instruments currently address this issue from different viewpoints : the United Nations Vienna Convention against Illicit Traffic in Narcotic Drugs and Psychotropic Substances (hereinafter "Vienna Convention"), and the Statement of Principles of the Basel Committee on Banking Regulations and Supervisory Practices (hereinafter Basel Statement of Principles), concerning the "prevention of criminal use of the banking system for the purpose of money laundering".

a) The Vienna Convention

This Convention, which was adopted in Vienna on December 20, 1988, focuses on drug trafficking in general, including of course, but not exclusively, drug money laundering. On this last issue, it lays firm ground for further progress in the following directions :

- it creates an obligation to criminalize the laundering of money derived from drug trafficking, thereby facilitating judicial cooperation and extradition in this field, which today are hampered, given the principle of dual criminality, by the fact that many countries do not presently criminalize money laundering ;

- several parts of the Vienna Convention deal with international cooperation. Its implementation would substantially facilitate international investigations ;

- it makes extradition between signatory States applicable in money laundering cases ;

- it sets out principles to facilitate cooperative administrative investigations ;

- it sets forth the principle that banking secrecy should not interfere with criminal investigations in the context of international cooperation.

More than eighty countries have signed this convention, including all Task Force countries. So far, only China, Senegal, the Bahamas and Nigeria have ratified it. Twenty ratifications are necessary for this convention to be brought into force. Given the complexity of the ratification and implementation process, in some countries, its entry into force could take several years.

----
(1) The Committee of Ministers to the Member States of the Council of Europe adopted on June 27, 1980, a recommendation concerning measures against the transfer and the sheltering of criminally originated funds.

b) <u>The Basel Statement of Principles</u>

This document, which was agreed to on December 12, 1988, and stated that public confidence in banks may be undermined through their association with criminals, outlines some basic principles with a view to combat money laundering operations through the banking system, in the following directions :

- customer identification ;

- compliance with laws and regulations pertaining to financial transactions, and refusal to assist transaction which appear to be associated with money laundering ;

- cooperation with law enforcement authorities, to the extent permitted by regulations relating to customer confidentiality.

All Task Force countries, except Australia, Austria, and Spain, were part of the group that agreed to the Basel Statement of Principles. The bank regulators and supervisors of these three countries however have expressed that they consider this Statement as also applicable to their supervised banking systems.

Although it is not in itself a legally binding document, various formulas have been used to make its principles an obligation, notably a formal agreement among banks that commits them explicitly (Austria, Italy, Switzerland), a formal indication by bank regulators that failure to comply with these principles could lead to administrative sanctions (France, United Kingdom), or legally binding texts with a reference to these principles (Luxemburg).

In spite of the fact that the Statement of Principles is a recent text, and furthermore that it was very recently established as an obligation for banks, practical measures have already been taken in many countries, such as the appointment of a compliance officer in each bank, in charge of the application of the internal programs against money laundering. Most Task Force countries have set detailed guidelines for banks, making the Principles precise and practical obligations.

It should be noted that certain of these Principles have been applied in most countries for a long time, as for instance the principles of customer identification, and retaining of a record of transactions.

B - NATIONAL PROGRAMS

Awareness of the problem of money laundering is recent. However, national programs to combat it are already in place in some Task Force countries, although much remains to be done in most of them.

The group agreed to the following working definition to describe the process of money laundering conduct or behaviour :

----
(1) Most delegates consider that the final paragraph of the definition, drawn from the Vienna Convention, does not describe money laundering per se, but an economic aspect of crime which must be addressed in any comprehensive scheme against money laundering, whereas a few delegates understand this paragraph as being included in the concept of money laundering.

- the conversion or transfer of property, knowing that such property is derived from a criminal offense, for the purpose of concealing or disguising the illicit origin of the property or of assisting any person who is involved in the commission of such an offense or offenses to evade the legal consequences of his action ;

- the concealment or disguise of the true nature, source, location, disposition, movement, rights with respect to, or ownership of property, knowing that such property is derived from a criminal offense ;

- the acquisition, possession or use of property, knowing at the time of receipt that such property was derived from a criminal offense or from an act of participation in such offense (1).

1 - Money laundering offense

Money laundering is already a specific criminal offense in seven Task Force countries (Australia, Canada, France, Italy, Luxemburg, United Kingdom, United States), and there is a pending legislation to create this offence in four additional Task Force countries (Belgium, Germany, Sweden, Switzerland). In the other Task Force countries (Netherlands, Spain, Austria, Japan), there is currently no specific money laundering offense, although, for some of them the general legislation pertaining to the proceeds of crime covers money laundering offenses.

Some differences appear in the scienter requirements, whereas most countries only criminalize intentional money laundering, other countries also criminalize negligence leading to money laundering.

The criminal penalties for these offenses are heavy fines, imprisonment up to 20 years, and sometimes prohibitions against engaging in certain professions.

2 - Freezing, seizure and confiscation of assets

Most Task Force countries have provisional measures concerning freezing, seizure, and/or procedures for asset confiscation relating to drug offenses. However, not all the countries that have established money laundering offenses permit these procedures in relation to money laundering.

The definition of property subject to freezing, seizure and confiscation is generally similar from one country to another, because, in most countries, it also extends to all proceeds of crime, which would normally cover indirect as well as direct profits or proceeds of drug trafficking. In a few countries, it also extends to the property laundered, the instrumentalities used in the crime, or property of corresponding value.

Most Task Force countries allow freezing, seizure or confiscation of assets related to drug trafficking in execution of a formal request of a foreign state, in the framework of their domestic laws, or provided a treaty exists, and subject to additional conditions. Nevertheless, the existing domestic laws and mutual legal assistance treaties do not provide for each Task Force country to obtain freezing, seizure or confiscation of drug related assets in all other member countries.

3 - Bank secrecy laws and reporting requirements

a) Customer identification

None of the Task Force countries allows anonymous accounts, although Austria allows limited forms of anonymous bearer accounts. Most Task Force countries require the identification of customers using safe deposit facilities. Only in some Task Force members (Australia, Luxemburg, Sweden, Switzerland) does the obligation to identify extend to the beneficial owners.

b) Internal records of transactions

All countries' banks must keep account books and records of transactions, for the purpose of prudential supervision, statistics and tax control. In a few countries, banks must also retain internal records of transactions (either all transactions, and/or large cash transactions and/or international transactions), for the purpose of combatting money laundering and other crimes.

The conditions of access of law enforcement authorities to these records are extremely varied among countries. In most cases, judicial proceedings are necessary to overcome bank secrecy rules.

c) Detection of suspicious transactions

The detection of suspicious transactions occurring through the financial system, in Task Force countries having specific detection programs, is broadly based on different systems, which can be complementary.

The responsibility for initially detecting suspicious financial flows falls mainly to financial institutions themselves. In some countries, such as Canada, banks have taken on this responsibility ; in other countries, such as the UK, banks have been indirectly obliged to take on this responsibility in order to avoid possible prosecution for money laundering ; while in other countries, such as the US and Australia, this responsibility has been imposed by regulation. The banker, to avoid the risk of being involved in money laundering operations, sets up internal programs to detect suspicious transactions, and declares his suspicions to the competent authorities. Under either system, when banks bring a questionable transaction to the attention of these authorities, they will be protected against judicial actions brought by their customers for failure to respect banking confidentiality. These systems also require confidential relations between bankers and these authorities. Although these systems are recent, the number of declarations -from several hundreds to several thousands each year- received by the competent authorities of countries which apply them, is an indication of their efficiency. In most other Task Force countries, bank secrecy rules do not allow bankers to make such declarations. In some other countries where the reporting of suspicious transactions is mandatory, such as the United States, failure to report suspicious transactions carries administrative penalties.

In addition to mandatory suspicious transaction reporting, competent administrative authorities in two countries rely on the gathering and analysis of systemactic information related to cash movements. This is the system in place in the United States and Australia. In this system, financial institutions report routinely all deposits, transfers and withdrawals of cash over $ 10,000. These reports, together with report of international important transfers of cash and similar instruments over $ 10,000, are fed into a computerized database, with an artificial intelligence system, enabling the detection of questionable transactions. In the United-States, about 6 millions reports are made annually under this system, with a cost for the financial institutions estimated at US $ 17 for each report. In the US, currency reports serve a number of purposes beyond identifying suspicious transactions. The reports are used in many ways to support investigations, prosecution and confiscation.

*

Although recent, there are signs that these programs against money laundering, in countries having such programs, have effective results, by creating increased risks for money launderers. For instance, in the United-States, money laundering "commissions" asked by launderers, which amounted to 2 to 4 % per transaction in the early 1980's, commonly reach 6 to 8 % now.

Recommendation
numbers

III - RECOMMENDATIONS

A - GENERAL FRAMEWORK OF THE RECOMMENDATIONS

Many of the current difficulties in international cooperation in drug money laundering cases are directly or indirectly linked with a strict application of bank secrecy rules, with the fact that, in many countries, money laundering is not today an offense, and with insufficiencies in multilateral cooperation and mutual legal assistance.

Some of these difficulties will be alleviated when the Vienna Convention is in effect in all the signatory countries, principally because this would open more widely the possibility of mutual legal assistance in money laundering cases. Accordingly, the group unanimoulsy agreed as its first recommendation that **each country should, without further delay, take steps to fully implement the Vienna Convention, an proceed to ratify it.**[1]

1

Concerning bank secrecy, it was unanimously agreed that **financial institutions secrecy laws should be conceived so as not to inhibit implementation of the recommendations of this group.**

2

Finally, **an effective money laundering enforcement program should include increased multilateral cooperation and mutual legal assistance in money laundering investigations and prosecutions and extradition in money laundering cases, where possible.**

3

Nevertheless, this should not be the end point of our efforts to fight this phenomenon. Additional measures are necessary, for at least two reasons :

- the need for rapid and tough actions

As the purpose of the Vienna Convention is the fight against drug trafficking in general, including of course, but not exclusively, the fight against drug money laundering, some countries could have difficulties in ratifying and implementing it for reasons that are not related to the issue of money laundering. It remains crucial, whatever the difficulties may be on legal and technical grounds, to ratify and implement the Convention fully and without delay.

Rapid progress on the issue of money laundering is necessary. Hence, the Task Force's recommendations include important steps that are implied by this Convention. Furthermore, even on the topics mentioned by the Vienna Convention, it seemed to the group that the growing dimension and increasing awareness of the problem of money laundering, would justify a reinforcement of its provisions applicable to money laundering issues.

----

[1] However the Task Force did not undertake to determine what steps would be adequate to meet the requirements of the Vienna Convention. So, the adoption of the proposals and recommendations of the Task Force would not necessarily constitute full compliance with the obligations assumed by Task Force countries as parties to the U.N. Vienna Convention.

- the need for practical measures.

Any discrepancy between national measures to fight money laundering can be used potentially by traffickers, who would move their laundering channels to the countries and financial systems where no or weak regulations exist on this matter, making more difficult the detection of funds of criminal origin. To avoid such a risk, these national measures, particularly those concerning the diligence of financial institutions, have to be conceived in a way that builds upon and enhances the Basel Statement of Principles, and to be harmonized in their most practical aspects, which is not provided for in the Statement.

On these bases, we recommend action steps that, in our view, could constitute a minimal standard in the fight against money laundering, for the countries participating in this Task Force, as well as for other countries. Some of these recommendations reflect the view of a majority of delegates, rather than unanimity, so that they are not limited to the weakest existing solution in the participating countries on each topic. Cases where a minority held a significantly different view are also mentioned. Accordingly, the minimal standard we recommend can be viewed as rather ambitious. Nevertheless, it should in no way prevent individual countries from adopting or maintaining more stringent measures against money laundering. Furthermore, as money laundering techniques evolve, anti-money laundering measures must evolve too : our recommendations will probably need periodic reevaluation.

These action steps against money laundering focus on improvements of national legal systems (B), enhancement of the role of the financial system (C), and the strengthening of international cooperation (D).

B - IMPROVEMENT OF NATIONAL LEGAL SYSTEMS
TO COMBAT MONEY LAUNDERING

1 - Definition of the criminal offense of money laundering

4 **Each country should take such measures, as may be necessary, including legislative ones, to enable it to criminalize drug money laundering as set forth in the Vienna Convention.**

However, the laundering of drug money is frequentely associated with the laundering of other criminal proceeds. Given the difficulty to bring evidence of drug money laundering specifically, an extension of the scope of this offense, for instance to the most serious offenses, such as arms trafficking, etc., might facilitate its prosecution.

5 **Accordingly, each country should consider extending the offense of drug money laundering to any other crimes for which there is a link to narcotics ; an alternative approach is to criminalize money laundering based on all serious offenses, and/or on all offenses that generate a significant amount of proceeds, or on certain serious offenses.**

6
The group agreed that, as provided in the Vienna Convention, the offense of money laundering should apply at least to knowing money laundering activity, including the concept that knowledge may be inferred from objective factual circumstances. Some delegates consider that the offense of money laundering should go beyond the Vienna Convention on this point to criminalize activity where a money launderer should have known the criminal origin of the laundered funds. As already mentioned, a few countries would impose criminal sanctions for negligent money laundering activity.

7
In addition, the group recommends that, where possible, corporations themselves -not only their employees- should be subject to criminal liability.

2 - Provisional measures and confiscation

The Vienna Convention provides for provisional measures and confiscation in case of drug trafficking and laundering of drug money. These measures are a necessary condition to an effective fight against drug money laundering, notably because they facilitate the execution of sentences and help reduce the financial attractiveness of money laundering.

8
Accordingly, countries should adopt measures similar to those set forth in the Vienna Convention, as may be necessary, including legislative ones, to enable their competent authorities to confiscate property laundered, proceeds from, instrumentalities used in or intended for use in the commission of any money laundering offense, or property of corresponding value.

Such measures should include the authority to : 1) identify, trace, and evaluate property which is subject to confiscation ; 2) carry out provisional measures, such a freezing and seizing, to prevent any dealing, transfer, or disposal of such property and 3) take any appropriate investigative measures.

In addition to confiscation and criminal sanctions, countries also should consider monetary and civil penalties, and/or proceedings including civil proceedings, to void contracts entered by parties, where parties knew or should have known that as a result of the contract, the state would be prejudiced in its ability to recover financial claims, e.g., through confiscation or collection of fines and penalties.

C - ENHANCEMENT OF THE ROLE OF THE FINANCIAL SYSTEM

In addressing the subject of money laundering, the group has kept in mind the necessity to weigh the impact of its recommendations on financial institutions, and to preserve the efficient operation of national and international financial systems.

1 - Scope of the following recommendations

The entry of cash into the financial system is of crucial importance in the drug money laundering process. This may occur through the financial system (banks and other financial institutions), and also through certain other professions dealing with cash, which are unregulated or virtually unregulated in many countries.

9   Accordingly, the recommendations 12 to 29 of this paper should apply not only to banks, but also to non-bank financial institutions.

10   For maximum effectiveness, these recommendations need to cover as many organisations as possible that receive large value cash payments in the course of their business. Therefore, the appropriate national authorities should take steps to ensure that these recommendations are implemented on as broad a front as is pratically possible.

11   Nevertheless, excessive variation among the national lists for these non-bank financial institutions and other professions dealing with cash, subject to the following recommendations, could potentially facilitate the activity of money launderers. To avoid that, some delegates prefer that a common, minimum list of these financial institutions and professions be accepted by all the countries. As examples of non-bank financial institutions, savings societies including postal savings societies, loan societies, building societies, security brokers and dealers, credit card companies, check cashers, transmitters of funds by wire, money changers / bureaux de change, sales finance companies, consumer loan companies, leasing companies, factoring companies, and gold dealers were mentioned.

It was agreed that, a working group should further examine the possibility of establishing a common minimal list of non bank financial institutions and other professions dealing with cash subject to these recommendations.

2 - Customer identification and record keeping rules

Crucial in the fight against money laundering through the financial system, are the ability of financial institutions to screen undesirable customers, and the ability for law enforcement authorities to conduct their enquiries on the basis of reliable documents about the transactions and the identity of clients.

12   Hence, financial institutions should not keep anonymous accounts or accounts in obviously fictitious names : they should be required (by law, by regulations, by agreements between supervisory authorities and financial institutions or by self-regulatory agreements among financial institutions) to identify, on the basis of an official or other reliable identifying document, and record the identity of their clients, either occasional or usual, when establishing business relations or conducting transactions (in particular opening of accounts or passbooks, entering into fiduciary transactions, renting of safedeposit boxes, performing large cash transactions).

Furthermore, layering of funds of illicit origin is often facilitated by nominee accounts in financial institutions and shareholdings in companies, where beneficial ownership is disguised.

13   Hence, financial institutions should take reasonable measures to obtain information about the true identity of the persons on whose behalf an account is opened or a transaction is conducted if there are any doubts as to whether these clients or customers are not acting on their own behalf, in particular, in the case of domiciliary companies (i.e. institutions, corporations, foundations, trusts, etc., that do not conduct any commercial or manufactoring business or any other form of commercial operation in the country where their registered office is located).

14   Financial institutions should maintain, for at least five years, all necessary records on transactions, both domestic or international, to enable them to comply swiftly with information requests from the competent authorities. Such records must be sufficient to permit reconstruction of individual transactions (including the amounts and types of currency involved, if any) so as to provide, if necessary, evidence for prosecution of criminal behaviour.

       Financial institutions should keep records on customer identification (e.g. copies or records of official identification documents like passports, identity cards, driving licenses or similar documents), account files and business correspondence for at least five years after the account is closed.

       These documents should be available to domestic competent authorities, in the context of criminal prosecutions and investigations.

3 - Increased diligence of financial institutions

       Identification of customers is generally not sufficient to allow financial institutions and law enforcement authorities to detect suspicious transactions.

15   Hence, financial institutions should pay special attention to all complex, unusual, large transactions, and all unusual patterns of transactions, which have no apparent economic or visible lawful purpose. The background and purpose of such transactions should, as far as possible, be examined, the findings established in writing, and be available to help supervisors, auditors and law enforcement agencies.

       Where financial institutions suspect that funds stem from a criminal activity, bank secrecy rules or other privacy laws which are presently enforced in most countries prohibit them to report their suspicions to the competent authorities. Thus, to avoid any involvement in money laundering operations, they have no other choice, in that case, than denying assistance, severing relations and closing accounts in accordance with the Basle Statement of Principles. The consequence is that these funds can flow through other, undetected channels, which would frustate the efforts of competent authorities in the fight against money laundering.

16   To avoid this risk, the following principle should be established : if financial institutions suspect that funds stem from a criminal activity, they should be permitted or required to report promptly their suspicions to the competent authorities. Accordingly, there should be legal provisions to protect financial institutions and their employees from criminal or civil liability for breach of any restriction on disclosure of information imposed by contract or by any legislative, regulatory or administrative provision, if they report in good faith, in disclosing suspected criminal activity to the competent authorities, even if they have not known precisely what the underlying criminal activity was, and regardless of whether illegal activity actually occured.

       There is a divergence of opinion within the Task Force on whether suspicious activity reporting should be mandatory or permissive. A few countries strongly believe that this reporting should be mandatory, possibly restricted to suspicions on serious criminal activities, and with administrative sanctions available for failure to report.

If financial institutions, while making these reports, warned at the same time their customers, the effect might be similar to a refusal to handle the suspected funds : the suspected customers and their funds would flow through undetected channels.

17   Hence, financial institutions, their directors and employees, should not, or, where appropriate, should not be allowed to, warn their customers when information relating to them is being reported to the competent authorities.

18   In the case of a mandatory reporting system, or in the case of a voluntary reporting system where appropriate, financial institutions reporting their suspicions should comply with instructions from the competent authorities.

19   In countries where no obligation of reporting these suspicions exist, when a financial institution develops suspicions about operations of a customer, and when the financial institution chooses to make no report to the competent authorities, it should deny assistance to this customer, sever relations with him and close his accounts.

The group also discussed what actions financial institutions should take when they learn from competent authorities, even in an informal way, that criminal proceedings, including international mutual assistance requests and/or appropriate freezing orders, are pending or imminent. Further examination of the intricate legal and practical aspects of this question would be useful, to avoid a premature withdrawal of funds which would unduly impair the criminal proceedings.

Staff in financial institutions are still only beginning, in most countries, to become aware of money laundering. This is of great help to money launderers. In some countries, complicity of staff may be also a problem.

20   Hence, financial institutions should develop programs against money laundering. These programs should include, as a minimum :

        a) the development of internal policies, procedures and controls, including the designation of compliance officers at management level, and adequate screening procedures to ensure high standards when hiring employees ;

        b) an ongoing employee training program ;

        c) an audit function to test the system.

4 - Measures to cope with the problem of countries with no or insufficient anti money laundering measures.

The strengthening of the fight against money laundering in some countries could lead to a simple move of the money laundering channels, to countries with insufficient money laundering measures, in a process akin to regulator shopping.

Frequently, a money laundering operation would involve the following stages :

- drugs cash proceeds would be exported from regulated countries to unregulated ones ;

- this cash would be laundered through the domestic formal or informal financial system of these havens ;

- the subsequent stage would be a return of these laundered funds to regulated countries with safe placement opportunities, particularly through wire transfers.

While sovereignty principles make it difficult to prevent this type of displacement of money laundering channels, and other laundering operations using regulation havens, the following principles should be applied by financial institutions in regulated countries :

21
- **financial institutions should give special attention to business relations and transactions with persons, including companies and financial institutions, from countries which do not or insufficiently apply these recommendations. Whenever these transactions have no apparent economic or visible lawful purpose, their background and purpose should, as far as possible, be examined, the findings established in writing, and be available to help supervisors, auditors and law enforcement agencies.**

22
- **financial institutions should ensure that the principles mentioned above are also applied to branches and majority owned subsidiaries located abroad, especially in countries which do not or insufficiently apply these recommendations, to the extent that local applicable laws and regulations permit. When local applicable laws and regulations prohibit this implementation, competent authorities in the country of the mother institution should be informed by the financial institutions that they cannot apply these recommendations.**

Within the context of relations between regulated and unregulated countries, the study of a system to monitor cash movements at the border is of special importance (see point 5 hereunder).

5 - Other measures to avoid currency laundering

It was recognised that the stage of drugs cash movements between countries is crucial in the detection of money laundering. A few delegates strongly support the proposal that a system of reporting of all large international transportations of currency or cash equivalent bearer instruments to a domestic central agency with a computerized data base available to domestic judicial or law enforcement authorities should be established for use in money laundering cases. But this opinion is not shared by the majority of the group.

23
Nevertheless, the group acknowledged that **the feasibility of measures to detect or monitor cash at the border should be studied, subject to strict safeguards to ensure proper use of information and without impeding in any way the freedom of capital movements.**

The detection of suspicious cash operations could potentially be also facilitated if law enforcement authorities were in a position to be informed and to analyze all large cash transactions occuring within their country.

For that purpose, one suggested solution is that these transactions be routinely reported by financial institutions to competent authorities.

However, the efficiency of such a system, which currently exists in two participating countries, is uncertain. The majority of the group was not convinced of the cost effectiveness of this system at this time, and expressed fears that it could lead financial institutions to feel less responsible for the fight against money laundering. On the other hand, it is the view of a few members that a comprehensive program to combat money laundering must include such a currency reporting system together with the reporting of international transportation of currency and currency equivalent instruments.

24 Nevertheless, the group agreed that countries should consider the feasibility and utility of a system where banks and other financial institutions and intermediaries would report all domestic and international currency transactions above a fixed amount, to a national central agency with a computerized data base, available to competent authorities for use in money laundering cases, subject to strict safeguards to ensure proper use of the information.

25 Furthermore, given the crucial importance of cash in drug trafficking and drug money laundering, and despite the fact that no clear correlation could be established between the cash intensiveness of a country's economy, and the role of this economy in international money laundering, countries should further encourage in general the development of modern and secure techniques of money management, including increased use of checks, payment cards, direct deposit of salary checks, and book entry recording of securities, as a means to encourage the replacement of cash transfers.

6 - Implementation, and role of regulatory and other administrative authorities

Effective implementation of the above recommendations must be ensured.

But the authorities supervising banks and other financial institutions have currently, in many countries, no competence to participate in the fight against criminal activities, because their mission is primarily a prudential one, and because of professional secrecy or other rules.

26 Accordingly, in each member country, the competent authorities supervising banks or other financial institutions or intermediaries, or other competent authorities, should ensure that the supervised institutions have adequate programs to guard against money laundering. These authorities should cooperate and lend expertise spontaneously or on request with other domestic judicial or law enforcement authorities in money laundering investigations and prosecutions.

27 The effective implementation of the above mentioned recommendations in other professions dealing with cash is hampered by the fact that, in many countries, these professions are virtually unregulated. Hence, competent authorities should be designated to ensure an effective implementation of all these recommendations, through administrative supervision and regulation, in other professions dealing with cash as defined by each country.

28 The establishment of programs to combat money laundering in financial institutions and other professions dealing with cash, would require the support of these competent authorities, particularly to make these institutions and professions aware of facts that should normally lead to suspicions. Accordingly, the competent authorities should establish guidelines which will assist financial institutions in detecting suspicious patterns of behaviour by their customers. It is understood that such guidelines must develop over time, and will never be exhaustive. It is further understood that such guidelines will primarily serve as an educational tool for financial institutions' personnel.

29   Furthermore, the competent authorities regulating or supervising financial institutions should take the necessary legal or regulatory measures to guard against control of, or acquisition of a significant participation in financial institutions by criminals or their confederates.

The group acknowledged the risk that, outside the financial sector, industrial or commercial companies also could be acquired by criminals with the aim to use them for money laundering purposes.

D - STRENGTHENING OF
INTERNATIONAL COOPERATION

The study of practical cases of money laundering clearly demonstrated that money launderers conduct their activities at an international level, thus exploiting differences between national jurisdictions and the existence of international boundaries. Therefore, enhanced international cooperation between enforcement agencies, financial institutions, and financial institution regulators and supervisors to facilitate the investigations, and prosecution of money launderers, is critical.

1 - <u>Administrative cooperation</u>

a) <u>Exchange of general information</u>

A first step is to improve the knowledge of international flows of drug money, noticeably cash flows, and the knowledge of money laundering methods, to enable a better focus of international and national efforts to combat this phenomenon.

30   Accordingly, national administrations should consider recording, at least in the aggregate, international flows of cash in whatever currency, so that estimates can be made of cash flows and reflows from various sources abroad, when this is combined with central bank information. Such information should be made available to the IMF and BIS to facilitate international studies.

31   International competent authorities, perhaps Interpol and the Customs Cooperation Council, should be given responsibility for gathering and disseminating information to competent authorities about the latest development in money laundering and money laundering techniques. Central banks and bank regulators could do the same on their network. National authorities in various spheres, in consultation with trade associations, could then disseminate this to financial institutions in individual countries.

b) <u>Exchange of information relating to suspicious transactions</u>

Present arrangements for international administrative cooperation and international exchange of information relating to identified transactions, are aknowledged to be insufficient. At the same time, this exchange of information must be consistent with national and international provisions on privacy and data protection. Furthermore, several countries consider that exchange of information relating to individual money laundering cases should take place only in the context of mutual legal assistance.

32
It was agreed that each country should make efforts to improve a spontaneous or "upon request" international information exchange relating to suspicious transactions, persons and corporations involved in those transactions between competent authorities. Strict safeguards should be established to ensure that this exchange of information is consistent with national and international provisions on privacy and data protection.

2 - Cooperation between legal authorities

a) Basis and means for cooperation in confiscation, mutual assistance, and extradition

A necessary condition to improve mutual legal assistance on money laundering cases, is that countries acknowledge the offense of money laundering in other countries as an acceptable basis for mutual legal assistance. The group agreed that countries should consider extending the scope of the offence of money laundering to reach any other crimes for which there is a link to narcotics, or to all serious offenses, and let the definition for this wider money laundering offense open between different options. Furthermore, it agreed that :

- countries should adopt a definition covering the offense of drug money laundering compatible with the definition of the Vienna Convention.

33
- countries should try to ensure, on a bilateral or multilateral basis, that different knowledge standards in national definitions -i.e. different standards concerning the intentional element of the infraction- do not affect the ability or willingness of countries to provide each other with mutual legal assistance.

34
Furthermore, international cooperation should be supported by a network of bilateral and multilateral agreements and arrangements based on generally shared legal concepts with the aim of providing practical measures to affect the widest possible range of mutual assistance.

35
The current works in the framework of the Council of Europe, concerning international cooperation as regards search, seizure and confiscation of the proceeds from crime, could constitute the basis of an important multilateral agreement on this matter. Accordingly, countries should encourage international conventions such as the draft convention of the Council of Europe on confiscation of the proceeds from offenses.

b) Focus of improved mutual assistance on money laundering issues

Experience of international cooperation on money laundering issues shows that improvements are necessary on the following topics :

36
- Cooperative investigations - Cooperative investigations among appropriate competent authorities of countries, should be encouraged.

37
- Mutual assistance in criminal matters - There should be procedures for mutual assistance in criminal matters regarding the use of compulsory measures including the production of records by financial institutions and other persons, the search of persons and premises, seizure and obtaining of evidence for use in money laundering investigations and prosecutions and in related actions in foreign jurisdictions.

38
- Seizure and confiscation - There should be authority to take expeditious action in response to requests by foreign countries to identify, freeze, seize and confiscate proceeds or other property of corresponding value to such proceeds, based on money laundering or the crimes underlying the laundering activity.

39
- Coordination of prosecution actions - To avoid conflicts of jurisdiction, consideration should be given to devising and applying mechanisms for determining the best venue for prosecution of defendants in the interests of justice in cases that are subject to prosecution in more than one country. Similarly, there should be arrangements for coordinating seizure and confiscation proceedings which may include the sharing of confiscated assets.

40
- Extradition - Countries should have procedures in place to extradite, where possible, individuals charged with a money laundering offense or related offenses. With respect to its national legal system, each country should recognize money laundering as an extraditable offense. Subject to their legal frameworks, countries may consider simplifying extradition by allowing direct transmission of extradition requests between appropriate ministries, extraditing persons based only on warrants of arrests or judgments, extraditing their nationals, and/or introducing a simplified extradition of consenting persons who waive formal extradition proceedings.

CONCLUSION

The delegates to the Financial Action Task Force agreed that the presidency of the Task Force would address this report to finance ministers of participating countries, which would submit it to their Heads of State or Government, and circulate it to other competent authorities.

The group agreed that decisions from the Summit of the Heads of State or Government of seven major industrial nations, which convened the Financial Task Force, would be crucial for the implementation of the recommendations and further work and studies. Political impetus would also be particularly necessary to crystallize strong coordinated overall international action, and to define the best ways to associate other countries, including drug producing countries, to the fight against money laundering.

While discussing the most adequate ways by which the follow-up to its works could be organized, the group emphasized that the wider the number of countries applying these recommandations (including countries which have weak or no regulations against money laundering) the greater their efficiency would be. It considered that a regular assessment of progress realized in enforcing money laundering measures would stimulate countries to give to these issues a high priority, and would contribute to a better mutual understanding and hence to an improvement of the national systems to combat money laundering.

DOCUMENT C

Report of the Caribbean Drug Money Laundering Conference
Oranjestad, Aruba, June 8-10, 1990 (Extracts)
Source: Foreign and Commonwealth Office, London

DELIBERATIONS AND RECOMMENDATIONS OF THE CONFERENCE

The Conference acknowledged that money laundering is an international problem affecting individual countries and that to combat this problem requires an international approach involving cooperation among all countries.

The Conference recognized and appreciated that the principles laid down in the 40 recommendations of the G-15 Financial Action Task Force on money laundering and the following 21 complementary recommendations developed by the experts are designed to address the money laundering problem.

Anti Money Laundering Authority

1.   Adequate resources need to be dedicated to fighting money laundering and other drug related financial crimes. In countries where experience in combating money laundering and other drug related financial crimes is limited, there need to be competent authorities which specialize in money laundering investigations and prosecutions and related forfeiture actions, advise financial institutions and regulatory authorities on anti-money laundering measures, and receive and evaluate suspicious transaction information from financial institutions and regulators and currency reports, if required, to be filed by individuals or institutions.

Crime of Money Laundering

2.   Consistent with recommendation **5** of the **Financial Action Task Force** and recognizing that the objectives of combating money laundering are shared by the members of this Conference, each country in determining for itself what crimes ought to constitute predicate offences, should be fully aware of the practical evidentiary complications which may arise if money laundering is made an offence only with respect to certain very specific predicate offences.

3.   In accordance with the **Vienna Convention,** each country should, subject to its constitutional principles and the basic concepts of its legal system, criminalize conspiracy or association to engage in, and aiding and abetting drug trafficking, money laundering and other serious drug-related offences and subject such activities to stringent criminal sanctions.

4.   When criminalizing money laundering, the national legislature should consider:

a.   whether money laundering should only qualify as an offence in cases where the offender actually knew that he was dealing with funds derived from crime or whether it should also qualify as an offence in cases where the offender ought to have known that this was the case;

b.   whether it should be relevant that the predicate offence may have been committed outside the territorial jurisdiction of the country where the laundering occurred;

c.   whether it is sufficient to criminalize the laundering of illegally obtained funds, or whether other property which may serve as a means of payment should also be covered.

5.   Where it is not otherwise a crime, countries should consider enacting statutes which criminalize the knowing payment, receipt or transfer, or attempted payment, receipt or transfer of property known to represent the proceeds of drug trafficking or money laundering, where the recipient of the property is a public official, political candidate, or political party. In countries where it is already a crime, countries should consider the imposition of enhanced punishment or other sanctions, such as forfeiture of office.

Attorney-Client   Privilege

6.   The fact that a person acting as a financial advisor or nominee is an attorney, should not in and of itself be sufficient reason for such person to invoke an attorney-client privilege.

Confiscation

7.   Confiscation measures should provide for the authority to seize, freeze and confiscate, at the request of a foreign state, property in the jurisdiction in which such property is located regardless of whether the owner of the property or any persons who committed the offence making the property subject to confiscation are present or have ever been present within the jurisdiction.

8.　　　　Countries should provide for the possibility of confiscating any property which represents assets which have been directly or indirectly derived from drug offences or related money laundering offenses (property confiscation), and may also provide for a system of pecuniary sanctions based on an assessment of the value of assets which have been directly or indirectly derived from such offences. In the latter case, the pecuniary sanctions concerned might be recoverable from any asset of the convicted person which may be available (value confiscation).

9.　　　　Confiscation measures may provide that all or part of any property confiscated be transferred directly for use by competent authorities, or be sold and the proceeds of such sales deposited into a fund dedicated to the use by competent authorities in anti-narcotics and anti-money laundering efforts.

10.　　　　Confiscation measures should also apply to narcotic drugs and psychotropic substances, precursor and essential chemicals, equipment and materials used or destined for the illicit manufacture, preparation, distribution and use of narcotic drugs and psychotropic substances.

Disposition of Confiscated Chemicals and Property

11.　　　　Serious problems may arise for some countries concerning the final disposition of precursor and essential chemicals, equipment or materials once confiscated, and which were originally produced elsewhere. Countries should work cooperatively with a view towards seeking appropriate solutions to such problems.

Administrative Authorities

12.　　　　In order to implement effectively the recommendations of the **Financial Action Task Force,** each country should have a system that provides for bank and other financial institutions supervision, including:
　　　1)　　licensing of all banks, including offices, branches, and agencies of foreign banks whether or not they take deposits or otherwise do business in the country (so-called offshore shell banks), and
　　　2) the periodic examination of institutions by authorities to ensure that the institutions have adequate anti-money laundering programs in place and are following the implementation of other recommendations of the **Financial Action Task Force.**

Similarly, in order to implement the recommendations of the **Financial Action Task Force,** there needs to be effective regulation, including licensing and examination, of institutions and businesses such as securities brokers and dealers, bureaux de change and casinos, which offer services that make them vulnerable to money laundering.

13.   Countries need to ensure that there are adequate border procedures for inspecting merchandise and carriers, including private aircraft, to detect illegal drug and currency shipments.

Recordkeeping

14.   In order to ensure implementation of the recommendations of the **Financial Action Task Force,** countries should apply appropriate administrative, civil or criminal sanctions to financial institutions which fail to maintain records for the required retention period. Financial institution supervisory authorities must take special care to ensure that adequate records are being maintained.

Currency Reporting

15.   Countries should consider the feasibility and utility of a system which requires the reporting of large amounts of currency over a certain specified amount received by businesses other than financial institutions either in one transaction or in a series of related financial transactions. These reports would be analysed routinely by competent authorities in the same manner as any currency report filed by financial institutions. Large cash purchases of property and services such as real estate and aircraft are frequently made by drug traffickers and money launderers and, consequently, are of similar interest to law enforcement. Civil and criminal sanctions would apply to businesses and persons who fail to file or falsely file reports or structure transactions with be intent to evade the reporting requirements.

Administrative Cooperation

16.   In furtherance of recommendation **30** of the **Financial Action Task Force,** information acquired about international currency flows should be shared internationally and disseminated, if possible through the services of appropriate international or regional organizations, or on existing international networks. Special agreements may also be concluded for this purpose.

International Cooperation

17.   Efforts should be made to encourage the use of the
Organization of American States (OAS) for the elaboration of
regional international Conventions on cooperation in criminal matters.
Initiatives entrusted to the **OAS** might include the drafting of a
multilateral Convention on mutual legal assistance in criminal matters
for the countries of the region and, similarly, the drafting of a Convention
on confiscation of the proceeds from crime.

18.   Member States of the **OAS** should consider signing the **OAS
Convention on Extradition,** concluded at Caracas on February 25, 1981.

19.   Each country should endeavor to ensure that its laws and other
measures regarding drug trafficking and money laundering, and bank
regulation as it pertains to money laundering, are to the greatest extent
possible as effective as the laws and other measures of all other
countries in the region .

Training and Assistance

20.   As a follow-up, there should be regular meetings among
competent judicial, law enforcement and supervisory authorities of the
countries of the **Caribbean** and **Central American** region in order to
discuss experiences in the fight against drug money laundering and
emerging trends and techniques.

21.   In order to enable countries with small economies and
limited resources to develop appropriate drug money laundering
prevention programs, other countries should consider widening the
scope of their international technical assistance programs, and to pay
particular attention to the need of training and otherwise
strengthening the quality and preserving the integrity of judicial, legal
and law enforcement systems.

CONCLUSION

The delegates agreed either to refer the 40 recommendations of the G-15 Financial Action Task Force on money laundering, as well as the 21 recommendations listed in this Report to their respective governments for consideration with a view toward implementation or to recommend the acceptance and implementation thereof to the extent that they have not already done so.

The Conference acknowledged that the implementation of some of the recommendations might entail for countries with small economies the employment of human and financial resources beyond their actual capability. In order to determine the extent of such resource requirements, it was suggested that a needs survey should be conducted in each country and the findings thereof centrally collected with the Chairman of the Aruba Drug Money Laundering Conference by 30 September 1990 for joint consideration and the design of an appropriate program of action.

It was further agreed by the delegates that each country would report on the decision of their respective governments regarding the 40 recommendations of the G-15 Financial Action Task Force on money laundering, as well as the 21 recommendations listed in this Report to the Chairman of the Aruba Drug Money Laundering Conference by 31 December 1990.

DOCUMENT D

Financial Action Task Force on Money Laundering
Report, 1990-1991, Paris 13 May, 1991
Source: H.M.Treasury, London

The delegations agreed to continue FATF for a period of five years, with a decision to review progress after three years, and to reconsider the continuing need, mission, and work program for this specialized group.

The group agreed to four ongoing tasks for FATF-3 and its successors : (1) self-reporting and mutual assessment (monitoring and surveillance) on the adoption and implementation of FATF recommendations by all members ; (2) coordination and oversight of efforts to encourage non-members to adopt and implement the recommendations ; (3) making further recommendations and evaluations of counter-measures while serving as a forum for considering developments in money laundering techniques domestically and worldwide, and for the exchange of information on enforcement techniques to combat money laundering ; and (4) standing ready to facilitate cooperation between organizations concerned with combatting money laundering and between individual countries or territories.

The decision to continue was taken as part of a critical political commitment to implementation of the recommendations each member government has endorsed. Members agreed to continue the self-evaluation process begun in FATF-2 to measure their progress in implementing the 40 recommendations, and, in a decision that underscores the great importance attached to this process, the members agreed to initiate a process of mutual evaluation. The decision was that each member would normally be subject to being evaluated on progress measures three years after endorsing the FATF-1 recommendations.

These decisions, perhaps unique to bodies of this kind, assure the global community that the major financial center countries are truly determined to adopt and implement effective countermeasures against money laundering.

The self-evaluation process begun in 1991 utilized a compliance grid which produced comprehensive evaluation of progress on legal and financial matters, although this was to some extent subjective, given the current lack of harmonization of laws and therefore of responses It was encouraging that the majority of members have substantially implemented the FATF-1 recommendations on legal matters. Substantial progress has also been made on complying with the recommendations relative to the role of the financial system, and strengthening international cooperation, but some countries need to make a greater effort in these matters.

FATF-3 will see a refinement and extension of the self-evaluation process, with an emphasis that goes beyond ratification of international conventions such as the Vienna an Strassburg convention and adoption of laws, to implementation and practice.

FATF-2 proved a useful forum for discussing the wide range of issues not yet concluded as action recommendations, issues which will be further explored by FATF-3. The legal issues group discussed possible refinements of existing recommendations, including those involving predicate crimes, corporate criminal liability, mutual legal assistance, and asset sharing. Similarly, the financial cooperation group, which included special presentations by financial enforcement officials of money laundering typologies and investigative practices, took note of the increasing use of non-bank and non-traditional financial institutions and other businesses and professions to convert the proceeds of drug and other crime. The group noted the need to continue monitoring new money laundering practices, and called for further work on developing a common action plan with respect to non-bank financial institutions and other businesses and professions.

A third working group charged with planning the future of FATF, which proposed an extension of the mutual evaluation process, also developed the plan of succession to the FATF Presidency, and outlined procedures for establishing a Secretariat within an existing international organization. The recommendation was that FATF Presidency be supported in the future by a steering group, and would work with and through this Secretariat. The members agreed to negotiate the creation of a specialized Secretariat with the Organization for Economic Cooperation and Development (OECD).

Finally, FATF-2 proposed that the organization, acting through its Secretariat, and drawing upon the expertise of its members, should attempt to help guide the provision of technical assistance between members or to non-members, upon request by either, subject to the availability of resources among the members who agree to provide such assistance.

INTRODUCTION

In July 1989, in Paris, the Heads of State or Government of the seven major industrialized countries, and the president of the Commission of the European Communities, convened a Financial Action Task Force, the FATF, under French presidency, with the aim of fighting money laundering. In addition to summit participants (United States, Japan, Germany, France, United Kingdom, Italy, Canada, and the Commission of the European Communities), eight countries (Sweden, Netherlands, Belgium, Luxembourg, Switzerland, Austria, Spain and Australia), joined the Task Force in order to enlarge its expertise and also to reflect the views of other countries particularly concerned by, or having particular experience in the fight against money laundering, at the national or international level.

In April 1990, the Task force issued a report with a comprehensive progam of forty recommendations to fight money laundering. This report was endorsed by the Finance ministers or other competent ministers of all FATF members in May 1990.

At the Houston Summit of the Heads of State or Government of the seven major industrialized countries, in July 1990, the Task Force was, as agreed at the May meeting of Task Force Finance Ministers, reconvened for a second year, still under the chairmanship of France, to assess and facilitate the implementation of the forty recommendations, and to complement them where appropriate. It was agreed that all OECD and financial center countries that would subscribe to the recommendations of the Task Force should be invited to participate in this exercise. All other countries were invited to participate in the fight against money laundering and to implement the recommendations of the FATF. It was agreed that the report of the second FATF should be completed before the next meeting of the Heads of State or Government of the Seven.

In addition to the initial members, experts of Denmark, Finland, Greece, Ireland, New Zealand, Norway, Portugal, Turkey, Hong Kong and the Gulf Cooperation Council participated in some or all the meetings, together with law enforcement specialists of Interpol and the Customs Cooperation Council. Almost all these participants(*) subsequently endorsed the report. and thus qualified for membership of the FATF.

Five series of meetings were held in Paris. More than 160 experts from various ministries, law enforcement authorities, and bank supervisory and regulatory agencies, met and worked together during six months. To facilitate the work of the Task Force, and to take advantage of the expertise of its participants, three working groups were created, which focused respectively on the implementation of recommendations relating to legal matters (working-group 1, presidency : United States), on the implementation of recommendations pertaining to the role of financial systems and international cooperation (working-group 2, presidency : Belgium), and on external mobilization and follow-up (working-group 3, presidency : United Kingdom). Their comprehensive reports constitute the key background material of this report.

Building upon this work, this report gives an assessment of the implementation of existing recommendations (part I), provides an overview of the geographical extension of the FATF program against money laundering (part II), and proposes guidelines as regards the follow-up to the second FATF (part III).

(*) The designations employed in this report do not imply the expression of any opinion whatsoever on the part of the group concerning the legal status of any country, territory, city or area, or of its authorities, or concerning the delimitation of its frontiers or boundaries.

I - ASSESSMENT OF THE IMPLEMENTATION,
AND ENHANCEMENTS TO THE EXISTING RECOMMENDATIONS

A - LEGAL MATTERS

On the mutual legal assistance matters, the group assessed the implementation of FATF recommendations 4 through 8 and 32 through 40 and discussed possible enhancements to existing recommendations.

Of particular concern to the group was that the recommendations be implemented in a way that would maximize cooperation in international money laundering cases.

1 - Global overview of the implementation

A legal issues surveillance grid was established, on the basis of answers by participants to a standardized questionnaire. Participants also provided a narrative explanation of the status of implementation. The participants were also requested to indicate how the differences in the scope and application of money laundering offences might affect mutual legal assistance.

All the FATF-1 participants have responded to the compliance grid and questionnaire.

All new participating countries and territories also responded.

However, the Task Force noted that, to some extent, the compliance grid format resulted in a subjective measure of progress of uncertain reliability, because there has been no harmonization of the national answers.

Nevertheless, it is encouraging that the vast majority of the answers to the surveillance grid are positive, (A : measure already implemented, or B : measure soon to be implemented) and that very few answers "C" (measure whose implementation is not foreseen) were obtained.

The majority of FATF-1 members have substantially implemented the full range of FATF recommendations within the scope of legal questions. Most of these countries have added legislation or taken other steps in 1990 which places them in the substantial implementation category. It is encouraging to note that several new participants are in a similar situation.

A limited number of nations are still evaluating how best to effect implementation and have not introduced legislation or taken other steps towards implementation.

2 - Ways to facilitate the implementation of some recommendations

The Task Force discussed how to solve the difficulties that are still obstacles to a fully efficient international cooperation to combat money laundering. It has examined how to improve domestic legislation, as required by recommendations 4 to 8, in order to facilitate the mutual legal assistance (recommendations 32 through 40).

The FATF is based or the premise that meaningful progress against money laundering can only be made through international cooperation, by minimizing both the barriers that remain in domestic laws and their effects on mutual assistance. It is clear that progress still needs to be made in these directions.

It was agreed that countries should periodically review their legislation and make whatever modifications that may be required to respond to changes in money laundering methods.

The Task Force determined to put forward refinements or extensions of existing recommendations, as discussed below.

a) <u>Recommendation 4</u> (Working definition of money laundering)

This definition, based on the relevant provision of the Vienna Convention, is an important step to the harmonisation of legislation. All the participants who answered the surveillance grid are, or should be very soon, in compliance with recommendation 4.

b) <u>Recommendation 5</u> (Predicate crimes)

Recommendation 5 provides in part that "...each country should consider extending the offense of drug money laundering to any other crimes for which there is a link to narcotics..." while recommendations 5 also sets forth the alternative possibility of criminalizing based on all or specified serious crimes.

Very few countries have in fact enacted specific money laundering legislation in which all or most serious proceeds- generating offenses were included as predicate crimes. **Nonetheless, two international documents have been or are about to be completed which intersect with recommendation 5.** Specifically, the Council of Europe convention on laundering, tracing, seizure and confiscation of proceeds of crime, and the European Communities proposed directive on the prevention of use of the financial system for the purpose of money laundering, on which a common position was reached on 14 February, 1991, and which will be finalized in the near future.

The Council of Europe convention requires parties to adopt measures to enable confiscation of the proceeds of any criminal offense. With respect to money laundering, it allows parties to declare that the offense of money laundering is limited to specified predicate offenses.

The common position on the EEC directive provides for money laundering to cover drug offenses and any other serious criminal activities designated as such for the purposes of this Directive by each member state.

Given the pervasiveness of money laundering in many fields of criminal activity, few countries expressed the sentiment that was expressed in FATF-1 that money laundering should be limited to drug crimes. Hence, important progress towards consensus was made in FATF-2 on this issue, although no agreement was reached on the scope of the predicates.

c) <u>Recommendation 7</u> (Corporate criminal liability)

Recommendation 7 provides in pertinent part "... where possible, corporations themselves - not only their employees - should be subject to criminal liability". There was extensive discussion on this point. **There was general agreement that the concept of corporate criminal liability, or at least, the availability of stringent civil or administrative actions is an important part of an effective anti-money laundering program.** Yet, almost half of the FATF member countries do not have corporate criminal liability law and a number of these countries have only limited authority to respond with civil or administrative actions with respect to criminal offenses by corporations. It was observed that constitutional or fundamental legal principles precluded a country from enacting corporate criminal sanctions. In other instances, it was simply a matter of no legislation having been enacted to criminalize corporate conduct. **The intention to continue to study the issue with a positive mind was generally expressed.**

d) <u>Recommendations 33 to 40</u> (Mutual legal assistance and other forms of cooperation)

Most participants soon should be able to provide mutual legal assistance to each other in international money laundering cases. But the improvement of this cooperation depends in furtherhand also on the adaptation of the domestic legislation

Most FATF members have developed a network of bilateral and multilateral conventions to facilitate mutual legal assistance, as required by recommendation 34. Austria generally prefers multilateral agreements. Japan does not plan at this stage to develop bilateral or multilateral agreements, but notes that, in its case, the conclusion of such bilateral or multilateral agreements are not prerequisite in rendering legal assistance.

Recommendations 37 and 38 (compulsory measures to be ordered by the way of mutual assistance, such as identifying the proceeds from a narcotic offence forfeiture, seizure...), will be applied very largely by all the states in the near future, as well as recommendation 40 dealing with extradition.

However, the issue of corporate criminal liability and differences in criminal offenses led to a lengthy discussion on the concern about how the manner in which countries implement the FATF recommendations could actually inhibit mutual legal assistance in money laundering cases and cooperation in related extradition and confiscation matters.

Differences in criminal offenses of money laundering very often create difficulties in implementing recommendations 32 through 38, which reinforce the need for a comprehensive mutual legal assistance system for money laundering and asset confiscation.

In a significant number of countries, the application of the principle of dual criminality would in all likelihood preclude extradition and mutual legal assistance if the request relates to a predicate not covered by the money laundering offense in the requested country. In the view of several countries, this result indicates another reason to enact money laundering offenses that cover a wide range of predicate offenses or all serious crimes.

It also was noted that in many countries the perpetrator of a crime cannot be prosecuted for laundering the proceeds of his crime. As far as possible, differences in approach to the liability of the perpetrator of the underlying offense should not inhibit the provision of assistance.

On the other hand, differences in corporate liability would affect mutual legal assistance in only a few countries. It was felt that a country that does not have corporate criminal liability should strive to honor a request for assistance in a case in which the requesting country is prosecuting a corporation for money laundering, e.g., by resorting to civil or administrative actions available under its laws.

Finally, it was pointed out that with respect to the different forms of international cooperation in criminal matters (mutual legal assistance, extradition, asset confiscation, etc.), different standards of dual criminality might evolve in national or international legislation or practice commensurate with the object and purpose of each specific type of cooperation.

For the purposes of mutual legal assistance, it was felt that participants should have an attitude of some flexibility in relation to the issue of dual criminality. Difficulties in practice, should not affect their readiness to provide one another with mutual legal assistance (apart from extradition).

To the extent that dual criminality remains a problem in progress towards facilitating mutual legal assistance and cooperation, the harmonization of domestic legislations may be the surest way in the longer run. In the shorter term, bilateral and multilateral agreements in these areas are probably more achievable.

e) Recommendation 39 and international asset sharing

Recommendation 39 encourages arrangements for coordinating seizure and confiscation proceedings which may include the sharing of confiscated assets. Actually, very few cases of sharing of assets confiscated in international money laundering operations have occurred. This may result, among other reasons, from the difficulty in determining the "fair" share to be given to other countries. Public accounting rules may also discourage this.

Ways to further facilitate the implementation of recommendation 39, with regard to international asset sharing, remains a matter for further discussion in the FATF.

B - ENHANCEMENT OF THE ROLE OF THE FINANCIAL SYSTEM, AND STRENGTHENING OF INTERNATIONAL COOPERATION

The group has assessed the implementation of recommendations 9 to 32. Substantial progress has been made to implement most of them, but some participating countries, should still devote great efforts on the furtherance and the completion of this process in the months and years to come (section 1).

Money launderers have increasingly turned to non-traditional financial institutions or other businesses or professions to convert the proceeds of their illegal activities into legitimate funds - as countries have tightened their control on traditional financial institutions or professions. Action should be undertaken to address this situation along the lines sketched out in section 2 a), and new money laundering practices should be updated regularly, with great care.

Relations with countries which do not or insufficiently apply the FATF recommendations require periodic exchange of information among law enforcement authorities (section 2 b).

The administrative systems to detect money laundering receive more support when they apply to cash movements at the border than when they consist in reporting all currency movements (section 2 c).

In general, more comprehensive cooperation is needed among all authorities involved in the fight against money laundering. Considerable progress has still to be made to exchange information at all levels (section 2 d).

1 - <u>Global overview of the implementation.</u>

As with legal matters, a "surveillance" grid has been established on the basis of voluntary answers by countries to a questionnaire. It is a useful gauge, but only a first attempt to get a global view of the implementation, since all the answers were not harmonized. A more thorough surveillance will result from a detailed examination of each country, as proposed in section III. At this time, the uncertain reliability of the answers led the group to the opinion that any publication of the grid would be premature.

When assessing the implementation status of <u>recommendations 9 to 32</u> (enhancement of the role of financial system, and strengthening of international administrative cooperation), one has to give special attention to the answers of the 16 members of FATF-1, and to notice that only 18 recommendations (out of 24) are relevant for analysis, the remaining six calling for further study (n°s 11, 23, 24, 30, 31) or for an alternative aproach (rec. n° 19).

It is very encouraging that, one year after the recommendations of FATF-1 have been drafted, the vast majority of the answers to the surveillance grid by the FATF-1 members are positive of which roughly half are measures "already implemented" (A) and close to half "measures soon to be implemented"(B), no later than Jan 1, 1993 in most cases.

Another interesting feature of the answers is that most of the negative ones apply to three recommendations (n°s 21, 23 and 24) which are considered difficult to implement by most countries, and are discussed below in this report.

It should also be noted that the EC Directive, which will be approved by mid 1991 and implemented before January 1, 1993, enforces 15 of the recommendations among its member countries, the remaining ones (21 to 25, 30 to 32) being either outside the objectives of the directive or unnecessary in the case of EC members (Rec. 19).

In summary, the implementation of most of the recommendations 9 to 32 appears already fairly good among members of FATF-1, and few cases of non compliance should remain by year-end 1992.

As regards these juridictions which participated in FATF-2 before being formal "members", it proved difficult for some to provide a detailed report, although the majority did so and the majority of these respondants reported substantial implementation of the recommmentations.

2 - Ways of facilitating the implementation of certain recommendations

Law enforcement authorities of participating countries as well as representatives of Interpol and of the Customs Cooperation Council were invited to share, during a full-day meeting on March 15, their technical experience regarding the new money laundering practices they encounter, which countries or areas do not or insufficiently apply FATF recommendations, and the cooperation between them.

Their discussions helped to determine some ways of facilitating the implementation of recommendations 11, 21/22, 23/24, and 31/32.

a) New money laundering practices and implementation of recommendation 11.

As countries have significantly tightened their control on deposit taking financial institutions, money launderers have increasingly turned to other financial institutions and other professions and businesses which handle significant amonts of cash, to convert the proceeds of illegal activities into legitimate funds. It was noted that, as regards other financial institutions and professions, first steps have been taken.

Today, non-traditional financial institutions or other businesses or professions are involved in a growing number, possibly a majority, of money laundering cases, estimated from the number of seizures in the cases unveiled in some countries(*).

Non-traditional financial institutions or professions provide "bank-like" services, thus running the risk that they can be used by money launderers in ways similar to traditional financial institutions or professions, while not being subject to the same regulations and controls.

In order to facilitate a wider implementation of regulations against money laundering, a report was prepared on a typology of money laundering practices for non-traditional financial institutions or professions, by the US Customs Service on the basis of the information on actual cases made available by the United States, the United Kingdom and the Hong Kong competent authorities.

(*) Countries participating in the FATF process reported numerous incidents in which money launderers were utilizing the non-traditional systems within their respective countries. Examples of these incidents include : (a) cash from cocaine crack sales deposited into a bureaux de change, funds transferred abroad for collection in US dollars, funds collected abroad in US dollars ; (b) cash from drug sales used to purchases gambling chips in a casino, proceeds returned in the form of "winnings" through a casino check, casino check deposited into bank account represented as "winning" ; (c) drug cash used to purchase antique firearms and art from auction houses and private individuals abroad, property returned and sold through domestic auction houses, fund transferred abroad and then returned to purchase real estate ; and, (d) a solicitor accepting drug cash from drug trafficking client, placing the funds into the solicitor's trust account, the solicitor utilizing the funds in the trust account to purchase real estate in the solicitor's name on behalf of the drug trafficking client. Variants of these schemes abound.

The group, reflecting the opinion of law enforcement specialists, made it clear that the FATF should not try to make an exhaustive, single list of all non-traditional financial institutions or professions that might be involved in money laundering practices, but should rather seek to address them as a whole, and mention, as an example, some "high risk" professions or institutions that could possibly be used in the cash-placement stage of the money laundering process.

These professions or institutions can be classified under four broad headings :

1 - organizations whose prime function is to provide a form of financial service but which, at least in some FATF member countries, fall outside the scope of the regulated financial sector. For example, bureaux de change, cheque cashers and money transmission services, including those provided through correspondent relationships outside the formal banking sector.

2 - Organizations whose primary purpose is to offer some form of gambling activity. For example : casinos, lotteries and various games of chance.

3 - Organizations whose primary function is to buy and sell high value items. For example : precious metal and gem dealers, auction houses, real estate agents ; automobile, aeroplane and boat dealers.

4 - Professionals who, in the course of providing their professional services, offer, in some countries, client account facilities. For example : lawyers, accountants, notaries and certain travel agents.

This typology ought to facilitate the implementation of recommendation 11 with the degree of flexibility that is necessary from one country to another, given the differences in the use of cash and in the effective role of each profession.

Outside the formal financial sector, professions which provide any of the financial services listed in the annex of the Second Banking Coordination Directive of the European Community, as well as life-insurance coverage, should be subject as far as possible to recommendations 12-22 and 26-29. However, recommendation 27 is not intended to oblige member countries to establish one supervisory institution for each and any of these professions : the nature of regulations and the means to ensure compliance are to be decided by each country. The group considered that the organisations cited under heading n° 1 of the typology, and the professionals cited under heading n° 4 of the typology, belonged to this category. However, with respect to the professionals, law and practices relating to professional confidentiality restrict in many countries the possibility of implementing some recommendations.

Some other types of business or professions can also be used in the cash placement stage of money laundering, for instance those cited under headings n° 2 and 3 of the typology, although their effective role is different from one country to another. For such activities, it would be extremely difficult for governments to ensure across the board compliance with the relevant FATF recommendations. **But there are steps that governments could take to raise awareness among those businesses most at risk and to combat their being used by launderers : dialogue with professional organizations which represent them, issuance of guidance notes - especially on how to recognize suspicious transactions - and, for some of these professions as designated by each government, implementation of the customer identification and record keeping requirements above a specific size of transaction, and, where possible, implementation of a suspicious transaction reporting scheme.**

While offering such guidance to facilitate the implementation of recommendaticn 11 by governments, the group felt it wise not to add anything to the existing recommendations 9 to 11, considering that money laundering is an evolving process and that discrepancies in the actual field of activity for the same business exist between countries. With this in mind, the importance was stressed of identifying and regularly updating "vulnerable businesses/professions", i.e. businesses or professions with a potential for misuse by money launderers, and to exchange information about them. **To this end, it was suggested that, in the future, the FATF keep itself informed about the evolution of money laundering practices and exchange information about actual cases of money laundering.**

b) <u>Implementation of recommendations 21/22</u>.

The Group has thoroughly examined how useful it would be to refine recommendations 21 (relation with countries which do not or insufficiently apply these recommendations) and 22 (application of the recommendations to branches and majority owned subsidiaries located abroad).

The Group observed that one way to facilitate the implementation of recommendation 21 would be to establish an internationally agreed "black list" of countries which do not or insufficiently apply the FATF recommendations. But the group felt, and law enforcement authorities confirmed, that the FATF should not attempt to produce, for the time being, a public common minimal list. Each country will be in a position to decide which jurisdictions must receive special attention, based on the answers given by its own financial institutions in accordance with recommendation 22. The absence of any list of "regulatory havens" makes it difficult however for financial institutions to focus their special attention in the sense required by recommendations 21 and 22.

Geographical zones where money laundering schemes develop, or might develop, are, in some cases, well-known and, in any case, can be characterised by some criteria. Such criteria include the lack of any legal requirement for institutions or professions to maintain records for the identification of their clients or the transactions performed, the absence of a legal permission for law enforcement authorities to have access to these records, and the impossibility for them of communicating these records to law enforcement authorities of others countries.

c) <u>Administrative Systems to detect money laundering (recommendations 23, 24)</u>.

<u>Recommendation 23</u>

Some countries strongly support the implementation of measures to detect or monitor important cash movements at the border to address the problem of cross border shipments of illegal source currency, either through a system of mandatory reporting of these movements, or through the possibility of freezing suspected assets[*] or through any other means that does not restrict the freedom of capital movements. Other countries emphasize that the information gathered in such a fashion should only be used to fight money laundering practices. This issue should be addressed again in the future.

---

[*] This way of implementing recommendation 23 would consist in measures whereby cash, monetary instruments, precious metal/stones, and other valuable movable property, which are to be imported to or exported from their jurisdiction, may be seized/detained by the competent law enforcement/judicial authorities pending investigation and/or proceedings to freeze such property where there are reasonable grounds to believe that such property directly or indirectly represents the proceeds of a criminal activity.

Recommendation 24

A large majority of the participating countries continue to consider that the implementation of a system to report all important currency transactions is difficult to envisage. They feel that at least similar results can be attained through the less burdensome system of a properly implemented suspicious transactions reporting scheme. Countries which have a currency transactions reporting scheme believe that it is an essential complement to suspicious transactions reporting.

d) Cooperation between law enforcement authorities, outside mutual legal assistance, and ways to improve bilateral exchanges (rec 31 and 32).

Law enforcement authorities reported that they are sometimes faced with legal or technical difficulties when cooperating - such as the right to privacy, confidentiality privileges or the sensitivity of some countries to tax-related issues. It was pointed out that a number of international agreements already provide an adequate basis for cooperation, but that, even in cases where such agreements exist, satisfactory cooperation does not always exist in practice.

The reasons for these shortcomings range from differences in the definition of the predicate offense (underlying crime), sometimes the absence of personal relations with their counterparts, to refusals to answer the questions from another country. All these elements hamper the efficiency of bilateral cooperation among administrative authorities.

Strong efforts should therefore be made to improve the cooperation among law enforcement authorities, enabling a more efficient implementation of recommendations 31 and 32.

"Contact lists" should be made available for instance through the UNIDCP (United Nations International Drug Control Program). Countries should also communicate to each other intelligence information, either in the framework of a legally organized cooperation, or informally - in which case the information should be used according to guidelines to be specified(*).

If was felt that law enforcement authorities and other relevant experts should regularly meet to exchange their views about money laundering practices and geographical networks. Their findings should be reported to the FATF.

Interpol and the Customs Cooperation Council could have a special responsability for gathering and disseminating this information. In addition, to help identifying geographical networks involved in money laundering, the FOPAC (Fonds provenant des activités criminelles), a division of Interpol which collects data about proceeds of criminal activities, could provide a good basis for such exchanges, in cooperation with the CCC.

Furthermore, exchanges of information on suspicious transactions, persons or corporations, should take place between Interpol and the Customs Cooperation Council. This information should then be disclosed to their members at their request, with the appropriate level of confidentiality.

(*) The information passed on to authorities of other participating countries should be used only for anti-money laundering purposes, and for the investigation of the underlying offenses, and could be submitted to restrictions. In practice, informal exchanges could reveal themselves very useful for implementation of recommendations 31 and 32.

II – GEOGRAPHICAL EXTENSION OF THE FATF PROGRAM
AGAINST MONEY LAUNDERING

Money laundering channels, at least those on a broad scale, generally involve international operations. This enables money launderers to use differences in national laws, regulations and enforcement practices.

For instance, a money laundering operation could involve the following stages : money from illegal activities e.g. drugs cash proceeds would be exported from regulated countries to unregulated ones ; then the cash can be placed through the domestic formal financial system of these" regulatory havens" ; the subsequent stage could then be a return of these funds to regulated countries with safe layering and integration opportunities, particularly through wire transfers. Of course, informal financial systems in "regulatory havens" are also a cause of concern

This type of money laundering operation, based on cash shipments abroad, probably plays an important role. However, once drug cash has been introduced into the formal financial institution, other techniques may be used by launderers to transfer funds abroad, using offshore companies. For instance, using the technique of "double invoicing", goods may be purchased at inflated prices by domestic companies owned by money launderers, from offshore corporation which they also own. The difference between the price and true value can be deposited offshore and paid to the offshore company. It then can be repatriated at will. Variations of the "double invoicing" technique bound . Some regulatory havens make it easy to set up shell companies, and to keep company ownership anonymous in the hope of attracting both license revenue and business for their own firms.

When the funds are repatriated after laundering abroad, the detection of their criminal origin is extremely difficult. Even if detected, differences in national laws, regulations and enforcement practices seriously impair the efficiency of enquiries and law enforcement measures.

This has been the rationale behind the effort to extend worldwide the FATF program against money laundering, and to give special attention to relations with countries which have a significant financial system, but do not or insufficiently apply this program.

A - GEOGRAPHICAL EXTENSION

The Houston Summit recommended that "all OECD and financial center countries that subscribe to the recommendations of the Task Force should be invited to participate in the FATF", and appealed to "all other countries to participate in the fight against money laundering and to implement the recommendations of the FATF".

The first step to broaden the geographical coverage is an effort throughout the world to present and explain the FATF recommendations, with a view towards obtaining formal endorsements, and, as far as possible, universal effective implementation to these recommendations. This worldwide mobilization against money laundering was launched in three directions.

1 - OECD countries and other major financial centers

a) The nine OECD countries which had not participated in the FATF-1 (Denmark, Finland, Greece, Iceland, Ireland, New-Zealand, Norway, Portugal, Turkey), were invited to participate in the FATF-2, provided they accepted the existing recommendations. All these countries, except Iceland, took part to the meetings of FATF-2, in order to help them clarify what would be at stake if they endorsed the recommendations, and to share with them experiences in the field of fighting money laundering. A meeting, on December 17, was specially devoted to briefing them.

At this stage, **Denmark, Finland, Ireland, New-Zealand, Norway, Portugal and Turkey have endorsed the FATF recommendations, and thus qualified for membership.**

b) In addition, the FATF decided that the three most important off-shore banking centers and areas, Hong-Kong, Singapore and the Gulf, would be invited, under the same conditions, to participate.

Hong-Kong attended FATF meetings and participated actively. It endorsed the recommendations, thus qualifying for membership. It has already taken major steps to implement the recommendations.

In order to reach a number of financial center countries in the Gulf, it was decided to invite the **Gulf Cooperation Council** (composed of Saudi Arabia, Bahrain, the United Arab Emirates, Oman, Qatar and Kuwait) to participate, rather than invite the individual countries in the area at this time. A representative of the GCC did participate in one of the meetings, but because of the situation in area, has not been able to coordinate a decision on endorsement of the recommendations among the GCC member countries as yet. The GCC will continue to be invited to future sessions.

Singapore has yet to endorse the FATF-1 recommendations, and formally accept the invitation. However, discussions have commenced and hopefully, they will lead to Singapore endorsing the recommendations and joining the group. It is, of course, appropriate that a country which has such eminence as a financial centre should join in the international effort against money laundering which membership of the Task Force provides. Singapore representatives have recently informally indicated their intention to participate, on the same basis as others.

2 - <u>Other financial centers</u>

Specific countries or territories were identified as being particularly exposed to money laundering, due to the importance of their international financial activities, to their geographical location -territories close to important drug producing, transit or consuming countries-, or, in some cases, to the low degree of regulation of their financial system, or to the involvement of one or several of their financial institutions in past money laundering operations. Contacts with these financial centers were undertaken by FATF members having close ties with them, or being geographically close to them.

Some of these centres are related to FATF members. The Netherlands confirmed that their endorsement of the FATF recommendations also covered the **Netherlands Antilles and Aruba** and that the Kingdom had full responsibility for the territories. **Jersey, Guernsey** and the **Isle of Man** are Crown Dependencies of the United Kingdom. They have all introduced legislation to trace, freeze and confiscate the proceeds of drug trafficking, including the criminalisation of drugs money laundering. Guernsey and the Isle of Man have endorsed the recommendations of th. Task Force and Jersey has confirmed that it is fully committed to preventing the use of the Island by those engaged in drug money laundering.

The contacts with other financial centres led to the following results.

a) **Cayman Islands, Montserrat, Anguilla, British Virgin Islands, Turks and Caicos Islands and Bermuda,** which are all British Dependent Territories, have been sent the Task Force recommendations and encouraged to endorse them. They have been asked to provide details of legislative and other measures which they have taken or are intending to take to combat money laundering. They have all introduced legislation to trace, freeze and confiscate the proceeds of drug trafficking, including the criminalisation of drugs money laundering. The legislation is very similar to that in the UK. They have confirmed, in general terms, that they support the FATF recommendations. They are currently working on detailed responses to the recommendations and considering the need for administrative measures in the context of local budgets and resource constraints.

b) **Gibraltar** - The authorities in Gibraltar, which is also a British Dependent Territory, have been sent the FATF report and encouraged to endorse its recommendations. They, also, are working on a detailed response which will describe the legislative and administrative measures that they have already taken, and are intending to take, to combat money laundering.

c) **Liechtenstein** - Liechtenstein is an independent state with special relationship to Switzerland mainly due to treaties on customs and monetary policy. Switzerland assumes however no responsibilities for Liechtenstein in regard to almost all of the issues in the scope of the FATF. According to its own assessment, Liechtenstein already applies a large number of the FATF recommendations. The majority of the rest will be implemented by or in connection with the planned bill criminalizing money laundering inspired by the Swiss legislation and entering the parliamentary process this year.

d) **Monaco** - Monaco is an independent state with a special relationship with France. It is preparing for the near future a complete set of texts, very close to the French ones, to fight money laundering.

The government of Monaco has officially expressed its intention to implement the FATF recommendations.

e) **Andorra** - Andorra is a territory under co-principality of the President of the French Republic and the bishop of Seo d'Urgell, Spain. The Bishop co-prince has been officially informed by the Spanish authorities of the 40 recommendations and has received an offer to get the necessary explanatory background. Following a request by the French co-prince, the Bishop of Seo d'Urgell has officially agreed to incorporate the FATF recommendations into local regulations. The implementation will have to take into account the specificities of the status of Andorra. Andorra has taken steps to give effect to provisions of the Vienna Convention. At this stage, bank regulations in Andorra are incomplete, and there is no banking supervisory authority. However, Andorran banks have established a code of conduct. The implementation of the FATF recommendations in Andorra will be conducted in cooperation with the relevant Andorran bodies, with a close involvement of the French authorities, and of the Spanish competent authorities upon request.

These contacts with financial centers will have to be continued, in order to obtain from those who have not done so a formal endorsement of the recommendations, to help the implementation if necessary, and to ensure that this implementation is effective. Furthermore, other financial centers might be identified in the future as requiring the same approach.

3 - <u>Regional mobilization</u>

In order to provide for the widest coverage of the FATF program, other countries or territories were or will be contacted through a process of mobilization on a regional basis. This process, launched by the FATF and undertaken by various countries or regional organisations, is only a first step. As with the financial centers, the aim is to assess where the countries or territories of the regional area stand in the fight against money laundering, to obtain as soon as possible full endorsement of the recommendations by most of them, to help implement these recommendations if necessary, and to ensure that this implementation is effective.

This first step takes the form of meetings associating some FATF members, and most or all countries or territories of the region concerned. In these meetings, the FATF report is presented in detail (it had been already transmitted in June 1990 to all countries having an embassy in Paris by the FATF secretariat) and the regional countries and territories express their views on the report.

The meeting for <u>Asia</u> was organised by Japan, together with the Economic and Social Commission of the United Nations for Asia and the Pacific (ESCAP). It was held in Tokyo on February 13 to 15, 1991. Forty five countries or territories (see list in Annex) sent delegates to this meeting. The general feeling was that the success of the fight against money laundering depends crucially on the harmonization of national programs. The participants called for an early endorsement of the FATF report by the countries and areas concerned.

The meeting for countries of <u>**central and eastern Europe**</u> was organised by the Commission of the European Communities, in Brussels, on March 4, 1991. Poland, Czechoslovakia, Hungary, Bulgaria, Romania and Yugoslavia sent delegates, together with several FATF members. These countries expressed their readiness to fight money laundering, and shared the view that the design of their new financial systems should include from the beginning regulations in this regard. However, some countries expressed reservations regarding the declarations of suspicious transactions : it was underlined that strong bank secrecy was essential to obtain the confidence of the population in the new financial system, because in the old system, a general obligation existed to report any suspicion of any illegal activity. The delegates will encourage their governments to endorse as soon as possible the FATF recommendations.

A meeting of the <u>**Carribbean Islands and Central American States**</u> (see list in Annex), was organised in Aruba as early as June 1990. The experts welcomed the FATF report, added some recommendations to address specific regional issues, and urged their governments to endorse and implement the FATF program. A second meeting should take place in Kingston, Jamaïca, in June 1991, with a view to formally endorsing the FATF report.

A meeting for __Africa__ (see in annex list of participating countries) has taken place in Abidjan, Ivory Coast, on May 9, 1991, just after the annual meeting of the African Development Bank. During this meeting, it appeared clearly that it was in the interest of all african countries to participate in the fight against money laundering. Participants welcomed the FATF recommendations, and will submit them to their governments for endorsement.

A meeting with countries of __Latin America__ , organized at the initiative of the United States under the auspices of the Organization of American States, will take place in Washington on May 21 to 24.

This process of regional mobilization will have to be pursued in the future, in a flexible way, with a view to ensuring, as far as possible, world-wide implementation of the FATF program. This will require formal endorsements of the report, as well as follow-up procedures to ensure that the implementation is effective. For many countries, technical assistance might also be necessary.

B - MEASURES DIRECTED AT NON COOPERATIVE COUNTRIES

1 - The problem of "regulatory havens" and non cooperative countries or territories and existing measures to address it

The issue of how to cope with the problem of countries with no or insufficient anti- money laundering measures, was adressed in last year's report of FATF, through recommendations 21 (special attention by financial institutions to transactions and business relations with persons located in "regulatory havens"), 22 (extension of the vigilance principles applicable to financial institutions, to their branches and subsidiaries located abroad) and 23 (detection or monitoring of cash at the border).

There was also general agreement that the wider the geographical extension of the FATF program, the easier the measures to deal with non cooperative countries or territories could be implemented. For instance, to be able to implement satisfactorily recommendation 21, financial institutions would need to know which countries or territories are to be considered as "regulatory havens", in order to focus their vigilance on a small number of transactions and business relations.

In the process of geographical extension of the recommendations, it appeared clearly that some countries or territories could remain reluctant to join in the international effort against money laundering. The motivations for this reluctance are generally easy to understand. Some jurisdictions who wish to establish a financial services industry as a supplementary source of income for the national finances - through the sale of authorization for shell companies and banking licenses - and to create employment for the population, use their lack of regulations as a competitive advantage. In addition, there are administrative costs in applying anti-money laundering sanctions. "Regulatory havens" may therefore be motivated by a wish to supplement their budgetary receipts, gain a marketing advantage for their financial services industry, or avoid imposing a cost on their financial services industry, or any combinatuion of all three. Finally, extreme cases, where governments cooperate with their financial institutions in large scale money laundering operations, cannot be excluded.

These kinds of motivations to avoid taking measures against money laundering, reflect clearly a short term view : a money laundering operation, once detected, can put at risk the whole financial system in these countries or territories, through the loss of credibility and confidence.

However, the problem of "regulatory havens" and non cooperative countries or territories in the fight against money laundering remains crucial, and deserves special attention.

2 - Additional measures

Some non cooperative countries or territories can already be identified, in particular those having denied assistance, in enquiries about international money laundering operations. The FATF devoted a special meeting to an exchange of views on this matter (see par. I-B 2b) : it was agreed that no "black list" of non cooperative countries or jurisdictions would be established, and that the results of this exchange of views would principally serve, at this stage, to help national efforts against money laundering. In order to lead these countries to more cooperative behaviour, it was felt that, for the time being, public and peer pressure could be sufficient, although FATF members could of course decide to go further on an individual basis, provided the Task Force was kept informed.

Public pressure could be exercised, in a "soft" way, through the publication of a "white list" of countries or territories which have implemented FATF recommendations and can thus be considered as fully participating to the international effort against money laundering. This publication would also facilitate national efforts to detect suspicious transactions. However, it was felt that it was too early to make a definitive assessment of which countries have satisfactorily implemented the FATF. This procedure cannot be envisaged before all countries have been given time to implement the FATF program, as a consequence of the geographical mobilization program described above, and before a thorough review of the degree and quality of this implementation has been conducted, through the assessment process descibed under part III-A. Furthermore, although a narrow majority of task force members would favor this course, there is at this stage no consensus on it.

Should this peer and public pressure prove insufficient, additional measures might be envisaged in the future.

Several types of measures were mentioned. For instance, an upgrading of the implementation of recommendation 21 might be considered, in order to submit all transfers/payments with these jurisdictions to a specific examination, which would at least increase the cost of transactions with them and thus compensate for the competitive advantage of the financial institutions located in the non cooperative country or territory. A systematic declaration to competent authorities of these transfers/payments might also be considered. The efficiency of these measures would of course be greater, if they were decided and implemented in a coordinated way, within the FATF.

III - FOLLOW-UP TO THE SECOND FATF

The group discussed arrangements which could ensure a full implementation of its program. The consensus was to maintain the group for the time being, to conduct four tasks :

1 - self-reporting and mutual assessment (monitoring and surveillance) on the adoption and implementation of FATF recommendations by all members ;

2 - co-ordination and oversight of efforts to encourage non-members to adopt and implement the recommendations ;

3 - making further recommendations and evaluations of counter-measures while serving as a forum for considering developments in money laundering techniques domestically and worlwide and for the exchange of information on enforcement techniques to combat money laundering ;

4 - standing ready to facilitate co-operation between organisations concerned with combating money laundering and between individual countries or territories.

A - FUTURE ROLE OF THE FATF

1 - <u>Process of future assessments</u>

a) Assessment among FATF members

The procedures adopted this year to assess the implementation among task force members, helped to determine guidelines for future assessments.

In the future, the essential objective should be to maintain the informality which the FATF has adopted and to avoid a rigid bureaucratic approach. The procedure could be for FATF members to complete answers to a standard questionnaire each year concerning the status of their implementation of the FATF recommendations. Surveillance grids could be used -provided they would be filled in a harmonized way, that is two countries in the same situation would give the same answer-, but FATF members would have to supply information supporting their responses on implementation status and the effect of their measures as well as explain their co-ordinated strategy against money laundering against the background of their particular characteristics. Consideration might also be given to more detailed surveillance grids, focusing on the key elements of the core recommendations.

The responses to the questionnaires would be circulated to all members by a Secretariat. The Secretariat would simultaneously circulate a summary of the various responses. This would form the self-reporting stage of the procedure.

There would then be a yearly meeting of the FATF members to consider the responses and discuss any problems arising out of them. Individual members would be chosen for examination by the FATF with the examination carried out by selected other members of the FATF, according to an agreed protocol for examination and agreed selection criteria. The objective would be to examine every FATF member by the end of 1996. Each year the FATF would select the members to be examined in the following year. Unless they wished to be examined earlier, members would not be subject to being examined until three years after their endorsement of the FATF-1 recommendations, except if the group decides otherwise, in exceptional circumstances. Each year a final assessment report would be prepared by the Secretariat under the supervision of the FATF. This would complete the mutual assessment process.

Assessment reports concerning individual countries would in principle not be published, but executives summaries would be.

During FATF meetings, particular questions related to FATF tasks might be discussed. Regular yearly meetings could be augmented by special meetings by agreement of the FATF. Working groups could also be established by the FATF if required.

b) Mobilisation and assessment in non member countries or territories

The contacts with "other financial centers" and "regional areas", as described above (part II-B : "geographical coverage") could be continued, for the time being, along the following lines : they would be pursued by individual FATF members, or in appropriate cases by steering groups of FATF members with the support of the Presidency/secretariat. Relevant FATF members would remain responsible for their associated or dependant territories as appropriate. Individual FATF members, or regional steering groups in appropriate cases, would also maintain contact with non-member financial centers and regionals areas. Reports would be made on developments in the relevant countries or territories. The annual meetings of the FATF would provide the opportunity to review progress and consider solutions to any problems.

An important part of this assessment process would be, upon request, the provision of technical assistance, in particular in drafting laws and regulations, and adapting bank supervisory and law enforcement authorities' structures. This could be provided by individual task force members, or by the secretariat, within the limits of its ressources.

Non-FATF members which subscribed to the FATF-1 recommendations, might join in the self-reporting process and complete the questionnaire on their adoption and implementation of the FATF recommendations. Such jurisdictions would be invited to attend the meetings at which their reports are discussed.

2 - Other tasks

In addition to the ongoing self-reporting/mutual assessment and co-ordination/oversight work, the FATF should also keep under review developments in money laundering trends and techniques and share information on legal, financial and enforcement counter-measures. Issues with regional or global implications could be discussed at the annual FATF meetings and consideration might be given to the development of further recommendations where appropriate.

FATF meetings will also provide the opportunity for informal exchange of information between members.

In this regard, the FATF would not be used as a formal intermediary for exchanges of information relating to suspicious transactions, or persons and corporations involved in these transactions ("hot information") : the exchange of "hot information" should take place, either bilaterally or through multilateral existing institutions, according to FATF recommendations. However, should difficulties arise in this matter, either between FATF participants, or between participants and non-participants, there should be a possibility for task force members to raise this issue in the FATF, in order to enable it to find a solution acceptable for all parties.

B - INSTITUTIONAL ARRANGEMENTS

The FATF could continue to function as an ad hoc group for the time being, reporting to finance Ministers or other competent Ministers and authorities. It should remain as flexible and informal as it is now. The question of the continuation of the FATF, and of its statute and future works should be addressed again in three years.

1 - Presidency

The FATF would continue to meet under the Presidency of an individual member. The Presidency would rotate on a yearly basis. The Presidency might run from 1 September to 31 August with the FATF making an annual report to Ministers or other competent authorities, enabling the FATF to report to suitable Ministerial and international fora in May-July. The President would be chosen by the FATF, taking into account as much as possible geographical locations and membership of various international groupings. A steering group would be set up including representatives of the Presidency, the Presidency for the last year and the next year, plus the chairmen of working groups, if any.

2 - Secretariat

The OECD could be invited to act as a secretariat for the FATF. The criteria used for this choice were : experience in areas related to those covered by the FATF ; multi-disciplinary nature ; and compatibility with the aims of the FATF. The OECD has confirmed that it has no difficulty in acting as a secretariat for a body which contains non-OECD members. The group is also grateful to UNIDCP for its offer to provide secretariat facilities.

The OECD would limit itself to secretariat functions, collating, co-ordinating and summarising responses from FATF members and supporting the FATF presidency. It could conduct studies by further decision of the FATF. It would not become involved in any enforcement activity.

The size and cost of this secretariat should be extremely limited, probably in the range of 2 to 4 millions francs each year. The burden sharing between FATF participants might be based on the standard OECD contribution formula. Countries, which are in a position to do so, might consider paying their contribution with a part of the funds stemming from assets seized in money laundering operations involving international cooperation.

3 - Future membership of the FATF

The FATF membership should not be further widened, in order to preserve the efficiency of the Task Force. However, countries who were invited to participate in this year, but who did not endorse the recommendations, would still be able to join.

Competent international organisations could be invited to participate as observers, at the discretion of the Presidency. They include the UNIDCP, the IMF, Interpol and the Customs Cooperation Council, the Bank of International Settlements and related committees, and the Council of Europe. Regional organisations wishing to play a role in the fight against money laundering could also be invited.

CONCLUSION

Relevant Ministers or other competent authorities of member jurisdictions will circulate this report to their Heads of State or Government. Their decisions, as well as further guidance from the Summit of the Heads of State or Government of the seven major industrial nations, will be crucial as regards the follow-up to the task force.

In order to ensure the success of the FATF program against money laundering, a high degree of mobilization in industrial and other financial center countries or territories is essential. This implies that those countries or territories which have not done so already, fully implement without delay the recommendations. This implies also the pursuit of the external mobilization effort which has been launched by the FATF-2, and a reinforcement of joint actions to deal with non cooperative countries or territories, in order to ensure that no financial center can put at risk the effectiveness of the fight against drug trafficking and other serious crimes.

The political commitment to fight money laundering, which enabled the establishment of an internationally agreed far-reaching program against money laundering in a record time, does not permit any abatement in the efforts of the Task Force, until the success of this program has been ensured. This success will provide a decisive contribution to the fight against criminal activities and above all against drug trafficking, and will improve the soundness of the international financial system.

CHAPTER II

INITIATIVES UNDERTAKEN
BY THE UNITED NATIONS

DOCUMENT A

1987 United Nations International Conference on Drug Abuse and Illicit Trafficking: Comprehensive Outline of Future Activities in Drug Abuse Control (extracts)

Source: (1987) 26 International Legal Materials

Introduction

1.   The Comprehensive Multidisciplinary Outline of Future Activities in Drug Abuse Control is a repertory of recommendations addressed to Governments and to organizations setting forth practical measures which can contribute to the fight against drug abuse and to the suppression of illicit trafficking. At the national level, it is for each Government to determine which of the recommendations could be useful in its country in the light of economic and social conditions and to the extent consistent with national law. The Comprehensive Multidisciplinary Outline is not and was not designed to be a formal legal instrument; it does not create either rights or obligations of an international character. Its purpose will be achieved when the text is used as a handbook by national authorities and by interested organizations as a source of ideas to be selected and translated into action appropriate to local circumstances in the manner considered fit by these authorities and organizations. The text is accordingly drafted in non-mandatory style as a working guide, rather than as a package to be accepted in its entirety.

2.   The recommendations have been drafted in terms fully consistent with the principal international instruments concerned with drug abuse control, that is, the Single Convention on Narcotic Drugs, 1961, as amended by the 1972 Protocol Amending the Single Convention on Narcotic Drugs, and the 1971 Convention on Psychotropic Substances of 1961. (sic.)

3.   In addition, with a view to safeguarding the principle of

the sovereignty of the State and the primacy of the fundamental
principles of the law and constitution of the State, many recommendations include a proviso concerning respect for these principles.

Background

4.   Throughout recorded history, substances to relieve suffering
and to alter moods have been known and used in human societies.
The ambivalence of these substances - they are indispensable for
the relief of pain and suffering, but addictive and destructive
when misused or abused - led societies from earliest times to
make rules restricting their use to religious or curative purposes and entrusting them only to priests or to healers and
doctors.

5.   Since the mid-nineteenth century, drug abuse has been
spreading in many countries as a result of a number of factors.
The causes are many and vary in intensity; they include, in
particular, the increased availability of products, the expansion
of communications, socio-economic factors, migration and rapid
urbanization, changes in attitudes and in the sense of values and
the ruthless exploitation of fellow human beings by criminals.

6.   In order to deal with the increase in drug abuse, the community of nations has since the early twentieth century gradually
evolved global control mechanisms intended to limit the availability of drugs for abuse, because it was quickly realized that
no single country could succeed alone in preventing drug abuse
and illicit trafficking. Between 1912 and 1972, no less than 12
multilateral drug control treaties were concluded. Under the
auspices of the United Nations, the Single Convention on Narcotic
Drugs, 1961, as amended by the 1972 Protocol, consolidated most
of the earlier instruments, and the 1971 Convention on Psychotropic Substances created a system of international control for a
number of previously uncontrolled psychoactive substances.
During this period, the main effort was directed to the gradual
devising and reinforcing of a network of administrative controls,
having as its primary object the regulation of the supply and

movement of drugs with a view to limiting their manufacture and import to the quantities required for legitimate medical and scientific purposes. Governments have also increasingly recognized the need to co-operate in the fight against the illicit production and manufacture of and traffic in drugs and accordingly to furnish to the international control organs, established first under the auspices of the League of Nations and then included in the United Nations system, periodic reports on their application of the international instruments and to submit to international supervision for their common benefit.

7. As gaps in the international control system were progressively closed, it became more generally apparent that the mechanisms originally created for the introduction of international supply control were not in themselves a sufficient response to the current needs of the international community.

8. Without prejudice to the importance of continuing administrative control of narcotic drugs and psychotropic substances and of international co-operation in the fight against the illicit traffic, counter-offensives of another dimension are now needed at the national and international levels to respond to the threat drug abuse poses not only to millions of persons but also to whole population groups and even to societies and economies in some countries. To take up the challenge it is necessary to intensify not only measures and programmes directed against the illicit production of and trafficking in drugs but also the activities undertaken to prevent the illicit demand for drugs and to further the treatment and eventual social reintegration of drug addicts.

9. Many heads of State or Government have recently directed their personal attention to launching such counter-offensives, and the Secretary-General of the United Nations, addressing the Economic and Social Council on 24 May 1985, noted that the moment had arrived for the international community to expand its efforts in a global undertaking that would be more concerted and more comprehensive. He envisaged a truly world-wide effort to contain the plague of illicit drugs and thus proposed that a world con-

ference be convened at the ministerial level in 1987 to deal with all aspects of drug abuse. Significant progress has already been achieved by the international community in building up defences against the production of addictive drugs and the illicit traffic in and abuse of those drugs. Building on this foundation of international co-operation developed over nearly 80 years, the international community is now concerting efforts to expand the United Nations work in the field of drug abuse control and in the fight against illicit trafficking in drugs.

10. The political will on the part of the international community to take urgent, effective and concerted action to deal with the disturbing situation created by drug abuse and the illicit drug traffic was reflected in the decision of the General Assembly to convene the International Conference on Drug Abuse and Illicit Trafficking (hereinafter referred to as "the Conference") in 1987 (General Assembly resolution 40/122 of 13 December 1985). The Assembly gave the Conference an ambitious mandate, encompassing the full range of issues relevant to the fight against drug abuse, illicit trafficking and related criminal activities at the national, regional and international levels. It directed the Conference to adopt a "comprehensive multidisciplinary outline of future activities which focuses on concrete and substantive issues directly relevant to the problems of drug abuse and illicit trafficking" (paragraph 4(a)). This mandate transcends the traditional concern with the control of the supply of and the illicit traffic in drugs and calls for a commitment by the Governments of all States to reinforce their individual efforts and to intensify and expand the scope of international co-operation into new areas.

Structure of the Comprehensive Multidisciplinary Outline of Future Activities in Drug Abuse Control

11. The Outline comprises four chapters, covering the main elements involved in the fight against drug abuse and illicit trafficking and the subjects included in the agenda of the Conference: the prevention and reduction of illicit demand; the control of supply; action against illicit trafficking; and treatment and rehabilitation.

12. Each chapter indicates specific targets, particularizing the objective to be attained and the action to be taken at the national level (by Governments, professional associations, academic institutions, non-governmental organizations, communities, parents and individuals); at the regional level (by regional inter-governmental and non-governmental organizations and bodies); and at the international level (by international organizations, especially those of the United Nations system).

13. The catalogue of proposed actions is not exhaustive, nor does it follow any particular order of priority. At the national level, it would be for each State to determine its own order of priority among the targets, in the light of its own needs and resources. While all the targets are applicable to most countries, the modalities for the suggested courses of action are not necessarily applicable in each instance. Any action should be considered within the socio-economic context of the country concerned and may need to be adapted to the particular cultural, social, political or legal setting in order to be successfully applied. In particular, due account being taken of the constitutional system, legislative and regulatory provisions and court practice may need to be adapted and revised in order to give full effect to national efforts.

III. SUPPRESSION OF ILLICIT TRAFFICKING

Introduction

223. Drug trafficking is sophisticated and complex. A wide variety of drugs is involved, and they may be of external or domestic origin. The illicit traffic in drugs not only violates national drug laws and international conventions, but may in many cases also involve other antisocial activities, such as organized crime, conspiracy, bribery, corruption and intimidation of public officials, tax evasion, banking law violations, illegal money transfers, criminal violations of import or export regulations, crimes involving firearms, and crimes of violence. Narcotics are now frequently used instead of money as the medium of exchange

for trading in weapons and other contraband, and some large drug-
trafficking networks have gained virtual control of certain
areas. Because of the far-reaching consequences of the illicit
drug trade, even the integrity and stability of certain Governments have been threatened. This wide range of illegal activities presents an equally wide range of openings for imaginative
law enforcement action, including action recognizing the need to
develop and implement law enforcement programmes relating to
subjects identified in the draft convention against illicit drug
trafficking and to give emphasis to the recommendations of the
Interregional Meeting of Heads of Nations Drug Law Enforcement
Agencies, as reflected in the report of the Meeting (A/41/559).

224. Action on the lines suggested in chapter I, concerning the
prevention and reduction of illicit demand, and in chapter II, on
the elimination of illicit supply, would obviously go a long way
towards suppressing illicit trafficking.

225. In addition, however, it is necessary to ensure vigorous
enforcement of the law in order to reduce the illicit availability of drugs, deter drug related crime, and contribute to drug
abuse prevention by creating an environment favourable to efforts
for reducing illicit supply and demand. The challenge is to
overcome the obstacles posed by the complexity of international
transactions, the covert nature of the drug traffic and the large
sums of money to be made from illicit drugs in proportion to
their often low bulk. Co-ordination of activities and co-operation among national agencies within each country and between
countries are vital for the achievement of the objective.

226. Many Governments have initiated innovative methods for
disrupting drug-trafficking organizations. These successful
initiatives may usefully be shared with other Governments, where
applicable, and can be adapted to the particular situation in a
given area or region.

227. Special emphasis should be placed on supplementing the
activities of the police and customs authorities by increasing
the effectiveness of the criminal justice system in the arrest,

prosecution and appropriate sentencing of convicted traffickers. The support of the full range of non-governmental organizations that have an interest in law enforcement and judicial matters should also be enlisted. Mutual legal and judicial assistance between national jurisdictions should be fostered and facilitated, as should co-operation between law enforcement agencies. Assets gained from the illicit drug trade should be made liable to seizure, as should the instruments used in trafficking. The extradition from one country of persons accused of drug offences in another country should be facilitated to the extent that it is not incompatible with the existing national legislation of the countries concerned.

228. An important step now being taken by the international community in this regard is the drafting of a new convention against illicit traffic in narcotic drugs and psychotropic substances, which is being prepared under the auspices of the Commission on Narcotic Drugs at the request of the General Assembly and which it is hoped will be adopted in the near future. States are encouraged to take an active part in the elaboration of the new convention and to become parties to the convention once it has been adopted. Pending its entry into force, which may take some time, measures envisaged in the proposed new convention could be taken to the extent possible by, when necessary, the introduction of appropriate provisions into national law.

229. Ratification and effective implementation by all States of the international conventions relating to drug abuse control will greatly enhance the prospects of ridding the world of illicit drug trafficking.

230. The international intergovernmental bodies concerned should bring to the attention of Governments any deficiencies noted in the operation of the international drug control system (e.g. leakages into illicit channels), and invite them to suggest or consider making (as the case may be) efforts to remedy the shortcomings at the national, regional and international levels.

Target 17. Disruption of major trafficking networks

The problem

231. Timely information on the criminal activities of traffickers is required in order that they can be identified and caught. Such information is often available in the records of organizations such as banks, air, road, rail and maritime transportation companies, managements of ports and airports, free-port authorities, courier services, money changers and financial and investment houses. Personnel in all organizations concerned should be trained to recognize the value to law enforcement authorities of such information.

232. The object is to channel all pertinent information to the appropriate law enforcement agencies promptly so that traffickers can be identified and caught. It is therefore necessary to strengthen co-operation between law enforcement agencies within each State and, under bilateral agreements, between these and their counterparts in other States, enhance training of law enforcement personnel (in skill and integrity) and enlist the assistance of the non-governmental sector in gathering information.

233. For this purpose, States parties that have not yet done so are urged to designate the co-ordinating agency envisaged in article 35(a) of the 1961 Convention and article 21(a) of the 1971 Convention, which should be given the necessary authority to co-ordinate the actions set forth below.

Suggested courses of action

At the national level

234. Having due regard to the national administrative and legal system, the agency could gather from all government agencies information useful for drug law enforcement and, subject to respect for privacy and confidentiality, ensure that this information is communicated promptly to the appropriate law enforce-

ment agency; this requirement could, if necessary, be spelt out in appropriate laws and regulations.

235. The ministry or authority concerned could be made responsible for arranging training for the personnel of all such agencies to enable them to recognize and to transmit promptly to the appropriate agency any information useful for the purpose of identifying traffickers and detecting their activities.

236. The appropriate agency could approach air and rail transport firms and shipping and trucking firms which operate internationally, and/or the associations of such firms, urging them to review their procedures for the purpose not only of safeguarding their services against misuse by traffickers (see also target 24) but also of ensuring that information about any trafficking operation whatsoever is reported promptly.

237. Legislative bodies could consider enacting legislation applying penalties to transport companies that are aware of such misuse and illicit traffic and do not take prompt and adequate steps to correct and report it or are reckless or grossly negligent in this regard. Legislation providing in such circumstances for the seizure and immobilization of transport equipment used in drug trafficking could be enacted if not already in effect (see also target 23).

238. Subject to the limitations necessitated by the constitutional, legal and administrative system, the appropriate ministry or other national authority responsible for financial matters should ensure that any suspect activity by banks, money changers, financial and investment houses and courier and related services is promptly reported to the ministry or authority concerned and to the drug law enforcement agency. Similarly, in cases where information held by the tax authorities might assist investigations, this information could be made accessible to the drug law enforcement agency. Any amendment needed in banking and corporate secrecy laws should be in terms conducive to the discovery of drug-related offences. With the support or advice of the

ministry or authority, training courses might be arranged for the staff of banking and financial institutions, so that they can learn how to recognize suspect transactions. The movement of unusually large amounts of cash or negotiable instruments, the deposit of exceptionally large amounts of cash in banks, the unreported maintenance of accounts abroad by nationals or residents in cases where such amounts are required to be reported, and large unexplained accumulations of wealth of obviously illicit origin should by law be liable to penalties if there is evidence of "laundering" or concealment of funds connected with illicit drug trafficking.

239. The appropriate ministry or other appropriate authority at the local level could establish standards of conduct and integrity for law enforcement agencies and officers that are involved in drug law enforcement. All States should ensure that an appropriate legal framework with penal sanctions is enacted (if they do not already exist) to support the criminal prosecution and punishment of corruption offences.

240. The appropriate national authorities could, with due regard for the fundamental principles of the national legal system, make use of all modern techniques of investigation in the fight against organized international drug trafficking, including corruption offences by public officials.

241. If in the course of investigating suspect activities a government agency discovers evidence of a connection between illicit drug trafficking and illicit arms trafficking or international organized criminal activities, it should promptly inform other national authorities accordingly and communicate relevant particulars to the authority concerned in the country that is the probable target of the illicit traffic or organized criminal activity in question.

At the regional and international levels

242. The ministries concerned and national law enforcement agencies should, as appropriate, under international treaties and

bilateral agreements co-operate closely with their counterparts in other States and in liaison with ICPO/Interpol when appropriate with a view to enhancing the effectiveness of their law enforcement action to suppress the illicit drug traffic. For this purpose, they could establish and maintain channels of communication between their respective law enforcement agencies, by means of which information can be exchanged without delay.

243. States should endeavour, directly or through the appropriate international organizations, to establish regional and international agreements strengthening co-operation in the fight against the illicit drug traffic.

244. Bilateral and multilateral assistance should be sought, where needed, for the purpose of financing programmes of technical co-operation and assistance and improving channels of communication for the transmission of information relating to the fight against the illicit drug traffic.

245. With the co-operation of ICPO/Interpol and CCC, when appropriate, the Division of Narcotic Drugs should continue to organize regular regional and interregional training courses to train personnel of law enforcement and related agencies and officials of national tourist agencies and to promote co-operation among these agencies in the fight against the illicit drug traffic.

246. Since the operations of drug trafficking gangs may vary from region to region, information available on profiles and methods of operation could be gathered by national authorities at the regional level in co-operation with ICPO/Interpol and CCC, when appropriate, to be used by States as well as by international agencies and entities concerned.

247. In countries where it is known or suspected that the "informal" or "parallel" sector of the economy accounts for a significant share of the national product and of international trade, the appropriate ministry or authority might investigate the ways in which the illicit production of and traffic in drugs contribute to the "informal" economic activities and take counteraction.

The ministry or the authority concerned may wish to communicate the relevant information to other countries, in the region or elsewhere, which are known destinations of the illicit cross-border drug traffic or of the flight of assets representing earnings of traffickers from unlawful transactions.

248. If conclusive evidence comes to light of illicit trafficking being carried on by means of the misuse of the diplomatic bag or of the diplomatic status, or of the consular status, it is open to the Government of the receiving State to take measures for halting this traffic and for dealing with the diplomatic or consular staff involved in strict conformity with the provisions of the Vienna Conventions on Diplomatic and Consular Relations.

The Conference draws the attention of the International Law Commission to possible misuse of the diplomatic bag for illicit drug trafficking, so that the Commission could study the matter under the topic relating to the status of the diplomatic bag.

Target 20. Mutual judicial and legal assistance

The Problem

257. The multinational aspects of illicit trafficking in drugs greatly complicate law enforcement, investigation and judicial counteraction. Witnesses, documents and other evidence are often scattered in States other than the State in which persons accused of drug-related offences are brought to trial, and the detailed rules concerning the production of evidence can create difficulties for judicial bodies. Subject to the limitations of the constitutional, legal and administrative system, needed mutual legal assistance includes, for example:

    (a) Taking evidence, including compelling testimony;

    (b) Serving judicial documents;

    (c) Executing requests for searches and seizures;

    (d) Examining objects, sites and conveyances;

(e) Locating or identifying witnesses or suspects;

(f) Verifying in narcotics laboratories the illegal nature of substances seized;

(g) Exchanging information and objects;

(h) Providing relevant documents and records, including bank, financial, corporate and business records: existing bank secrecy laws are being used in many instances to obstruct co-operation and the provision of information needed for the investigation of allegations of drug-related offences.

Suggested courses of action

At the national level

258. The appropriate authorities could suggest that, in conformity with the relevant bilateral and multilateral agreements, the greatest possible measure of mutual judicial assistance should be provided in judicial proceedings, including investigations and prosecutions relating to illicit trafficking offences, making or proposing any necessary modifications in the legislation, regulations or procedures. Legislative provisions could be enacted as required, granting broad powers to the courts to assist courts in other jurisdictions in gathering evidence in accordance with the laws of the requested State and, to the greatest extent possible, in conformity with the laws of the requesting State.

259. Each State could ensure that the appropriate agency or responsible authority has the capacity to receive requests for mutual legal assistance and to address such requests to other States. The agency or authority of the requested State should have capacity to recommend that requests for mutual legal assistance be executed in accordance with the procedural requirement specified in the request in so far as they are not incompatible with the law of the requested State.

At the regional and international levels

260. The appropriate ministries or authorities could, in co-operation with ministries of foreign affairs, initiate action to enter into regional or international agreements that would serve the purposes described above. A number of States have entered into or are negotiating bilateral and regional agreements for these purposes. Many such agreements relax the rules governing bank secrecy in drug trafficking cases, thus reducing the number of "safe havens" available to traffickers.

261. The Secretary-General of the United Nations should be requested by the Commission on Narcotic Drugs to issue periodically lists of the national agencies or authorities designated by States parties to facilitate legal and judicial co-operation.

262. The Secretary-General should also be requested to publish a compendium of the bilateral and regional agreements on mutual legal assistance entered into by States, and States should report the conclusion of such agreements to the Secretary-General, if the Parties deem this to be appropriate.

263. In view of the paramount importance of timely intelligence in the fight against illicit trafficking, Governments would be able to intensify their efforts against these illicit activities if they possessed efficient channels of communication enabling them to track movements of traffickers promptly. For this purpose they may find it useful to enter into multilateral, bilateral or regional arrangements providing for the reciprocal exchange of relevant information among law enforcement agencies, including those of transit States. The latter may request assistance from the United Nations Fund for Drug Abuse Control and bilateral and multilateral assistance programmes in establishing or expanding their communications network for this purpose.

264. In cases where they consider it desirable with a view to strengthening international or regional peace and security and building confidence, interested Governments might envisage the

conclusion of formal agreements (in so far as these do not already exist) that contain provisions for pursuing the fight against illicit drug trafficking. Such agreements might envisage, <u>inter</u> <u>alia</u>, reciprocal training courses for officials, greater ease of communication between authorities, the establishment of direct telex links etc.

265. States whose systems of law and rules of evidence and procedure are much alike may wish to consider entering into agreements for the transfer of criminal proceedings as appropriate and for the reciprocal recognition of judicial decisions concerning drug-related offences. In such cases, the provisions of such an agreement might specify that the order of the court in one State party to the agreement is enforceable in another State party, provided that in cases where a sentence is imposed the respect of the convicted person's fundamental human rights is guaranteed in the place where the sentence is to be served.

<u>Target 23. Forfeiture of the instruments and proceeds of illicit drug trafficking</u>

<u>The problem</u>

278. In line with the provisions of article 37 of the 1961 Convention and article 22, paragraph 3, of the 1971 Convention referring to objects directly associated with the commission of a drug trafficking offence, most national, criminal or civil legal systems make provision for the seizure and forfeiture of the tools and devices actually used in committing the offence. Most of such existing provisions, however, cannot be construed as being applicable to assets acquired by means of the proceeds resulting from drug trafficking.

279. The volume of the property and money transactions, and especially of cash transfers, related to drug trafficking has increased so greatly that these transactions affect some national economies in their entirety. The increased use by traffickers and their associates of complex corporate structures and intricate business transactions involving banks, trust companies,

firms dealing in real estate and other financial institutions has
added to the difficulty of seizing assets obtained as a result of
trafficking in drugs. Because bank, tax and investment legislation varies from country to country, traffickers and their accom-
plices can find loopholes in national laws and procedures and can
quickly adapt laundering schemes and techniques to hide their
ill-gotten gains.

Suggested courses of action

  At the national level

280. Within the scope of the fundamental principles of the national legal systems, the legislature, ministries or other authorities concerned, university law faculties, research institutes and like academic bodies could review the national legislation and regulations and consider the desirability of proposing
any necessary modifications that would facilitate and ensure the
seizure, freezing, and forfeiture of the objects knowingly used
in trafficking and the proceeds thereof, including objects knowingly acquired with those proceeds.

281. The law could provide that, where it has been determined by
appropriate judicial or administrative procedures that specific
assets were acquired by means of the proceeds of trafficking,
title to all such assets is forfeited. If some of these assets
are located in another State, the State in which the action was
initiated could assist that other State in seizing those assets.

282. States could in their legislation and regulations authorize
their judicial or other authorities concerned to accede to appropriate requests for such actions from other States where the
offence may have been committed.

283. Associations of banks, investment houses and like institutions should devise codes of conduct whereby their members would
pledge themselves to assist the authorities in tracing the proceeds of trafficking activities. Subject to respect for the
fundamental principles of national laws, the legislation could

provide that the personnel and/or management of such firms will be liable to fines or other penalties if they knowingly participate in or facilitate schemes for concealing information relating to such transactions.

284. Subject to the limitations of the constitutional, legal and administrative system, the ministry concerned may wish to carry out, or cause to be carried out for the purpose of detecting the sources of illicit supply of drugs and of reducing that supply, an investigation into the income levels of persons suspected of serving as channels of supply. The investigators should be directed to look for evidence in the records of the tax authorities, motor vehicle licensing authorities, land registry, public register of companies and any other accessible statistical or financial records that may disclose a gap between declared income and ostentatious expenditure.

285. The ministry or other authority concerned should consider the desirability and possibility of establishing a special fund whose resources would be mobilized to serve the cause of the fight against the illicit drug traffic and drug abuse. The assets of the fund might be constituted from, for example, voluntary contributions, special governmental allocations, monies or property seized in connection with the prosecution and conviction of drug traffickers.

286. The distribution of the value of the proceeds of seizure and forfeiture could be a matter for agreement between the States concerned. Each State could empower an appropriate agency to establish a trust fund for holding such forfeited property.

At the regional and international levels

287. The Division of Narcotic Drugs in co-operation with ICPO/Interpol and CCC, assisted, as appropriate, by the United Nations Fund for Drug Abuse Control, should encourage the exchange of information about trans-border laundering schemes and techniques and of experience with the training of staff of law enforcement agencies and of financial institutions.

288. In cases where bilateral or multilateral agreements are negotiated for the purpose of promoting international trade, economic co-operation, cultural exchanges or for like purposes, the representatives of the States negotiating such agreements might consider the advisability of inserting in these instruments provisions designed to prevent legitimate transactions under the agreements from being used as vehicles for the laundering of gains from illicit drug trafficking, illicit drug manufacture and illicit cultivation of narcotic plants.

DOCUMENT B

United Nations Convention Against Illicit Traffic in Narcotic Drugs and Psychotropic Substances
Adopted in Vienna on 19 December 1988

Source: Home Office, London

The Parties to this Convention,

Deeply concerned by the magnitude of and rising trend in the illicit production of, demand for and traffic in narcotic drugs and psychotropic substances, which pose a serious threat to the health and welfare of human beings and adversely affect the economic, cultural and political foundations of society,

Deeply concerned also by the steadily increasing inroads into various social groups made by illicit traffic in narcotic drugs and psychotropic substances, and particularly by the fact that children are used in many parts of the world as an illicit drug consumers market and for purposes of illicit production, distribution and trade in narcotic drugs and psychotropic substances, which entails a danger of incalculable gravity,

Recognizing the links between illicit traffic and other related organized criminal activities which undermine the legitimate economies and threaten the stability, security and sovereignty of States,

Recognizing also that illicit traffic is an international criminal activity, the suppression of which demands urgent attention and the highest priority,

Aware that illicit traffic generates large financial profits and wealth enabling transnational criminal organizations to penetrate, contaminate and corrupt the structures of government, legitimate commercial and financial business, and society at all its levels,

Determined to deprive persons engaged in illicit traffic of the proceeds of their criminal activities and thereby eliminate their main incentive for so doing,

Desiring to eliminate the root causes of the problem of abuse of narcotic drugs and psychotropic substances, including the illicit demand for such drugs and substances and the enormous profits derived from illicit traffic,

Considering that measures are necessary to monitor certain substances, including precursors, chemicals and solvents, which are used in the manufacture of narcotic drugs and psychotropic substances, the ready availability of which has led to an increase in the clandestine manufacture of such drugs and substances,

Determined to improve international co-operation in the suppression of illicit traffic by sea,

Recognizing that eradication of illicit traffic is a collective responsibility of all States and that, to that end, co-ordinated action within the framework of international co-operation is necessary,

Acknowledging the competence of the United Nations in the field of control of narcotic drugs and psychotropic substances and desirous that the international organs concerned with such control should be within the framework of that Organization,

Reaffirming the guiding principles of existing treaties in the field of narcotic drugs and psychotropic substances and the system of control which they embody,

Recognizing the need to reinforce and supplement the measures provided in the Single Convention on Narcotic Drugs, 1961, that Convention as amended by the 1972 Protocol Amending the Single Convention on Narcotic Drugs, 1961, and the 1971 Convention on Psychotropic Substances, in order to counter the magnitude and extent of illicit traffic and its grave consequences,

Recognizing also the importance of strengthening and enhancing effective legal means for international co-operation in criminal matters for suppressing the international criminal activities of illicit traffic,

Desiring to conclude a comprehensive, effective and operative international convention that is directed specifically against illicit traffic and that considers the various aspects of the problem as a whole, in particular those aspects not envisaged in the existing treaties in the field of narcotic drugs and psychotropic substances,

Hereby agrees as follows:

Article 1

DEFINITIONS

Except where otherwise expressly indicated or where the context otherwise requires, the following definitions shall apply throughout this Convention:

(a) "Board" means the International Narcotics Control Board established by the Single Convention on Narcotic Drugs, 1961, and that Convention as amended by the 1972 Protocol Amending the Single Convention on Narcotic Drugs, 1961;

(b) "Cannabis plant" means any plant of the genus Cannabis;

(c) "Coca bush" means the plant of any species of the genus Erythroxylon;

(d) "Commercial carrier" means any person or any public, private or other entity engaged in transporting persons, goods or mails for remuneration, hire, or any other benefit;

(e) "Commission" means the Commission on Narcotic Drugs of the Economic and Social Council of the United Nations;

(f) "Confiscation", which includes forfeiture where applicable, means the permanent deprivation of property by order of a court or other competent authority;

(g) "Controlled delivery" means the technique of allowing illicit or suspect consignments of narcotic drugs, psychotropic substances, substances in Table I and Table II annexed to this Convention, or substances substituted for them, to pass out of, through or into the territory of one or more countries, with the knowledge and under the supervision of their competent authorities, with a view to identifying persons involved in the commission of offences established in accordance with article 3, paragraph 1 of the Convention;

(h) "1961 Convention" means the Single Convention on Narcotic Drugs, 1961;

(i) "1961 Convention as amended" means the Single Convention on Narcotic Drugs, 1961, as amended by the 1972 Protocol Amending the Single Convention on Narcotic Drugs, 1961;

(j) "1971 Convention" means the Convention on Psychotropic Substances, 1971;

(k) "Council" means the Economic and Social Council of the United Nations;

(l) "Freezing" or "seizure" means temporarily prohibiting the transfer, conversion, disposition or movement of property or temporarily assuming custody or control of property on the basis of an order issued by a court or a competent authority;

(m) "Illicit traffic" means the offences set forth in article 3, paragraphs 1 and 2, of this Convention;

(n) "Narcotic drug" means any of the substances, natural or synthetic, in Schedules I and II of the Single Convention on Narcotic Drugs, 1961, and that Convention as amended by the 1972 Protocol Amending the Single Convention on Narcotic Drugs, 1961;

(o) "Opium poppy" means the plant of the species Papaver somniferum L;

(p) "Proceeds" means any property derived from or obtained, directly or indirectly, through the commission of an offence established in accordance with article 3, paragraph 1;

(q) "Property" means assets of every kind, whether corporeal or incorporeal, movable or immovable, tangible or intangible, and legal documents or instruments evidencing title to, or interest in, such assets;

(r) "Psychotropic substance" means any substance, natural or synthetic, or any natural material in Schedules I, II, III and IV of the Convention on Psychotropic Substances, 1971;

(s) "Secretary-General" means the Secretary-General of the United Nations;

(t) "Table I" and "Table II" mean the correspondingly numbered lists of substances annexed to this Convention, as amended from time to time in accordance with article 12;

(u) "Transit State" means a State through the territory of which illicit narcotic drugs, psychotropic substances and substances in Table I and Table II are being moved, which is neither the place of origin nor the place of ultimate destination thereof.

Article 2

SCOPE OF THE CONVENTION

1. The purpose of this Convention is to promote co-operation among the Parties so that they may address more effectively the various aspects of illicit traffic in narcotic drugs and psychotropic substances having an international dimension. In carrying out their obligations under the Convention, the Parties shall take necessary measures, including legislative and administrative measures, in conformity with the fundamental provisions of their respective domestic legislative systems.

2. The Parties shall carry out their obligations under this Convention in a manner consistent with the principles of sovereign equality and territorial integrity of States and that of non-intervention in the domestic affairs of other States.

3. A Party shall not undertake in the territory of another Party the exercise of jurisdiction and performance of functions which are exclusively reserved for the authorities of that other Party by its domestic law.

Article 3

OFFENCES AND SANCTIONS

1. Each Party shall adopt such measures as may be necessary to establish as criminal offences under its domestic law, when committed intentionally:

(a) (i) The production, manufacture, extraction, preparation, offering, offering for sale, distribution, sale, delivery on any terms whatsoever, brokerage, dispatch, dispatch in transit, transport, importation or exportation of any narcotic drug or any psychotropic substance contrary to the provisions of the 1961 Convention, the 1961 Convention as amended or the 1971 Convention;

(ii) The cultivation of opium poppy, coca bush or cannabis plant for the purpose of the production of narcotic drugs contrary to the provisions of the 1961 Convention and the 1961 Convention as amended;

(iii) The possession or purchase of any narcotic drug or psychotropic substance for the purpose of any of the activities enumerated in (i) above;

(iv) The manufacture, transport or distribution of equipment, materials or of substances listed in Table I and Table II, knowing that they are to be used in or for the illicit cultivation, production or manufacture of narcotic drugs or psychotropic substances;

(v) The organization, management or financing of any of the offences enumerated in (i), (ii), (iii) or (iv) above;

(b) (i) The conversion or transfer of property, knowing that such property is derived from any offence or offences established in accordance with subparagraph (a) of this paragraph, or from an act of participation in such offence or offences, for the purpose of concealing or disguising the illicit origin of the property or of assisting any person who is involved in the commission of such an offence or offences to evade the legal consequences of his actions;

    (ii) The concealment or disguise of the true nature, source, location, disposition, movement, rights with respect to, or ownership of property, knowing that such property is derived from an offence or offences established in accordance with subparagraph (a) of this paragraph or from an act of participation in such an offence or offences;

(c) Subject to its constitutional principles and the basic concepts of its legal system:

    (i) The acquisition, possession or use of property, knowing, at the time of receipt, that such property was derived from an offence or offences established in accordance with subparagraph (a) of this paragraph or from an act of participation in such offence or offences;

    (ii) The possession of equipment or materials or substances listed in Table I and Table II, knowing that they are being or are to be used in or for the illicit cultivation, production or manufacture of narcotic drugs or psychotropic substances;

    (iii) Publicly inciting or inducing others, by any means, to commit any of the offences established in accordance with this article or to use narcotic drugs or psychotropic substances illicitly;

    (iv) Participation in, association or conspiracy to commit, attempts to commit and aiding, abetting, facilitating and counselling the commission of any of the offences established in accordance with this article.

2. Subject to its constitutional principles and the basic concepts of its legal system, each Party shall adopt such measures as may be necessary to establish as a criminal offence under its domestic law, when committed intentionally, the possession, purchase or cultivation of narcotic drugs or psychotropic substances for personal consumption contrary to the provisions of the 1961 Convention, the 1961 Convention as amended or the 1971 Convention.

3. Knowledge, intent or purpose required as an element of an offence set forth in paragraph 1 of this article may be inferred from objective factual circumstances.

4. (a) Each Party shall make the commission of the offences established in accordance with paragraph 1 of this article liable to sanctions which take into account the grave nature of these offences, such as imprisonment or other forms of deprivation of liberty, pecuniary sanctions and confiscation.

(b) The Parties may provide, in addition to conviction or punishment, for an offence established in accordance with paragraph 1 of this article, that the offender shall undergo measures such as treatment, education, aftercare, rehabilitation or social reintegration.

(c) Notwithstanding the preceding subparagraphs, in appropriate cases of a minor nature, the Parties may provide, as alternatives to conviction or punishment, measures such as education, rehabilitation or social reintegration, as well as, when the offender is a drug abuser, treatment and aftercare.

(d) The Parties may provide, either as an alternative to conviction or punishment, or in addition to conviction or punishment of an offence established in accordance with paragraph 2 of this article, measures for the treatment, education, aftercare, rehabilitation or social reintegration of the offender.

5. The Parties shall ensure that their courts and other competent authorities having jurisdiction can take into account factual circumstances which make the commission of the offences established in accordance with paragraph 1 of this article particularly serious, such as:

(a) The involvement in the offence of an organized criminal group to which the offender belongs:

(b) The involvement of the offender in other international organized criminal activities;

(c) The involvement of the offender in other illegal activities facilitated by commission of the offence;

(d) The use of violence or arms by the offender;

(e) The fact that the offender holds a public office and that the offence is connected with the office in question;

(f) The victimization or use of minors;

(g) The fact that the offence is committed in a penal institution or in an educational institution or social service facility or in their immediate vicinity or in other places to which school children and students resort for educational, sports and social activities;

(h) Prior conviction, particularly for similar offences, whether foreign or domestic, to the extent permitted under the domestic law of a Party.

6. The Parties shall endeavour to ensure that any discretionary legal powers under their domestic law relating to the prosecution of persons for offences established in accordance with this article are exercised to maximize the effectiveness of law enforcement measures in respect of those offences and with due regard to the need to deter the commission of such offences.

7. The Parties shall ensure that their courts or other competent authorities bear in mind the serious nature of the offences enumerated in paragraph 1 of this article and the circumstances enumerated in paragraph 5 of this article when considering the eventuality of early release or parole of persons convicted of such offences.

8. Each Party shall, where appropriate, establish under its domestic law a long statute of limitations period in which to commence proceedings for any offence established in accordance with paragraph 1 of this article, and a longer period where the alleged offender has evaded the administration of justice.

9. Each Party shall take appropriate measures, consistent with its legal system, to ensure that a person charged with or convicted of an offence established in accordance with paragraph 1 of this article, who is found within its territory, is present at the necessary criminal proceedings.

10. For the purpose of co-operation among the Parties under this Convention, including, in particular, co-operation under articles 5, 6, 7 and 9, offences established in accordance with this article shall not be considered as fiscal offences or as political offences or regarded as politically motivated, without prejudice to the constitutional limitations and the fundamental domestic law of the Parties.

11. Nothing contained in this article shall affect the principle that the description of the offences to which it refers and of legal defences thereto is reserved to the domestic law of a Party and that such offences shall be prosecuted and punished in conformity with that law.

Article 4

JURISDICTION

1. Each Party:

(a) Shall take such measures as may be necessary to establish its jurisdiction over the offences it has established in accordance with article 3, paragraph 1, when:

  (i) The offence is committed in its territory;

  (ii) The offence is committed on board a vessel flying its flag or an aircraft which is registered under its laws at the time the offence is committed;

(b) May take such measures as may be necessary to establish its jurisdiction over the offences it has established in accordance with article 3, paragraph 1, when:

  (i) The offence is committed by one of its nationals or by a person who has his habitual residence in its territory;

  (ii) The offence is committed on board a vessel concerning which that Party has been authorized to take appropriate action pursuant to article 17, provided that such jurisdiction shall be exercised only on the basis of agreements or arrangements referred to in paragraphs 4 and 9 of that article;

(iii) The offence is one of those established in accordance with article 3, paragraph 1, subparagraph (c)(iv), and is committed outside its territory with a view to the commission, within its territory, of an offence established in accordance with article 3, paragraph 1.

2. Each Party:

(a) Shall also take such measures as may be necessary to establish its jurisdiction over the offences it has established in accordance with article 3, paragraph 1, when the alleged offender is present in its territory and it does not extradite him to another Party on the ground:

(i) That the offence has been committed in its territory or on board a vessel flying its flag or an aircraft which was registered under its law at the time the offence was committed; or

(ii) That the offence has been committed by one of its nationals;

(b) May also take such measures as may be necessary to establish its jurisdiction over the offences it has established in accordance with article 3, paragraph 1, when the alleged offender is present in its territory and it does not extradite him to another Party.

3. This Convention does not exclude the exercise of any criminal jurisdiction established by a Party in accordance with its domestic law.

Article 5

CONFISCATION

1. Each Party shall adopt such measures as may be necessary to enable confiscation of:

(a) Proceeds derived from offences established in accordance with article 3, paragraph 1, or property the value of which corresponds to that of such proceeds;

(b) Narcotic drugs and psychotropic substances, materials and equipment or other instrumentalities used in or intended for use in any manner in offences established in accordance with article 3, paragraph 1.

2. Each Party shall also adopt such measures as may be necessary to enable its competent authorities to identify, trace, and freeze or seize proceeds, property, instrumentalities or any other things referred to in paragraph 1 of this article, for the purpose of eventual confiscation.

3. In order to carry out the measures referred to in this article, each Party shall empower its courts or other competent authorities to order that bank, financial or commercial records be made available or be seized. A Party shall not decline to act under the provisions of this paragraph on the ground of bank secrecy.

4. (a) Following a request made pursuant to this article by another Party having jurisdiction over an offence established in accordance with article 3, paragraph 1, the Party in whose territory proceeds, property, instrumentalities or any other things referred to in paragraph 1 of this article are situated shall:

(i) Submit the request to its competent authorities for the purpose of obtaining an order of confiscation and, if such order is granted, give effect to it; or

(ii) Submit to its competent authorities, with a view to giving effect to it to the extent requested, an order of confiscation issued by the requesting Party in accordance with paragraph 1 of this article, in so far as it relates to proceeds, property, instrumentalities or any other things referred to in paragraph 1 situated in the territory of the requested Party.

(b) Following a request made pursuant to this article by another Party having jurisdiction over an offence established in accordance with article 3, paragraph 1, the requested Party shall take measures to identify, trace, and freeze or seize proceeds, property, instrumentalities or any other things referred to in paragraph 1 of this article for the purpose of eventual confiscation to be ordered either by the requesting Party or, pursuant to a request under subparagraph (a) of this paragraph, by the requested Party.

(c) The decisions or actions provided for in subparagraphs (a) and (b) of this paragraph shall be taken by the requested Party, in accordance with and subject to the provisions of its domestic law and its procedural rules or any bilateral or multilateral treaty, agreement or arrangement to which it may be bound in relation to the requesting Party.

(d) The provisions of article 7, paragraphs 6 to 19 are applicable mutatis mutandis. In addition to the information specified in article 7, paragraph 10, requests made pursuant to this article shall contain the following:

   (i) In the case of a request pertaining to subparagraph (a)(i) of this paragraph, a description of the property to be confiscated and a statement of the facts relied upon by the requesting Party sufficient to enable the requested Party to seek the order under its domestic law;

   (ii) In the case of a request pertaining to subparagraph (a)(ii), a legally admissible copy of an order of confiscation issued by the requesting Party upon which the request is based, a statement of the facts and information as to the extent to which the execution of the order is requested;

   (iii) In the case of a request pertaining to subparagraph (b), a statement of the facts relied upon by the requesting Party and a description of the actions requested.

(e) Each Party shall furnish to the Secretary-General the text of any of its laws and regulations which give effect to this paragraph and the text of any subsequent changes to such laws and regulations.

(f) If a Party elects to make the taking of the measures referred to in subparagraphs (a) and (b) of this paragraph conditional on the existence of a relevant treaty, that Party shall consider this Convention as the necessary and sufficient treaty basis.

(g) The Parties shall seek to conclude bilateral and multilateral treaties, agreements or arrangements to enhance the effectiveness of international co-operation pursuant to this article.

5. (a) Proceeds or property confiscated by a Party pursuant to paragraph 1 or paragraph 4 of this article shall be disposed of by that Party according to its domestic law and administrative procedures.

(b) When acting on the request of another Party in accordance with this article, a Party may give special consideration to concluding agreements on:

   (i) Contributing the value of such proceeds and property, or funds derived from the sale of such proceeds or property, or a substantial part thereof, to intergovernmental bodies specializing in the fight against illicit traffic in and abuse of narcotic drugs and psychotropic substances;

   (ii) Sharing with other Parties, on a regular or case-by-case basis, such proceeds or property, or funds derived from the sale of such proceeds or property, in accordance with its domestic law, administrative procedures or bilateral or multilateral agreements entered into for this purpose.

6. (a) If proceeds have been transformed or converted into other property, such property shall be liable to the measures referred to in this article instead of the proceeds.

(b) If proceeds have been intermingled with property acquired from legitimate sources, such property shall, without prejudice to any powers relating to seizure or freezing, be liable to confiscation up to the assessed value of the intermingled proceeds.

(c) Income or other benefits derived from:

   (i) Proceeds;

   (ii) Property into which proceeds have been transformed or converted; or

   (iii) Property with which proceeds have been intermingled

shall also be liable to the measures referred to in this article, in the same manner and to the same extent as proceeds.

7. Each Party may consider ensuring that the onus of proof be reversed regarding the lawful origin of alleged proceeds or other property liable to confiscation, to the extent that such action is consistent with the principles of its domestic law and with the nature of the judicial and other proceedings.

8. The provisions of this article shall not be construed as prejudicing the rights of bona fide third parties.

9. Nothing contained in this article shall affect the principle that the measures to which it refers shall be defined and implemented in accordance with and subject to the provisions of the domestic law of a Party.

Article 6

EXTRADITION

1. This article shall apply to the offences established by the Parties in accordance with article 3, paragraph 1.

2. Each of the offences to which this article applies shall be deemed to be included as an extraditable offence in any extradition treaty existing between Parties. The Parties undertake to include such offences as extraditable offences in every extradition treaty to be concluded between them.

3. If a Party which makes extradition conditional on the existence of a treaty receives a request for extradition from another Party with which it has no extradition treaty, it may consider this Convention as the legal basis for extradition in respect of any offence to which this article applies. The Parties which require detailed legislation in order to use this Convention as a legal basis for extradition shall consider enacting such legislation as may be necessary.

4. The Parties which do not make extradition conditional on the existence of a treaty shall recognize offences to which this article applies as extraditable offences between themselves.

5. Extradition shall be subject to the conditions provided for by the law of the requested Party or by applicable extradition treaties, including the grounds upon which the requested Party may refuse extradition.

6. In considering requests received pursuant to this article, the requested State may refuse to comply with such requests where there are substantial grounds leading its judicial or other competent authorities to believe that compliance would facilitate the prosecution or punishment of any person on account of his race, religion, nationality or political opinions, or would cause prejudice for any of those reasons to any person affected by the request.

7. The Parties shall endeavour to expedite extradition procedures and to simplify evidentiary requirements relating thereto in respect of any offence to which this article applies.

8. Subject to the provisions of its domstic law and its extradition treaties, the requested Party may, upon being satisfied that the circumstances so warrant and are urgent, and at the request of the requesting Party, take a person whose extradition is sought and who is present in its territory into custody or take other appropriate measures to ensure his presence at extradition proceedings.

9. Without prejudice to the exercise of any criminal jurisdiction established in accordance with its domestic law, a Party in whose territory an alleged offender is found shall:

(a) If it does not extradite him in respect of an offence established in accordance with article 3, paragraph 1, on the grounds set forth in article 4, paragraph 2, subparagraph (a), submit the case to its competent authorities for the purpose of prosecution, unless otherwise agreed with the requesting Party;

(b) If it does not extradite him in respect of such an offence and has established its jurisdiction in relation to that offence in accordance with article 4, paragraph 2, subparagraph (b), submit the case to its competent authorities for the purpose of prosecution, unless otherwise requested by the requesting Party for the purposes of preserving its legitimate jurisdiction.

10. If extradition, sought for purposes of enforcing a sentence, is refused because the person sought is a national of the requested Party, the requested Party shall, if its law so permits and in conformity with the requirements of such law, upon application of the requesting Party, consider the enforcement of the sentence which has been imposed under the law of the requesting Party, or the remainder thereof.

11. The Parties shall seek to conclude bilateral and multilateral agreements to carry out or to enhance the effectiveness of extradition.

12. The Parties may consider entering into bilateral or multilateral agreements, whether ad hoc or general, on the transfer to their country of persons sentenced to imprisonment and other forms of deprivation of liberty for offences to which this article applies, in order that they may complete their sentence there.

Article 7

MUTUAL LEGAL ASSISTANCE

1. The Parties shall afford one another, pursuant to this article, the widest measure of mutual legal assistance in investigations, prosecutions and judicial proceedings in relation to criminal offences established in accordance with article 3, paragraph 1.

2. Mutual legal assistance to be afforded in accordance with this article may be requested for any of the following purposes:

(a) Taking evidence or statements from persons;

(b) Effecting service of judicial documents;

(c) Executing searches and seizures;

(d) Examining objects and sites;

(e) Providing information and evidentiary items;

(f) Providing originals or certified copies of relevant documents and records, including bank, financial, corporate or business records;

(g) Identifying or tracing proceeds, property, instrumentalities or other things for evidentiary purposes.

3. The Parties may afford one another any other forms of mutual legal assistance allowed by the domestic law of the requested Party.

4. Upon request, the Parties shall facilitate or encourage, to the extent consistent with their domestic law and practice, the presence or availability of persons, including persons in custody, who consent to assist in investigations or participate in proceedings.

5. A Party shall not decline to render mutual legal assistance under this article on the ground of bank secrecy.

6. The provisions of this article shall not affect the obligations under any other treaty, bilateral or multilateral, which governs or will govern, in whole or in part, mutual legal assistance in criminal matters.

7. Paragraphs 8 to 19 of this article shall apply to requests made pursuant to this article if the Parties in question are not bound by a treaty of mutual legal assistance. If these Parties are bound by such a treaty, the corresponding provisions of that treaty shall apply unless the Parties agree to apply paragraphs 8 to 19 of this article in lieu thereof.

8. Parties shall designate an authority, or when necessary authorities, which shall have the responsibility and power to execute requests for mutual legal assistance or to transmit them to the competent authorities for execution. The authority or the authorities designated for this purpose shall be notified to the Secretary-General. Transmission of requests for mutual legal assistance and any communication related thereto shall be effected between the authorities designated by the Parties; this requirement shall be without prejudice to the right of a Party to require that such requests and communications be addressed to it through the diplomatic channel and, in urgent circumstances, where the Parties agree, through channels of the International Criminal Police Organization, if possible.

9. Requests shall be made in writing in a language acceptable to the requested Party. The language or languages acceptable to each Party shall be notified to the Secretary-General. In urgent circumstances, and where agreed by the Parties, requests may be made orally, but shall be confirmed in writing forthwith.

10. A request for mutual legal assistance shall contain:

(a) The identity of the authority making the request;

(b) The subject matter and nature of the investigation, prosecution or proceeding to which the request relates, and the name and the functions of the authority conducting such investigation, prosecution or proceeding;

(c) A summary of the relevant facts, except in respect of requests for the purpose of service of judicial documents;

(d) A description of the assistance sought and details of any particular procedure the requesting Party wishes to be followed;

(e) Where possible, the identity, location and nationality of any person concerned;

(f) The purpose for which the evidence, information or action is sought.

11. The requested Party may request additional information when it appears necessary for the execution of the request in accordance with its domestic law or when it can facilitate such execution.

12. A request shall be executed in accordance with the domestic law of the requested Party and, to the extent not contrary to the domestic law of the requested Party and where possible, in accordance with the procedures specified in the request.

13. The requesting Party shall not transmit nor use information or evidence furnished by the requested Party for investigations, prosecutions or proceedings other than those stated in the request without the prior consent of the requested Party.

14. The requesting Party may require that the requested Party keep confidential the fact and substance of the request, except to the extent necessary to execute the request. If the requested Party cannot comply with the requirement of confidentiality, it shall promptly inform the requesting Party.

15. Mutual legal assistance may be refused:

(a) If the request is not made in conformity with the provisions of this article;

(b) If the requested Party considers that execution of the request is likely to prejudice its sovereignty, security, ordre public or other essential interests;

(c) If the authorities of the requested Party would be prohibited by its domestic law from carrying out the action requested with regard to any similar offence, had it been subject to investigation, prosecution or proceedings under their own jurisdiction;

(d) If it would be contrary to the legal system of the requested Party relating to mutual legal assistance for the request to be granted.

16. Reasons shall be given for any refusal of mutual legal assistance.

17. Mutual legal assistance may be postponed by the requested Party on the ground that it interferes with an ongoing investigation, prosecution or proceeding. In such a case, the requested Party shall consult with the requesting Party to determine if the assistance can still be given subject to such terms and conditions as the requested Party deems necessary.

18. A witness, expert or other person who consents to give evidence in a proceeding or to assist in an investigation, prosecution or judicial proceeding in the territory of the requesting Party, shall not be prosecuted, detained, punished or subjected to any other restriction of his personal liberty in that territory in respet of acts, omissions or convictions prior to his departure from the territory of the requested Party. Such safe conduct shall cease when the witness, expert or other person having had, for a period of fifteen consecutive days, or for any period agreed upon by the Parties, from the date on which he has been officially informed that his presence is no longer required by the judicial authorities, an opportunity of leaving, has nevertheless remained voluntarily in the territory or, having left it, has returned of his own free will.

19. The ordinary costs of executing a request shall be borne by the requested Party, unless otherwise agreed by the Parties concerned. If expenses of a substantial or extraordinary nature are or will be required to fulfil the request, the Parties shall consult to determine the terms and conditions under which the request will be executed as well as the manner in which the costs shall be borne.

20. The Parties shall consider, as may be necessary, the possibility of concluding bilateral or multilateral agreements or arrangements that would serve the purposes of, give practical effect to, or enhance the provisions of this article.

Article 8

TRANSFER OF PROCEEDINGS

The Parties shall give consideration to the possibility of transferring to one another proceedings for criminal prosecution of offences established in accordance with article 3, paragraph 1, in cases where such transfer is considered to be in the interests of a proper administration of justice.

Article 9

OTHER FORMS OF CO-OPERATION AND TRAINING

1. The Parties shall co-operate closely with one another, consistent with their respective domestic legal and administrative systems, with a view to enhancing the effectiveness of law enforcement action to suppress the commission of offences established in accordance with article 3, paragraph 1. They shall, in particular, on the basis of bilateral or multilateral agreements or arrangements:

(a) Establish and maintain channels of communication between their competent agencies and services to facilitate the secure and rapid exchange of information concerning all aspects of offences established in accordance with article 3, paragraph 1, including, if the Parties concerned deem it appropriate, links with other criminal activities;

(b) Co-operate with one another in conducting enquiries, with respect to offences established in accordance with article 3, paragraph 1, having an international character, concerning:

   (i) The identity, whereabouts and activities of persons suspected of being involved in offences established in accordance with article 3, paragraph 1;

   (ii) The movement of proceeds or property derived from the commission of such offences;

   (iii) The movement of narcotic drugs, psychotropic substances, substances in Table I and Table II of this Convention and instrumentalities used or intended for use in the commission of such offences;

(c) In appropriate cases and if not contrary to domestic law, establish joint teams, taking into account the need to protect the security of persons and of operations, to carry out the provisions of this paragraph. Officials of any Party taking part in such teams shall act as authorized by the appropriate authorities of the Party in whose territory the operation is to take place; in all such cases, the Parties involved shall ensure that the sovereignty of the Party on whose territory the operation is to take place is fully respected;

(d) Provide, when appropriate, necessary quantities of substances for analytical or investigative purposes;

(e) Facilitate effective co-ordination between their competent agencies and services and promote the exchange of personnel and other experts, including the posting of liaison officers.

2. Each Party shall, to the extent necessary, initiate, develop or improve specific training programmes for its law enforcement and other personnel, including customs, charged with the suppression of offences established in accordance with article 3, paragraph 1. Such programmes shall deal, in particular, with the following:

(a) Methods used in the detection and suppression of offences established in accordance with article 3, paragraph 1;

(b) Routes and techniques used by persons suspected of being involved in offences established in accordance with article 3, paragraph 1, particularly in transit States, and appropriate countermeasures;

(c) Monitoring of the import and export of narcotic drugs, psychotropic substances and substances in Table I and Table II;

(d) Detection and monitoring of the movement of proceeds and property derived from, and narcotic drugs, psychotropic substances and substances in Table I and Table II, and instrumentalities used or intended for use in, the commission of offences established in accordance with article 3, paragraph 1;

(e) Methods used for the transfer, concealment or disguise of such proceeds, property and instrumentalities;

(f) Collection of evidence;

(g) Control techniques in free trade zones and free ports;

(h) Modern law enforcement techniques.

3. The Parties shall assist one another to plan and implement research and training programmes designed to share expertise in the areas referred to in paragraph 2 of this article and, to this end, shall also, when appropriate, use regional and international conferences and seminars to promote co-operation and stimulate discussion on problems of mutual concern, including the special problems and needs of transit States.

Article 10

INTERNATIONAL CO-OPERATION AND ASSISTANCE FOR TRANSIT STATES

1. The Parties shall co-operate, directly or through competent international or regional organizations, to assist and support transit States and, in particular, developing countries in need of such assistance and support, to the extent possible, through programmes of technical co-operation on interdiction and other related activities.

2. The Parties may undertake, directly or through competent international or regional organizations, to provide financial assistance to such transit States for the purpose of augmenting and strengthening the infrastructure needed for effective control and prevention of illicit traffic.

3. The Parties may conclude bilateral or multilateral agreements or arrangements to enhance the effectiveness of international co-operation pursuant to this article and may take into consideration financial arrangements in this regard.

Article 11

CONTROLLED DELIVERY

1. If permitted by the basic principles of their respective domestic legal systems, the Parties shall take the necessary measures, within their possibilities, to allow for the appropriate use of controlled delivery at the international level, on the basis of agreements or arrangements mutually consented to, with a view to identifying persons involved in offences established in accordance with article 3, paragraph 1, and to taking legal action against them.

2. Decisions to use controlled delivery shall be made on a case-by-case basis and may, when necessary, take into consideration financial arrangements and understandings with respect to the exercise of jurisdiction by the Parties concerned.

3. Illicit consignments whose controlled delivery is agreed to may, with the consent of the Parties concerned, be intercepted and allowed to continue with the narcotic drugs or psychotropic substances intact or removed or replaced in whole or in part.

Article 12

SUBSTANCES FREQUENTLY USED IN THE ILLICIT MANUFACTURE OF NARCOTIC DRUGS OR PSYCHOTROPIC SUBSTANCES

1. The Parties shall take the measures they deem appropriate to prevent diversion of substances in Table I and Table II used for the purpose of illicit manufacture of narcotic drugs or psychotropic substances, and shall co-operate with one another to this end.

2. If a Party or the Board has information which in its opinion may require the inclusion of a substance in Table I or Table II, it shall notify the Secretary-General and furnish him with the information in support of that notification. The procedure described in paragraphs 2 to 7 of this article shall also apply when a Party or the Board has information justifying the deletion of a substance from Table I or Table II, or the transfer of a substance from one Table to the other.

3. The Secretary-General shall transmit such notification, and any information which he considers relevant, to the Parties, to the Commission, and, where notification is made by a Party, to the Board. The Parties shall communicate their comments concerning the notification to the Secretary-General, together with all supplementary information which may assist the Board in establishing an assessment and the Commission in reaching a decision.

4. If the Board, taking into account the extent, importance and diversity of the licit use of the substance, and the possibility and ease of using alternate substances both for licit purposes and for the illicit manufacture of narcotic drugs or psychotropic substances, finds:

(a) That the substance is frequently used in the illicit manufacture of a narcotic drug or psychotropic substance;

(b) That the volume and extent of the illicit manufacture of a narcotic drug or psychotropic substance creates serious public health or social problems, so as to warrant international action,

it shall communicate to the Commission an assessment of the substance, including the likely effect of adding the substance to either Table I or Table II on both licit use and illicit manufacture, together with recommendations of monitoring measures, if any, that would be appropriate in the light of its assessment.

5. The Commission, taking into account the comments submitted by the Parties and the comments and recommendations of the Board, whose assessment shall be determinative as to scientific matters, and also taking into due consideration any other relevant factors, may decide by a two-thirds majority of its members to place a substance in Table I or Table II.

6. Any decision of the Commission taken pursuant to this article shall be communicated by the Secretary-General to all States and other entities which are, or which are entitled to become, Parties to this Convention, and to the Board. Such decision shall become fully effective with respect to each Party one hundred and eighty days after the date of such communication.

7. (a) The decisions of the Commission taken under this article shall be subject to review by the Council upon the request of any Party filed within one hundred and eighty days after the date of notification of the decision. The request for review shall be sent to the Secretary-General, together with all relevant information upon which the request for review is based.

(b) The Secretary-General shall transmit copies of the request for review and the relevant information to the Commission, to the Board and to all the Parties, inviting them to submit their comments within ninety days. All comments received shall be submitted to the Council for consideration.

(c) The Council may confirm or reverse the decision of the Commission. Notification of the Council's decision shall be transmitted to all States and other entities which are, or which are entitled to become, Parties to this Convention, to the Commission and to the Board.

8. (a) Without prejudice to the generality of the provisions contained in paragraph 1 of this article and the provisions of the 1961 Convention, the 1961 Convention as amended and the 1971 Convention, the Parties shall take the measures they deem appropriate to monitor the manufacture and distribution of substances in Table I and Table II which are carried out within their territory.

(b) To this end, the Parties may:

(i) Control all persons and enterprises engaged in the manufacture and distribution of such substances;

(ii) Control under licence the establishment and premises in which such manufacture or distribution may take place;

(iii) Require that licensees obtain a permit for conducting the aforesaid operations;

(iv) Prevent the accumulation of such substances in the possession of manufacturers and distributors, in excess of the quantities required for the normal conduct of business and the prevailing market conditions.

9. Each Party shall, with respect to substances in Table I and Table II, take the following measures:

(a) Establish and maintain a system to monitor international trade in substances in Table I and Table II in order to facilitate the identification of suspicious transactions. Such monitoring systems shall be applied in close co-operation with manufacturers, importers, exporters, wholesalers and retailers, who shall inform the competent authorities of suspicious orders and transactions.

(b) Provide for the seizure of any subtance in Table I or Table II if there is sufficient evidence that it is for use in the illicit manufacture of a narcotic drug or psychotropic substance.

(c) Notify, as soon as possible, the competent authorities and services of the Parties concerned if there is reason to believe that the import, export or transit of a substance in Table I or Table II is destined for the illicit manufacture of narcotic drugs or psychotropic substances, including in particular information about the means of payment and any other essential elements which led to that belief.

(d) Require that imports and exports be properly labelled and documented. Commercial documents such as invoices, cargo manifests, customs, transport and other shipping documents shall include the names, as stated in Table I or Table II, of the substances being imported or exported, the quantity being imported or exported, and the name and address of the exporter, the importer and, when available, the consignee.

(e) Ensure that documents referred to in subparagraph (d) of this paragraph are maintained for a period of not less than two years and may be made available for inspection by the competent authorities.

10. (a) In addition to the provisions of paragraph 9, and upon request to the Secretary-General by the interested Party, each Party from whose territory a substance in Table I is to be exported shall ensure that, prior to such export, the following information is supplied by its competent authorities to the competent authorities of the importing country:

(i) Name and address of the exporter and importer and, when available, the consignee;

(ii) Name of the substance in Table I;

(iii) Quantity of the substance to be exported;

(iv) Expected point of entry and expected date of dispatch;

(v) Any other information which is mutually agreed upon by the Parties.

(b) A Party may adopt more strict or severe measures of control than those provided by this paragraph if, in its opinion, such measures are desirable or necessary.

11. Where a Party furnishes information to another Party in accordance with paragraphs 9 and 10 of this article, the Party furnishing such information may require that the Party receiving it keep confidential any trade, business, commercial or professional secret or trade process.

12. Each Party shall furnish annually to the Board, in the form and manner provided for by it and on forms made available by it, information on:

(a) The amounts seized of substances in Table I and Table II and, when known, their origin;

(b) Any substance not included in Table I or Table II which is identified as having been used in illicit manufacture of narcotic drugs or psychotropic substances, and which is deemed by the Party to be sufficiently significant to be brought to the attention of the Board;

(c) Methods of diversion and illicit manufacture.

13. The Board shall report annually to the Commission on the implementation of this article and the Commission shall periodically review the adequacy and propriety of Table I and Table II.

14. The provisions of this article shall not apply to pharmaceutical preparations, nor to other preparations containing substances in Table I or Table II that are compounded in such a way that such substances cannot be easily used or recovered by readily applicable means.

Article 13

MATERIALS AND EQUIPMENT

The Parties shall take such measures as they deem appropriate to prevent trade in and the diversion of materials and equipment for illicit production or manufacture of narcotic drugs and psychotropic substances and shall co-operate to this end.

Article 14

MEASURES TO ERADICATE ILLICIT CULTIVATION OF NARCOTIC PLANTS AND TO ELIMINATE ILLICIT DEMAND FOR NARCOTIC DRUGS AND PSYCHOTROPIC SUBSTANCES

1. Any measures taken pursuant to this Convention by Parties shall not be less stringent than the provisions applicable to the eradication of illicit cultivation of plants containing narcotic and psychotropic substances and to the elimination of illicit demand for narcotic drugs and psychotropic substances under the provisions of the 1961 Convention, the 1961 Convention as amended and the 1971 Convention.

2. Each Party shall take appropriate measures to prevent illicit cultivation of and to eradicate plants containing narcotic or psychotropic substances, such as opium poppy, coca bush and cannabis plants, cultivated illicitly in its territory. The measures adopted shall respect fundamental human rights and shall take due account of traditional licit uses, where there is historic evidence of such use, as well as the protection of the environment

3. (a) The Parties may co-operate to increase the effectiveness of eradication efforts. Such co-operation may, inter alia, include support, when appropriate, for integrated rural development leading to economically viable alternatives to illicit cultivation. Factors such as access to markets, the availability of resources and prevailing socio-economic conditions should be taken into account before such rural development programmes are implemented. The Parties may agree on any other appropriate measures of co-operation.

(b) The Parties shall also facilitate the exchange of scientific and technical information and the conduct of research concerning eradication.

(c) Whenever they have common frontiers, the Parties shall seek to co-operate in eradication programmes in their respective areas along those frontiers.

4. The Parties shall adopt appropriate measures aimed at eliminating or reducing illicit demand for narcotic drugs and psychotropic substances, with a view to reducing human suffering and eliminating financial incentives for illicit traffic. These measures may be based, inter alia, on the recommendations of the United Nations, specialized agencies of the United Nations such as the World Health Organization, and other competent international organizations, and on the Comprehensive Multidisciplinary Outline adopted by the International Conference on Drug Abuse and Illicit Trafficking, held in 1987, as it pertains to governmental and non-governmental agencies and private efforts in the fields of prevention, treatment and rehabilitation. The Parties may enter into bilateral or multilateral agreements or arrangements aimed at eliminating or reducing illicit demand for narcotic drugs and psychotropic substances.

5. The Parties may also take necessary measures for early destruction or lawful disposal of the narcotic drugs, psychotropic substances and substances in Table I and Table II which have been seized or confiscated and for the admissibility as evidence of duly certified necessary quantities of such substances.

Article 15

COMMERCIAL CARRIERS

1. The Parties shall take appropriate measures to ensure that means of transport operated by commercial carriers are not used in the commission of offences established in accordance with article 3, paragraph 1; such measures may include special arrangements with commercial carriers.

2. Each Party shall require commercial carriers to take reasonable precautions to prevent the use of their means of transport for the commission of offences established in accordance with article 3, paragraph 1. Such precautions may include:

(a) If the principal place of business of a commercial carrier is within the territory of the Party:

(i) Training of personnel to identify suspicious consignments or persons;

(ii) Promotion of integrity of personnel;

(b) If a commercial carrier is operating within the territory of the Party:

(i) Submission of cargo manifests in advance, whenever possible;

(ii) Use of tamper-resistant, individually verifiable seals on containers;

(iii) Reporting to the appropriate authorities at the earliest opportunity all suspicious circumstances that may be related to the commission of offences established in accordance with article 3, paragraph 1.

3. Each Party shall seek to ensure that commercial carriers and the appropriate authorities at points of entry and exit and other customs control areas co-operate, with a view to preventing unauthorized access to means of transport and cargo and to implementing appropriate security measures.

Article 16

COMMERCIAL DOCUMENTS AND LABELLING OF EXPORTS

1. Each Party shall require that lawful exports of narcotic drugs and psychotropic substances be properly documented. In addition to the requirements for documentation under article 31 of the 1961 Convention, article 31 of the 1961 Convention as amended and article 12 of the 1971 Convention, commercial documents such as invoices, cargo manifests, customs, transport and other shipping documents shall include the names of the narcotic drugs and psychotropic substances being exported as set out in the respective Schedules of the 1961 Convention, the 1961 Convention as amended and the 1971 Convention, the quantity being exported, and the name and address of the exporter, the importer and, when available, the consignee.

2. Each Party shall require that consignments of narcotic drugs and psychotropic substances being exported be not mislabelled.

Article 17

ILLICIT TRAFFIC BY SEA

1. The Parties shall co-operate to the fullest extent possible to suppress illicit traffic by sea, in conformity with the international law of the sea.

2. A Party which has reasonable grounds to suspect that a vessel flying its flag or not displaying a flag or marks of registry is engaged in illicit traffic may request the assistance of other Parties in suppressing its use for that purpose. The Parties so requested shall render such assistance within the means available to them.

3. A Party which has reasonable grounds to suspect that a vessel exercising freedom of navigation in accordance with international law and flying the flag or displaying marks of registry of another Party is engaged in illicit traffic may so notify the flag State, request confirmation of registry and, if confirmed, request authorization from the flag State to take appropriate measures in regard to that vessel.

4. In accordance with paragraph 3 or in accordance with treaties in force between them or in accordance with any agreement or arrangement otherwise reached between those Parties, the flag State may authorize the requesting State to, inter alia:

(a) Board the vessel;

(b) Search the vessel;

(c) If evidence of involvement in illicit traffic is found, take appropriate action with respect to the vessel, persons and cargo on board.

5. Where action is taken pursuant to this article, the Parties concerned shall take due account of the need not to endanger the safety of life at sea, the security of the vessel and the cargo or to prejudice the commercial and legal interests of the flag State or any other interested State.

6. The flag State may, consistent with its obligations in paragraph 1 of this article, subject its authorization to conditions to be mutually agreed between it and the requesting party, including conditions relating to responsibility.

7. For the purposes of paragraphs 3 and 4 of this article, a Party shall respond expeditiously to a request from another Party to determine whether a vessel that is flying its flag is entitled to do so, and to requests for authorization made pursuant to paragraph 3. At the time of becoming a Party to this Convention, each Party shall designate an authority or, when necessary, authorities to receive and respond to such requests. Such designation shall be notified through the Secretary-General to all other Parties within one month of the designation.

8. A Party which has taken any action in accordance with this article shall promptly inform the flag State concerned of the results of that action.

9. The Parties shall consider entering into bilateral or regional agreements or arrangements to carry out, or to enhance the effectiveness of, the provisions of this article.

10. Action pursuant to paragraph 4 of this article shall be carried out only by warships or military aircraft, or other ships or aircraft clearly marked and identifiable as being on government service and authorised to that effect.

11. Any action taken in accordance with this article shall take due account of the need not to interfere with or affect the rights and obligations and the exercise of jurisdiction of coastal States in accordance with the international law of the sea.

Article 18

FREE TRADE ZONES AND FREE PORTS

1. The Parties shall apply measures to suppress illicit traffic in narcotic drugs, psychotropic substances and substances in Table I and Table II in free trade zones and in free ports that are no less stringent than those applied in other parts of their territories.

2. The Parties shall endeavour:

(a) To monitor the movement of goods and persons in free trade zones and free ports, and, to that end, shall empower the competent authorities to search cargoes and incoming and outgoing vessels, including pleasure craft and fishing vessels, as well as aircraft and vehicles and, when appropriate, to search crew members, passengers and their baggage;

(b) To establish and maintain a system to detect consignments suspected of containing narcotic drugs, psychotropic substances and substances in Table I and Table II passing into or out of free trade zones and free ports;

(c) To establish and maintain surveillance systems in harbour and dock areas and at airports and border control points in free trade zones and free ports.

Article 19

THE USE OF THE MAILS

1. In conformity with their obligations under the Conventions of the Universal Postal Union, and in accordance with the basic principles of their domestic legal systems, the Parties shall adopt measures to suppress the use of the mails for illicit traffic and shall co-operate with one another to that end.

2. The measures referred to in paragraph 1 of this article shall include, in particular:

(a) Co-ordinated action for the prevention and repression of the use of the mails for illicit traffic;

(b) Introduction and maintenance by authorized law enforcement personnel of investigative and control techniques designed to detect illicit consignments of narcotic drugs, psychotropic substances and substances in Table I and Table II in the mails;

(c) Legislative measures to enable the use of appropriate means to secure evidence required for judicial proceedings.

Article 20

INFORMATION TO BE FURNISHED BY THE PARTIES

1. The Parties shall furnish, through the Secretary-General, information to the Commission on the working of this Convention in their territories and, in particular:

(a) The text of laws and regulations promulgated in order to give effect to the Convention;

(b) Particulars of cases of illicit traffic within their jurisdiction which they consider important because of new trends disclosed, the quantities involved, the sources from which the substances are obtained, or the methods employed by persons so engaged.

2. The Parties shall furnish such information in such a manner and by such dates as the Commission may request.

Article 21

FUNCTIONS OF THE COMMISSION

The Commission is authorized to consider all matters pertaining to the aims of this Convention and, in particular:

(a) The Commission shall, on the basis of the information submitted by the Parties in accordance with Article 20, review the operation of this Convention;

(b) The Commission may make suggestions and general recommendations based on the examination of the information received from the Parties;

(c) The Commission may call the attention of the Board to any matters which may be relevant to the functions of the Board;

(d) The Commission shall, on any matter referred to it by the Board under article 22, paragraph 1(b), take such action as it deems appropriate;

(e) The Commission may, in conformity with the procedures laid down in article 12, amend Table I and Table II;

(f) The Commission may draw the attention of non-Parties to decisions and recommendations which it adopts under this Convention, with a view to their considering taking action in accordance therewith.

Article 22

FUNCTIONS OF THE BOARD

1. Without prejudice to the functions of the Commission under article 21, and without prejudice to the functions of the Board and the Commission under the 1961 Convention, the 1961 Convention as amended and the 1971 Convention:

(a) If, on the basis of its examination of information available to it, to the Secretary-General or to the Commission, or of information communicated by United Nations organs, the Board has reason to believe that the aims of this Convention in matters related to its competence are not being met, the Board may invite a Party or Parties to furnish any relevant information;

(b) With respect to articles 12, 13 and 16:

    (i) After taking action under subparagraph (a) of this article, the Board, if satisfied that it is necessary to do so, may call upon the Party concerned to adopt such remedial measures as shall seem under the circumstances to be necessary for the execution of the provisions of articles 12, 13 and 16;

    (ii) Prior to taking action under (iii) below, the Board shall treat as confidential its communications with the Party concerned under the preceding subparagraphs;

    (iii) If the Board finds that the Party concerned has not taken remedial measures which it has been called upon to take under this subparagraph, it may call the attention of the Parties, the Council and the Commission to the matter. Any report published by the Board under this subparagraph shall also contain the views of the Party concerned if the latter so requests.

2. Any Party shall be invited to be represented at a meeting of the Board at which a question of direct interest to it is to be considered under this article.

3. If in any case a decision of the Board which is adopted under this article is not unanimous, the views of the minority shall be stated.

4. Decisions of the Board under this article shall be taken by a two-thirds majority of the whole number of the Board.

5. In carrying out its functions pursuant to subparagraph 1(a) of this article, the Board shall ensure the confidentiality of all information which may come into its possession.

6. The Board's responsibility under this article shall not apply to the implementation of treaties or agreements entered into between Parties in accordance with the provisions of this Convention.

7. The provisions of this article shall not be applicable to disputes between Parties falling under the provisions of article 32.

Article 23

REPORTS OF THE BOARD

1. The Board shall prepare an annual report on its work containing an analysis of the information at its disposal and, in appropriate cases, an account of the explanations, if any, given by or required of Parties, together with any observations and recommendations which the Board desires to make. The Board may make such additional reports as it considers necessary. The reports shall be submitted to the Council through the Commission which may make such comments as it sees fit.

2. The reports of the Board shall be communicated to the Parties and subsequently published by the Secretary-General. The Parties shall permit their unrestricted distribution.

Article 24

APPLICATION OF STRICTER MEASURES THAN THOSE REQUIRED BY THIS CONVENTION

A Party may adopt more strict or severe measures than those provided by this Convention if, in its opinion, such measures are desirable or necessary for the prevention or suppression of illicit traffic.

Article 25

NON-DEROGATION FROM EARLIER TREATY RIGHTS AND OBLIGATIONS

The provisions of this Convention shall not derogate from any rights enjoyed or obligations undertaken by Parties to this Convention under the 1961 Convention, the 1961 Convention as amended and the 1971 Convention.

Article 26

SIGNATURE

This Convention shall be open for signature at the United Nations Office at Vienna, from 20 December 1988 to 28 February 1989, and thereafter at the Headquarters of the United Nations at New York, until 20 December 1989, by:

(a) All States;

(b) Namibia, represented by the United Nations Council for Namibia;

(c) Regional economic integration organizations which have competence in respect of the negotiation, conclusion and application of international agreements in matters covered by this Convention, references under the Convention to Parties, States or national services being applicable to these organizations within the limits of their competence.

Article 27

RATIFICATION, ACCEPTANCE, APPROVAL OR ACT OF FORMAL CONFIRMATION

1. This Convention is subject to ratification, acceptance or approval by States and by Namibia, represented by the United Nations Council for Namibia, and to acts of formal confirmation by regional economic integration organizations referred to in article 26, subparagraph (c). The instruments of ratification, acceptance or approval and those relating to acts of formal confirmation shall be deposited with the Secretary-General.

2. In their instruments of formal confirmation, regional economic integration organizations shall declare the extent of their competence with respect to the matters governed by this Convention. These organizations shall also inform the Secretary-General of any modification in the extent of their competence with respect to the matters governed by the Convention.

Article 28

ACCESSION

1. This Convention shall remain open for accession by any State, by Namibia, represented by the United Nations Council for Namibia, and by regional economic integration organizations referred to in article 26, subparagraph (c).

Accession shall be effected by the deposit of an instrument of accession with the Secretary-General.

2. In their instruments of accession, regional economic integration organizations shall declare the extent of their competence with respect to the matters governed by this Convention. These organizations shall also inform the Secretary-General of any modification in the extent of their competence with respect to the matters governed by the Convention.

Article 29

ENTRY INTO FORCE

1. This Convention shall enter into force on the ninetieth day after the date of the deposit with the Secretary-General of the twentieth instrument of ratification, acceptance, approval or accession by States or by Namibia, represented by the Council for Namibia.

2. For each State or for Namibia, represented by the Council for Namibia, ratifying, accepting, approving or acceding to this Convention after the deposit of the twentieth instrument of ratification, acceptance, approval or accession, the Convention shall enter into force on the ninetieth day after the date of the deposit of its instrument of ratification, acceptance, approval or accession.

3. For each regional economic integration organization referred to in article 26, subparagraph (c) depositing an instrument relating to an act of formal confirmation or an instrument of accession, this Convention shall enter into force on the ninetieth day after such deposit, or at the date the Convention enters into force pursuant to paragraph 1 of this article, whichever is later.

Article 30

DENUNCIATION

1. A Party may denounce this Convention at any time by a written notification addressed to the Secretary-General.

2. Such denunciation shall take effect for the Party concerned one year after the date of receipt of the notification by the Secretary-General.

Article 31

AMENDMENTS

1. Any Party may propose an amendment to this Convention. The text of any such amendment and the reasons therefor shall be communicated by that party to the Secretary-General, who shall communicate it to the other Parties and shall ask them whether they accept the proposed amendment. If a proposed amendment so circulated has not been rejected by any Party within twenty-four months after it has been circulated, it shall be deemed to have been accepted and shall enter into force in respect of a Party ninety days after that Party has deposited with the Secretary-General an instrument expressing its consent to be bound by that amendment.

2. If a proposed amendment has been rejected by any Party, the Secretary-General shall consult with the Parties and, if a majority so requests, he shall bring the matter, together with any comments made by the Parties, before the Council which may decide to call a conference in accordance with Article 62, paragraph 4, of the Charter of the United Nations. Any amendment resulting from such a Conference shall be embodied in a Protocol of Amendment. Consent to be bound by such a Protocol shall be required to be expressed specifically to the Secretary-General.

Article 32

SETTLEMENT OF DISPUTES

1. If there should arise between two or more Parties a dispute relating to the interpretation or application of this Convention, the Parties shall consult together with a view to the settlement of the dispute by negotiation, enquiry, mediation, conciliation, arbitration, recourse to regional bodies, judicial process or other peaceful means of their own choice.

2. Any such dispute which cannot be settled in the manner prescribed in paragraph 1 of this article shall be referred, at the request of any one of the States Parties to the dispute, to the International Court of Justice for decision.

3. If a regional economic integration organization referred to in article 26, subparagraph (c) is a Party to a dispute which cannot be settled in the manner prescribed in paragraph 1 of this article, it may, through a State Member of the United Nations, request the Council to request an advisory opinion of the International Court of Justice in accordance with article 65 of the Statute of the Court, which opinion shall be regarded as decisive.

4. Each State, at the time of signature or ratification, acceptance or approval of this Convention or accession thereto, or each regional economic integration organization, at the time of signature or deposit of an act of formal confirmation or accession, may declare that it does not consider itself bound by paragraphs 2 and 3 of this article. The other Parties shall not be bound by paragraphs 2 and 3 with respect to any Party having made such a declaration.

5. Any Party having made a declaration in accordance with paragraph 4 of this article may at any time withdraw the declaration by notification to the Secretary-General.

Article 33

AUTHENTIC TEXTS

The Arabic, Chinese, English, French, Russian and Spanish texts of this Convention are equally authentic.

Article 34

DEPOSITARY

The Secretary-General shall be the depositary of this Convention.

ANNEX

Table I	Table II
Ephedrine	Acetic anhydride
Ergometrine	Acetone
Ergotamine	Anthranilic acid
Lysergic acid	Ethyl ether
1-phenyl-2-propanone	Phenylacetic acid
Pseudoephedrine	Piperidine

The salts of the substances listed in this Table whenever the existence of such salts is possible.	The salts of the substances listed in this Table whenever the existence of such salts is possible.

DOCUMENT C

Report of the United States Delegation to the United Nations Conference for the adoption of a Convention Against Illicit Traffic in Narcotic Drugs and Psychotropic Substances
(extracts)
Source: 101st Congress, 1st Session, SENATE, Exec.Rept. 101-15

(Article 1 - DEFINITIONS)

Comments:

(a): The definition of "Board" is self-explanatory.

(b): The definition of "cannabis plant" is intentionally broad and is meant to cover all parts of the plant. It is identical to the definition contained in the Single Convention.

(c): The definition of "coca bush" is identical to the one in the Single Convention.

(d): The definition of "commercial carrier" is intended to be all-inclusive. The words "or other" were added before "entity" in order to make it as broad as possible and enable it to apply to entities that were neither public nor private. This definition is broad enough to encompass private aircraft.

(e): The definition of "Commission is self-explanatory.

(f): The definition of "confiscation" was included to ensure that the term is understood to mean the permanent, final deprivation of ownership of property by a court or other competent authority. The reference to the concept of forfeiture underscores that it is synonymous with that concept as used in United States law.

(g): The definition of "controlled delivery" was deemed necessary to clarify the obligations undertaken by Parties by operation of

Article 11, in particular because the use of this particular law enforcement technique is uncommon in some countries.

(h),(i)(j):   These definitions are self-explanatory; they were included to allow short-hand references to the earlier conventions.

(l): Although the concept of legally "freezing" or "seizing" property is almost universally recognized, this definition clarifies those concepts particularly for countries which have not yet enacted domestic forfeiture laws.   As used in the Convention, they are substantially synonymous with U.S. law.

(m): "Illicit traffic" was defined by reference to the offenses set forth in art. 3, paras. 1 and 2 to clarify that the personal possession offenses are also included.   In fact, the term is rarely used in the text of the Convention and most provisions generally refer to specific offenses listed in Article 3.

(n): The definition of "narcotic drug", together with the definition of "psychotropic substances", identifies the substances which are the subject of this Convention.   It includes all substances listed in the annexed Schedules, not only those which are pharmacologically narcotic.   All listed substances are "controlled substances" under United States law.

(o): The definition of "opium poppy" is identical to the one in the Single Convention.

(p): The term "proceeds" as used in this Convention includes all property derived or obtained from an offense listed in Article 3, paragraph 1, including profits thereof.   By contrast, the term "instrumentalities" means all property used or intended for use in an offense.

(q): "Property" is defined broadly to encompass intangible ownership rights as well as physical objects.

(r): The term "psychotropic substances" is defined by reference to the schedules adopted under the 1971 Convention. The United States is a party to that convention, and all of the substances on the schedules are "controlled substances" under United States law.

(s), (t): The definitions of "Secretary-General", "Table I" and "Table II" are self-explanatory.

(u): A definition of "transit state" was included to clarify the meaning of Article 10.

(Article 3 - OFFENCES AND SANCTIONS)

Comments

Article 3 is the cornerstone of the Convention. It sets forth two categories of substantive offenses which parties are either obligated or permitted to make criminal. It is designed to focus on the fundamental law enforcement measures necessary to combat the dual problems of international drug trafficking and money laundering. The article focuses and imposes the greatest international obligations on those offenses which have the most international impact. Therefore, although the Convention recognizes that the demand for narcotic drugs and psychotropic substances fuels illicit international trafficking, criminalizing personal use offenses is mandatory but subject to the constitutional principles and the basic concepts of each Party's legal system. Fewer international obligations are imposed on Parties to assist in the investigation and prosecution of these offenses. Domestic and international strategies for reducing the demand for illegal drugs are, for the most part, not the subject of the Convention.

Paragraph 1 and 2 of this article were carefully crafted to include a mandatory obligation on the part of the States Party to enact legislation criminalizing specific categories of narcotics and money laundering offenses. These mandatory offenses are not limited by the chapeau "subject to its constitutional principles and the basic concepts of its legal system". Making these categories of offenses mandatory was a significant accomplishment.

The specific narcotic drugs and psychotropic substances covered by these offenses are those substances and drugs under international control pursuant to the provisions of the Single and Psychotropic Substances Conventions. The United States is a party to both these Conventions. Our schedules of controlled substances include all drugs and substances under international control under both conventions. There are a few substances subject to control in the United States which are not controlled internationally.

Paragraph 1(a) is intended to be an all-inclusive list of illicit drug trafficking offenses. It was subdivided into subparagraphs (i) to (v) to clarify and distinguish the acts involved. Subparagraph (i) reproduces the list of criminal acts contained in the Single Convention with the exception of cultivation, possession, and purchase. Cultivation is covered separately in subparagraph (ii) because, of all the illicit narcotic drugs and psychotropic substances subject to international control, only marijuana, coca bushes and the opium poppy are cultivated. Possession and purchase were covered separately in subparagraph (iii). Possession, purchase and cultivation for personal use are also covered in paragraph 2.

Subparagraph (iv) includes the manufacture, transport or distribution of materials, equipment and substances in Tables I and II (precursor and essential chemicals) knowing that they are to be used to manufacture, cultivate or produce narcotic drugs or psychotropic substances. This provision is new and is intended to criminalize the acts of those who knowingly supply essential materials or chemicals to produce or cultivate illegal drugs.

Subparagraph (v) requires the criminalization of the financing, organizing, or managing of any of the acts listed in subparagraphs (i) to (iv). The negotiators believed that the inclusion of this subparagraph was extremely important to reach the highest levels of international drug trafficking. This provision is a significant step forward from the Single Convention which only addresses the financing of drug trafficking and limits the obligation to criminalize financing to the limitations of a Party's constitution, legal system and domestic law. This paragraph combines provisions of law separately designated in the U.S. Code including: 18 U.S.C. 1956 and 1957 (money laundering), 18 U.S.C. 1961 (RICO), and 21 U.S.C. 848 (CCE).

All of the offenses listed in paragraph 1(a) are presently criminal offenses under Title 21 of the United States Code. The distribution, transport, or manufacture of precursor or essential chemicals or materials or equipment knowing they are to be used in illicit drug offenses have been criminalized under the Anti-Drug Abuse Act of 1988 (Pub. L. 100-690).

Subparagraph (b) imposes an obligation on parties to criminalize illegal drug related money laundering. Much of the language is derived from the United States statutes on money laundering (see, e.g. 18 U.S.C. sections 1956-57). Two modifications were made in the U.S. statutes. First, the paragraphs relate only to property derived from offenses established in accordance with subparagraph (a), that is, illegal drug offenses. Second, because the Convention makes no attempt to impose currency reporting requirements, there are no references to actions to avoid such reporting requirements. The language "from an act of participation in such offense or offenses" was included in subparagraphs (b)(i) and (ii) to insure that the laundering of property derived from conspiracy offenses was included in the coverage of the offense. The language "or of assisting any person who is involved in the commission of such an offense or offenses to evade the legal consequences of his action" in paragraph (b)(i) is intended to ensure that it is an offense for a person to intentionally convert or transfer property knowing that property is derived from an illicit trafficking offense with the purpose of assisting a person involved in the offense to avoid forfeiture proceedings or discovery of his illicit trafficking and the subsequent criminal proceedings. Because the language of paragraph (b)(i) requires a specific intent to either convert or transfer property or to assist a person to evade discovery of his illegal actions or of the illicit source of his income, it is not intended and does not reach legitimate payment of attorney's fees. Thus, if an attorney received money for legitimate representation purposes, he/she could not be prosecuted if it turned out that the money was derived from a narcotics offense. The paragraph requires a "conversion or transfer" for the purpose of "concealing or disguising" assets or "evading the legal consequences of his action". The term "evasion" implies criminal purpose -- not legal avoidance through <u>bona fide</u> representation by counsel. Current United States money laundering laws, 18 U.S.C. 1956-57, satisfy United States obligations to establish these offenses.

Subparagraph (c) lists the permissive categories of offenses that the Parties are obligated to establish as offenses under their domestic law. The obligation to establish these offenses is qualified by the limiting chapeau, "subject to its constitutional principles and the basic concepts of its legal system". There were a number of reasons that the negotiators believed that the obligation to enact these offenses had to be limited. First, because some legal systems allow little or no discretion to the police and prosecutors, it was believed impossible to formulate offenses that all parties could agree to that would not sweep innocent conduct into its proscribed conduct. Second, some offenses, such as conspiracy offenses, are not titled the same nor do they involve exactly the same elements in various states; indeed, some legal systems specifically prohibit conspiracy offenses. Thus, although these are similarities between such offenses as criminal association and conspiracy, the legal concepts differ from legal system to legal system. Third, the United States negotiators were concerned that a literal reading of some of these offenses might create unconstitutional offenses in the United States. In particular, subparagraph (c)(iii) could be read to include conduct protected by the First Amendment. By limiting a Party's obligation to enact legislation to create offenses in these categories to the extent consistent with its constitutional principles and the basic concepts of its legal system, constitutional and definitional difficulties can be more easily eliminated.

The first subparagraph requires each Party to criminalize the acquisition, possession or use of property if the offender knew at the time of receipt of the property that it was derived from an Article 3, paragraph 1 offense. At the negotiations it was recognized that the limiting chapeau was important here because the conduct described could criminalize a purchase by a bona fide purchaser for value.

The second subparagraph, subparagraph (ii), requires parties to criminalize the possession of equipment, materials, and chemicals (substances in Tables I and II) if the offender knew that they were being used or intended for use in the illicit cultivation, manufacture or production of illicit narcotic drugs and psychotropic substances.

Subparagraph (iii) requires parties to criminalize the incitement or inducement of others to commit any other offense established according to Article 3. This offense is very broadly drawn and references not only other Article 3 paragraph 1 offenses, but all article 3 offenses. Thus it also includes inducement of others to purchase, possess or cultivate illegal drug for personal use.

Subparagraph (iv) includes an obligation to enact as criminal offenses such offenses as conspiracy and aiding and abetting offenses.

Paragraph 2 also represents a compromise among states on how severely to treat possession, purchase or cultivation of illicit narcotic drugs and psychotropic substances for personal use. While recognizing that personal use offenses should be treated as criminal offenses, the Parties qualified the obligation with the chapeau "subject to its constitutional principles and the basic concepts of its legal system." The placement of these offenses in a separate paragraph was deliberately done for two reasons.

First, in order to limit the international obligations in the articles on mutual legal assistance, forfeiture and extradition, it was believed necessary to separate personal use offenses from the trafficking offenses in paragraph 1 of Article 3. Because international assistance in extradition, mutual legal assistance and forfeiture are often expensive and time consuming procedures for both the requested and requesting Parties, the negotiators did not want to impose these obligations on Parties for offenses of a more minor nature. Second, the personal use offenses were separated to allow Parties to impose alternative sanctions such as treatment and rehabilitation programs rather than incarceration in appropriate cases.

Paragraph 3 is included to clarify that the requisite elements of knowledge, intent or purpose in the offenses described in this Article may be inferred from objective facts. The purpose of this paragraph is to state that the inclusion of those elements in the description of the offenses is not intended to change in any way the level or form of proof required by a Party's domestic law. Thus the paragraph affirms the possibility of proving these elements circumstantially.

Paragraph 4 is designed to obligate Parties to treat illicit drug offenses as serious offenses subject to such penalties as imprisonment, fines and forfeiture. At the same time the negotiators recognized that, for minor offenses or for simple possession offenses, rehabilitation or treatment programs may be provided as an alternative to imprisonment.

Paragraph 5 provides a non-exhaustive list of factors which courts or other competent authorities should be able to consider in deciding on the appropriate sanctions. Factors that the negotiators considered to make more serious the offense, or the offender's role in the offense, are traditional factors recognized as aggravating factors under United States law and practice. See Title 18, United States Code, Section 3553 and Chapter 3, Sentencing Guidelines. They include such factors as the involvement of an organized criminal group, the use of firearms or violence and the use or victimization of minors.

Paragraph 6 is a hortatory paragraph calling on Parties whose legal systems grant discretion in the prosecution of persons for Article 3 offenses to exercise this discretion in ways that maximize law enforcement and deter others from the commission of such offenses. United States law vests broad discretion in the Executive branch to initiate or forego prosecution. It is the obligation of the Executive branch to see that the laws of the United States be "faithfully executed." U.S. Const., Art. II, Sec.3. In exercising its discretion, United States law enforcement officials are guided by the "Principles of Federal Prosecution." See U.S. A.M. 9:27.000. Those principles call for a weighing of relevant factors, including the seriousness of the offense, the person's culpability and criminal history and the deterrent effect of prosecution.

Paragraph 7 requires Parties to ensure that their courts or other competent authorities consider the seriousness of paragraph 1 offenses and the existence of aggravating circumstances listed in paragraph 5 when considering the early release or parole of persons convicted of paragraph 1 offenses. The Sentencing Reform Act of 1984, implemented November 1, 1987, Title 18, United States Code, Section 3557 et seq. introduced determinate federal sentences and abolished parole. The seriousness of drug offenses is reflected in U.S. law in the mandatory minimum sentences to be imposed for many controlled substance violations. See, e.g., 21 U.S.C. SS 841, 846, 848.

Paragraph 8 requires each party to establish where appropriate a mechanism for tolling the statute of limitations for illicit trafficking offenses and to extend that limitation period when the alleged offender has evaded that Party's criminal justice authorities. The United States statute of limitations for non-capital felony controlled substances violations is five years. Unlike many other states, our limitation period is tolled by the filing of an indictment. Title 18, United States Code, Section 3282. Section 3290 of Title 18 also tolls the running of the statute of limitations if the person flees from justice. The limitations period may also be suspended for a period to allow the United States to obtain evidence in a foreign country. 18 U.S.C. S 3292. These provisions of U.S. law create appropriately long limitations periods.

Paragraph 9 directs Parties to take whatever measures are necessary and consistent with their domestic laws to ensure that persons accused or convicted appear at the necessary criminal proceedings. United States statutes on release and detention pending trial and sentence are designed to permit our courts to impose such conditions of bail as will reasonably assure a person's presence or to detain a person if no conditions will reasonably assure the appearance of the person. Title 18, United Sates Code, Section 3142 <u>et seq</u>.

Paragraph 10 states that for purposes of cooperation among Parties, offenses established pursuant to this Article shall not be considered fiscal offenses, political offenses or politically motivated offenses. This paragraph obligates Parties not to refuse to cooperate because their domestic law or a bilateral or multilateral treaty exempts fiscal, political or politically motivated offenses from any international obligations to cooperate. This paragraph clearly states that illegal drug and money laundering offenses are not, by definition, political or fiscal offenses. It also states that if a Party recognizes a limitation to its obligation to cooperate for offenses committed for political reasons, such as drug trafficking to raise money for a political group, that limitation shall not apply. This paragraph, however, in no way limits a Party's right to refuse to assist another Party because the request for assistance itself is made for political purposes rather than as part of a genuine investigation of illicit drug trafficking. Although there is universal agreement that drug trafficking offenses are not by their nature political offenses, narcotics money laundering offenses have been considered to be fiscal offenses. Traditionally, several states have not extradited offenders or provided mutual legal assistance for fiscal offenses. Thus, by increasing the availability of cooperation in drug money laundering investigations, this provision is extremely important.

Unfortunately, the constitutional law of a few states requires that the courts of those states determine whether or not an offense is a political offense. At the insistence of those states, the paragraph is qualified with the statement "without prejudice to the constitutional limitations and the fundamental domestic law of the Parties." It is understood, however, that the courts of those states will be guided by the principle contained in the paragraph of not viewing Article 3 offenses as political, politically motivated or fiscal offenses.

Paragraph 11 is included to clarify that the offenses established according to the Article will be described, prosecuted and punished in accord with a Party's domestic law. It also provides that the article is not intended to change the legal defenses to those offenses.

(Article 4 - JURISDICTION)

Comments:

Article 4 deals with a Party's obligation to establish its jurisdiction over illegal drug offenses. The negotiators believed that it was not enough to require parties to criminalize certain conduct; Parties also had to establish their jurisdiction to prosecute those offenses. Although recognizing a variety of conceptual bases for the exertion of criminal jurisdiction, the article does not resolve the inherent question of which Party's assertion of jurisdiction is preferred when there is an overlap of competing jurisdictions. The offenses that are the subject of the Convention are for the most part international offenses. Frequently drug trafficking acts occur in more than one state and more than one state has established its jurisdiction over one or more of the acts of illicit trafficking involved. A simple example where two states both have territorially based jurisdiction is the trafficker who transports drugs from state A over the border to state B. He commits an offense in two states, both of which have a territorial basis for exerting jurisdiction. According to the provisions of Articles 3 and 4, both State A and

State B, if they are Parties to the Convention, must have enacted laws criminalizing the trafficker's conduct as an offense. In State A the offender has committed an exportation offense, in State B an importation offense. Assuming that the drugs the trafficker transported were to be distributed, he has also possessed drugs with the intent to distribute them in both states. Both states must also establish jurisdiction over the acts which occurred in their territory. The article does not, however, give primacy to one or the other state's right to prosecute the offender.

Paragraph 1(a) obligates a Party to establish jurisdiction over offenses committed on its territory or aboard ships or aircraft registered under its laws or flying its flag. This provision is probably unnecessary since virtually every state has also established floating territorial jurisdiction, that is the jurisdiction of the flag or registry state over conduct on board its ships and aircraft. The unqualified inclusion of an obligation to establish territorial and floating territorial jurisdiction does indicate a certain preference for these types of jurisdiction.

Subparagraph (b) recognizes other bases for jurisdiction. A Party is not obligated to establish jurisdiction in the circumstances, but may do so if it chooses. The first listed is jurisdiction based on the fact that the offender is a national or habitual resident of a Party. Thus a Party may establish its jurisdiction over narcotics offenses committed anywhere in the world if committed by its nationals or habitual residents. Although the United States has the power to establish its criminal jurisdiction over acts of its nationals worldwide and has done so for certain criminal conduct, the United States has not done so for all violations involving controlled substances.

Subparagraph (b)(ii) is an important recognition of a Party's power to establish its jurisdiction over offenses of illicit traffic by sea. Thus a Party may proscribe these offenses whenever they occur without having to establish a jurisdictional nexus to the territory of the Party proscribing the offenses. Exercise of this proscriptive jurisdiction on board a foreign flag vessel, however, is limited to those situations where the enforcing Party is so authorized by the flag State. This subparagraph recognizes the jurisdiction necessary to implement the permissive provisions of Article 17. The United States recognizes this form of jurisdiction.

Subparagraph (b)(iii) recognizes as a permissive form of jurisdiction what is called the effects principle of jurisdiction, that is jurisdiction over an offense which, although committed outside the territory of the state establishing jurisdiction, has or is intended to have an effect within the territory of that state. This an extremely important provision for the United States. We recognize jurisdiction over the person who, outside the territory of the United States, orchestrates drug trafficking acts inside the United States.

Paragraph 2 of Article 4 must be read in connection with paragraph 9 of Article 6. Paragraph 2 is included to ensure that a Party has jurisdiction to proscribe offenses and jurisdiction to prosecute those offenses when that Party refuses to extradite. Several international agreements have recognized a virtually universal jurisdiction when extradition is refused. See, e.g., Convention for the Suppression of Unlawful Seizure of Aircraft ("Hijacking"), done at The Hague December 16, 1970, 22 U.S.T. 1641, TIAS 7192; Convention for the Suppression of Unlawful Acts against the Safety of Civil Aviation ("Sabotage"), done at Montreal September 23, 1971, 24 U.S.T. 564, TIAS 7570. These conventions include an obligation to prosecute any time extradition is refused. Noting that there are very few aircraft hijackings and aircraft sabotage offenses compared to the numerous illegal drug offenses worldwide, the negotiators agreed not to require Parties to this Convention to provide for such general jurisdiction. United States negotiators also opposed the extension of jurisdiction for philosophical and pragmatic reasons. Our policy is that drug trafficking offenses should be tried in the state injured by the trafficking, and, therefore, extradition to the injured state is far preferable to prosecution in a disinterested state. Second, a realistic appraisal of the feasibility of prosecution in a state which has not gathered the evidence in a form and procedure admissible in its courts mitigates against successful prosecution in virtually every instance.

Paragraph 2 requires a Party to establish its jurisdiction when it does not extradite an offender found in its territory because the offense occurred on its territory or on board a ship or aircraft registered under its law or flying its flag. It is also required to establish its jurisdiction when it refuses to extradite an offender found on its territory because that offender is its national. Article 6, paragraph 9 imposes a complementary obligation, when extradition is refused because the offense occurred in the territory of the Party from whom extradition is requested or the offense was committed by its national, to submit the case to its competent authorities for the purpose of prosecution.

Subparagraph (b) recognizes that a Party may also establish jurisdiction over Article 3, paragraph 1 offenses when the offender is present in its territory and it refuses to extradite him for any reason. This subparagraph imposes no obligation on a party to establish its jurisdiction when it refuses extradition for reasons other than those listed in subparagraph (a).

Paragraph 3 makes clear that this article in no way prohibits a party from exercising any criminal jurisdiction allowed by its domestic law.

(Article 5 - CONFISCATION)

Comments:

Article 5 embraces two sets of obligations. First, each Party must enact domestic laws to enable it to identify, trace, seize, freeze, and forfeit all manner of property derived from or used in offenses established in accordance with Article 3, paragraph 1, that is all drug trafficking and money laundering

offenses therein described. Second, the article requires each
Party to assist other Parties upon request to identify, trace,
seize, freeze or forfeit proceeds, property, instrumentalities or
any other things within its territory that was used or intended
for use in Article 3, paragraph 1 offenses in the territory of
the requesting Party. For many of the countries that
participated in the negotiation of this Convention, the
provisions of this article are innovative.

The article is titled "Confiscation" and the term
"confiscation" is used throughout rather than the term
"forfeiture". Confiscation was chosen because that is the term
used in the Single and Psychotropic Substances Conventions[1] and
because this is the term used by many European countries in their
forfeiture laws. The term is synonymous with the term forfeiture
used in U.S. law.

Paragraph 1 contains a broad obligation upon Parties to take
whatever measures are necessary to forfeit all proceeds derived
from drug trafficking or money laundering offenses as well as all
instrumentalities used in or intended for use in those offenses.
Subparagraphs (a) and (b) are intended to include all forms of
property that might be used or intended for use in or derived
from the covered offenses. It includes the drugs themselves as
well as materials, equipment or other instrumentalities.
Further, subparagraph (a) allows the option of forfeiting either
the proceeds of the offenses or, in their place, property which
has a corresponding value.[2]

----

1. Article 37 of the Single Convention states "[a]ny drugs,
   substances and equipment used in or intended for the
   commission of any of the offenses, referred to in article
   36, shall be liable to seizure and confiscation." Article
   22[3] of the Psychotropic Substances Convention contains a
   similar provision on the seizure and confiscation of
   psychotropic substances and equipment.

2. Title 21, U.S.C. Section 853 and Title 18, U.S.C. Section
   982 provides for the same possibility under the"substitute
   assets" provisions.

The law of the United States provides for the forfeiture of all categories of property contained within paragraph 1.[3] In addition, as noted above, U.S. forfeiture law provides for the substitution of assets in criminal forfeiture.[4]

Paragraph 2 requires Parties to take the necessary measures to allow their authorities to identify, trace, seize or freeze proceeds, property, instrumentalities or any other thing as the necessary preliminary steps toward the eventual forfeiture of that property.

Paragraph 3 obligates each Party to empower its courts or other authorities to order the production of or to seize business records, including bank records, needed to trace, identify, seize, and forfeit proceeds or instrumentalities. This paragraph includes an affirmative obligation on each Party to ensure that bank secrecy laws are not permitted to shield from discovery any

----

3. The laws of the United States include both civil and criminal forfeiture statutes. Title 21, United States Code, Section 881 subjects all controlled substances, proceeds derived from a controlled substances violation and instrumentalities used in or intended for use in a controlled substances violation to civil forfeiture. Title 21, United States Code, Section 853 provides that a person convicted of a Controlled Substances Act felony shall forfeit all proceeds derived from that felony and any property used in or intend for use in the commission of such felony. Title 18, United States Code, Section 981 provides that the gross receipts of a money laundering offense in violation of Title 18, United States Code, Section 1956 or 1957 shall be subject to civil forfeiture.

4. Section 853(p) of Title 21 provides that if any of the property subject to criminal forfeiture pursuant to the provisions of Section 853 "(1) cannot be located upon the exercise of due diligence; (2) has been transferred or sold to, or deposited with a third party; (3) has been placed beyond the jurisdiction of the court; (4) has been substantially diminished in value; or (5) has been commingled with other property which cannot be divided with difficulty; the court shall order the forfeiture of any other assets of the defendant up to the value of any property described in paragraphs (1) to (5)". Section 982 of Title 18 incorporates the provision on substitution of assets in Section 853(p) of Title 21 to the forfeiture of property involved in money laundering offenses.

of the requested materials needed to perfect the forfeiture order.   This provision and a similar provision in Article 7, paragraph 5 are intended to prevent bank secrecy laws from obstructing either forfeiture proceedings or the investigation and prosecution of trafficking offenses.   These provisions are among the most important in the Convention.

Paragraph 4(a) establishes two procedures for parties to seek assistance from other parties to forfeit proceeds or instrumentalities located in the requested Party's territory. The two alternative procedures reflect the different legal approaches to forfeiture taken by different states.   Alternative (a)(i) provides for the initiation of a forfeiture proceeding in the requested Party based upon the information provided by the requesting Party.   Alternative (a)(ii) is an exquatur-type proceeding in which the requested Party gives, in essence, full faith and credit to a forfeiture order duly entered in the requesting Party.   It was universally agreed among the negotiators that Parties should be obligated to assist one another by forfeiting the proceeds of trafficking found within their borders.   The difficulty presented was to ensure that Parties that used different procedures could avail themselves of one another's legal system.   Although the traditional rule was that one country would not enforce the criminal judgments, including forfeiture judgments of another country, some countries, in particular the United Kingdom, have enacted laws that permit them under certain circumstances to recognize and enforce a foreign forfeiture judgment.[5] Usually this judgment of forfeiture must be a final criminal judgment and is considered enforceable against any of the offender's assets.   Other countries are unable to enforce a foreign criminal judgment of forfeiture, but are able to proceed in rem against the proceeds or instrumentalities if a sufficient factual basis is provided to establish, to the satisfaction of its courts or other competent authorities, that the property is the proceeds or instrumentalities of trafficking offenses.

----

5.   Drug Trafficking Offenses Act of 1986, Section 26.

Recently enacted legislation in the United States expands the authority of the United States to forfeit the proceeds of foreign drug trafficking crimes. Title 18, United States Code Section 981(a)(1)(B) allows the forfeiture of property located within the United States "which represents the proceeds of an offense against a foreign nation involving the manufacture, importation, sale, or distribution of a controlled substance (as such term is defined for the purposes of the Controlled Substances Act) within whose jurisdiction such offense would be punishable by death or imprisonment for a term exceeding one year and which would be punishable under the laws of the United States by imprisonment for a term exceeding one year if such act or activity constituting the offense against the foreign nation had occurred within the jurisdiction of the United States."

Section 981 does not grant authority to forfeit instrumentalities used in or intended for use in foreign drug trafficking crimes. To fully implement Article 5 paragraph 4, Section 981 should be amended to include forfeiture of the instrumentalities of foreign drug offenses.

Subparagraph (b) requires Parties to assist one another in those proceedings leading to the forfeiture of the proceeds and instrumentalities of illicit trafficking. This provision is particularly important because it represents an international recognition of a change in the traditional rule that no state is obligated to aid another in the execution of penal laws respecting the enforcement of fines or forfeiture of criminal assets. U.S. law currently allows such assistance.

Section 1782 of Title 28, United States Code, empowers U.S. courts to order persons "to give . . . testimony or statements or to produce a document or other things for use in a proceeding in a foreign or international tribunal." This broad grant of authority to assist foreign tribunals is limited only in that a person may not be compelled to testify or to produce a document or other things in violation of any legally applicable privilege. Section 981(c) of Title 18 empowers the Attorney General or the

Secretary of the Treasury to seize and retain in their custody any property subject to forfeiture as the proceeds of a foreign drug felony pursuant to Section 981(a)(1)(B) pending final outcome of the forfeiture proceedings.

Subparagraph (c) states that the actions to be taken for forfeiture and the forfeiture decision shall be taken by the requested Party according to its domestic law, procedural rules and any treaties, agreements or arrangements to which it is a party. Thus, although a Party is obliged to assist another party to trace, identify, seize, freeze and forfeit proceeds and instrumentalities, it does so according to its own domestic laws and procedures. The article does not require Parties to make any changes in their substantive or procedural laws on forfeiture except to the extent necessary to allow the international assistance contemplated in subparagraphs (a) and (b). The burden of proof, notice requirements, and defenses to forfeiture are determined exclusively by domestic law. This subparagraph must be read, however, in conjunction with paragraph 3 which requires Parties to empower their courts to pierce bank secrecy. Subparagraph (c) does not permit a party to prevent either forfeiture proceedings or the antecedent proceedings that lead up to forfeiture because of their domestic bank secrecy laws.

Subparagraph (d) details the information to be included in a request for forfeiture assistance. It was the intent of the negotiators that subparagraph (d) provide guidance to Parties as to what information a requested party would need in order to execute a request. The subparagraph includes by reference the procedures outlined in the article on mutual legal assistance. In addition it provides for inclusion in the request of the specific information needed to execute a request for forfeiture. Once more the negotiators attempted to accommodate the two major approaches taken to international forfeiture. Subparagraph (i) describes the information which must be provided in a request to a Party that must initiate forfeiture proceedings by establishing the basis for forfeiture by presenting the facts of the foreign investigation. Subparagraph (ii) describes the information needed in the request if the request is to be executed by a party which is empowered by its law to recognize and give effect to a foreign forfeiture order.

Subparagraph (iii) lists the information that must be included in the request if the requesting Party is seeking assistance in identifying, tracing, seizing or freezing property.

Subparagraph (e) requires each Party to provide the Secretary General with copies of its laws and regulations governing forfeiture. This provision was included to enable the Secretary General, through his designee, to provide a clearing house of information on national forfeiture laws and regulations. The Single Convention and the Psychotropic Substances Convention have similar provisions.[6]

Paragraph (f) is an affirmative statement that if a treaty basis is necessary for a Party to assist another Party to identify, trace, seize, freeze and forfeit proceeds and instrumentalities, then this Convention provides the necessary and sufficient treaty basis. This paragraph can be contrasted to paragraph 3 of the Article 6. In Article 6, paragraph 3, Parties that need a treaty basis for extradition are given the option of considering the Convention as a sufficient basis.

Paragraph (g) recognizes that it is possible to improve on the provisions for cooperation in forfeiture through other agreements, treaties or arrangements. Parties are, therefore, directed to seek to conclude such agreements. It is the policy reflected in our law and our drug strategy that the government seek to conclude treaties and other agreements that facilitate international forfeiture.

Paragraph 5 addresses the question of what happens to the proceeds and property forfeited by a Party. After lengthy debate it was agreed that the disposal of forfeited assets would be

----

6.   See Article 18(i)(b), Single Convention; Article 16(a), Psychotropic Substances Convention.

determined by the law of the Party which confiscated those assets. Thus, the general rule stated in this paragraph is that each country shall dispose of assets it forfeits, either as proceeds or property of a domestic offense or at the request of another Party, according to its own domestic law or regulations on the disposition of forfeited assets. Many states, however, wanted to encourage sharing of forfeited assets either among the countries involved in the investigation and prosecution of the trafficking offenses or among Parties injured by the trafficking. Other countries, Brazil in particular, wanted to encourage Parties to contribute some or all of the forfeited assets to intergovernmental bodies such as United Nations Fund for Drug Abuse Control. Subparagraph (b) was included to encourage Parties to consider such contributions. The subparagraph imposes no obligation on a Party to share or to consider sharing, but does recognize that a Party may give special consideration to concluding agreements on such sharing. This provision is consistent with Title 18, United States Code, Section 981(i) which authorizes the Attorney General, with concurrence of the Secretary of State, equitably to transfer properly forfeited under the Controlled Substances Act to a foreign state, with which the U.S. has entered into an agreement, to reflect generally the contribution of that foreign country's participation in any acts which led to the seizure or forfeiture of the property. Title 19, U.S.C. Section 161a(c)(2) authorizes the Secretary of the Treasury to make similar transfers of property under Title 18, Title 31 and the customs laws.

Paragraph 6 was included to ensure that proceeds derived from and instrumentalities used in illegal trafficking could not escape forfeiture simply because their form had been changed or they had been commingled with other property. The fact that property had been converted, transformed or intermingled with legitimate property does not defeat its forfeiture. Subparagraph (c) provides that income or other benefits derived from illegally obtained proceeds or property shall also be forfeitable. This mirrors U.S. law which permits the forfeiture of property or property traceable thereto.

Paragraph 7 recognizes that some Parties reverse the burden of proof as to the origin of property subject to forfeiture. The paragraph does not require Parties to do so, but merely recognizes that if consistent with its domestic law, a Party may reverse the burden of proof. U.S. forfeiture laws which reference customs laws and procedures provide for the inversion of the burden of proof in some cases.

Paragraph 8 states that the provisions of the article shall not affect the rights of <u>bona fide</u> third parties. The paragraph does not attempt to define those rights. The rights of <u>bona fide</u> third parties are defined by the domestic law of each Party. Thus, this paragraph simply states that it was not the intention of the negotiators to inadvertently change the rights <u>bona fide</u> third parties have under the domestic law of a Party.

Paragraph 9 states that measures to be taken pursuant to this article shall be defined and implemented according to the domestic law of each Party.

(Article 6 - EXTRADITION)

COMMENT

The Article on extradition was one of the most difficult to negotiate. The negotiators wanted to go further than had been done in previous multilateral treaties on criminal offenses, but found it virtually impossible to accommodate the widely differing legal systems among over one hundred States. Many States saw extradition, particularly of their own nationals, to be directly tied to their concepts of sovereignty. Most wanted to retain some form of discretion as to whether or not they would extradite an offender to certain countries whose legal or political systems they distrusted.

The United States had hoped to include a broad obligation to extradite one's own nationals in this article. Unfortunately there was overwhelming opposition from countries which, for either political or legal reasons, would not accept any provision on the extradition of their nationals, even a hortatory provision. Thus, the article contains no provision on the extradition of nationals.

The structure of the first four paragraphs parallels similar provisions in the Single Convention and in the Psychotropic Substances Convention as well as language in other multilateral conventions on criminal conduct.[1] These provisions are designed to ensure that the criminal conduct which is the subject of those conventions is considered extraditable conduct by the Parties, whatever the nature of their extradition relationship.

Paragraph 1 defines the scope of the criminal conduct which is covered by the article. The article applies to all Article 3, paragraph 1 offenses. The negotiators intended that this provision would have a twofold effect. First, it ensures that all Article 3 paragraph 1 offenses are considered by all Parties to be extraditable offenses. Because all Parties are obligated to establish Article 3, paragraph 1 offenses as criminal offenses in their domestic law, any requirements of dual criminality, that is that the offense is criminal in both jurisdictions, in a Party's extradition law should be met. Although there has been almost universal recognition that illicit drug trafficking offenses are extraditable offenses, narcotics related money laundering is a new criminal offense for many states and has not been traditionally recognized as an extraditable offense. The universal recognition of narcotics related money laundering as an extraditable offense is one of the most important aspects of this article.

----

1.   Article 36(2)(b), Single Convention; Article 22(2)(b), Psychotropic Substances Convention; see also Article 8(1)-(3), Convention for the Suppression of Unlawful Seizure of Aircraft (Hague Convention) of December 16, 1970, 22 U.S.T. 1641; Article 8(1)-(3), Convention for the Suppression of Unlawful Acts against the Safety of Civil Aviation (Montreal Convention) of September 23, 1971, 24 U.S.T. 564.

Paragraph 1 also limits the scope of the article by eliminating from the scope of its applicability offenses which are clearly outside the purview of the Convention. Thus it states the obvious - that the provisions of the article to not apply to fraud offenses for example. It also excludes article 3, paragraph 2 offenses, thus excluding possession, cultivation and purchase for personal use. Because the United States negotiators believed that this Convention should focus on international drug traffic, they agreed to eliminate the numerous small offenses. Many of these offenses are punishable by terms of imprisonment of less than 1 year.[2] Traditionally, most extradition treaties do not cover offenses punishable by a term of imprisonment of less than 1 year.

Paragraph 2 amends existing bilateral treaties between Parties to include article 3, paragraph 1 offenses and requires Parties to include such offenses as extraditable offenses in all future extradition treaties between them. Extradition from the United States is conditional on the existence of a bilateral extradition treaty between the requesting country and the United States. That bilateral treaty may be amended by a multilateral treaty to include additional offenses. This provision is consistent with our law interpreting a similar provision in the Single Convention.[3] It is also consistent with our policy to include illegal drug and money laundering offenses as extraditable offenses in all future extradition treaties to be negotiated.

----

2. See 21 U.S.C. 844(b).

3. See Arnbjornsdottir-Mendler v. United States, 721 F.2d 679 (9th Cir. 1983) (extradition to Iceland based on old US/Denmark Treaty and Single Convention). The Single Convention has been very useful to supplement old bilateral treaties which do not require the extradition of drug offenders. For instance our current extradition treaty with Costa Rica which was negotiated at the turn of the century does not cover drug offenses. Nevertheless the United States and Costa Rica are parties to the Single Convention and its 1972 Protocol. We have obtained more than 20 drug offenders from Costa Rica since 1982.

Paragraph 3 recognizes that a Party which requires a treaty basis for extradition may consider this Convention as that required basis.   Although this provision will provide other States a sufficient legal basis for extradition, U.S. extradition law and practice requires a bilateral treaty.

The final sentence of paragraph 3 requires a Party which needs detailed legislation to use the Convention as an extradition treaty to consider enacting such legislation.   This provision is a new one not contained in any of the other multilateral criminal conventions.   It is an obligation only to consider, not necessarily to enact, such legislation.   The obligation is inapplicable to the United States because our inability to use this Convention as the basis for extradition in the absence of bilateral treaty is based, not on the absence of detailed legislation, but on our case law and the provisions of our extradition statute.

Paragraph 4 requires Parties which do not require a treaty basis for extradition to recognize article 3 paragraph 1 offenses as extraditable offenses between themselves.   This paragraph does not apply to the United States.[4]

Paragraph 5 states that extradition shall be subject to the law of the Requested Party.   The extradition procedures, the standard of proof, and the defenses to extradition are to be defined exclusively by the domestic law of the requested party. Paragraph 5 must be read, however, together with Article 3, paragraph 10 which amends bilateral extradition treaties to preclude the denial of extradition on the grounds that Article 3, paragraph 1 offenses are "fiscal", "political", or "politically motivated" offenses.

Paragraph 6 grants discretion to refuse extradition to the requested party if that party believes that there are substantial grounds to believe that the extradition would facilitate

----

4.   See 18 U.S.C. 3181, 3184.

prosecution or punishment for human or civil rights reasons. This paragraph must be read together with paragraph 5. Thus it does not change the defenses to extradition under United States law.

The United States delegation clarified on the record of the Conference, through a statement of explanation, that the use of the phrase "judicial or other competent authorities" in this paragraph grants Parties full discretion to determine for themselves, consistent with their domestic law, which branch of government, whether judicial, executive or legislative, is charged with making the decision to refuse extradition for humanitarian reasons. In some states, such as the United States, the relevant procedural law reserves the decision with regard to human rights to the Executive Branch of Government. There was no indication at the negotiations of any intent to require some states to alter their procedures in order to conform them to the procedures followed by others. Such an intent would be inconsistent with the intent of the Article, as explicitly mentioned in paragraph 7, which is to expedite as much as possible the extradition process for serious drug traffickers. Consistent with this spirit the committee adopted paragraph 5 which reserves the right of each party to determine the procedure to be followed within that party. Thus paragraph 6 does not alter the procedural law of the United States concerning the mechanism by which such decisions are made. Humanitarian defenses to extradition remain the province of the Executive Branch, in particular the Secretary of State.[5] See Sindona v. Grant, 619 F. 2d 167 (2d Cir. 1980); Peroff v. Hylton, 542 F. 2d 1247 (4th Cir. 1976); In Re Lincoln, 228 F. 70 (E.D.N.Y. 1915), aff'd per curriam 241 U.S. 651 (1915).

----

5. Some United States extradition treaties do provide that extradition may be refused for humanitarian grounds. See e.g. U.S./Finland treaty, TIAS 9626; United States/Sweden treaty, TIAS 5496. The provisions of those treaties clearly refer to the power of the executive branch of government, the branch which is responsible for negotiating and implementing the underlying treaty, to deny extradition based upon such humanitarian appeals.

Paragraph 7 contains a general hortatory provision encouraging Parties to attempt to simplify and expedite extradition procedures. This provision must be read in the context of a Party's domestic law. Thus for the United States, this paragraph contains no necessity of simplifying our evidentiary requirement of probable cause, but only that within the framework of that requirement, the United States should endeavour to simplify, if possible, our procedures. The United States fulfils this requirement in its ongoing efforts to negotiate new modern treaties.

Paragraph 8 is a permissive grant of authority to a Party to arrest provisionally and hold without bond a person whose extradition is sought pending the formal request for his extradition. This provision is subject to domestic law and bilateral treaties of a party. Title 18, United States Code, Section 3184 provides the statutory authority for the provisional arrest of a fugitive in the United States. This provision is dependent on the existence of a bilateral treaty. United States case law holds that bail is granted in extradition cases only upon a showing of special circumstances. Wright v. Henkel, 190 U.S. 40 (1903).

Paragraph 9 imposes an obligation on a Party to submit the case to its competent authorities for the purpose of prosecution if extradition is refused for certain circumstances. The paragraph must be read in tandem with Article 4, paragraph 2 which obligates Parties to extend their jurisdiction in certain instances when extradition is refused. This provision is an extradite or prosecute provision commonly referred to in civil law states as aut dedere aut judicare. Subparagraph (a) of paragraph 9 first imposes an obligation to submit for prosecution if extradition is refused because the offenses involved occurred on the territory of the Requested Party or on board a ship or aircraft registered under its law. The existence of United States territorial jurisdiction is not a ground for refusal of extradition under United States law. The second obligation to submit for prosecution occurs in those instances where extradition is refused because the offender is a national of the requested Party. The Supreme Court has held that the United States may extradite its nationals only in the absence of any limiting language in a bilateral treaty. <u>Charlton v. Kelly</u>, 229 U.S. 447 (1913). However, if an extradition treaty contains language which limits that authority, e.g., "neither party shall be bound to deliver up its own citizens", the Court has held that U.S. nationals may not be extradited unless the treaty also contains a positive grant of authority to surrender U.S. citizens. <u>Valentine v. United States ex rel Neidecker</u>, 299 U.S. 5, 7-12 (1936). Post-<u>Valentine</u> extradition treaties of the United States contain language such as "[N]either of the contracting Parties shall be bound to deliver up its own citizen under the stipulations of this Convention, <u>but the executive authority of each shall have the power to deliver them up, if, in its discretion, it is deemed proper to do so.</u>" (Emphasis added). Such a clause contains the necessary positive grant of authority to the Executive to extradite United States citizens.

Although all post-<u>Valentine</u> treaties contain such a clause, the United States does have several pre-<u>Valentine</u> treaties still in force that contain the limitation but lack the requisite grant of authority. In those rare instances, the United States, although obligated under a bilateral treaty to extradite, would be forced to refuse to extradite based on the nationality of the offender. Absent a statutory grant of discretion to the executive to extradite U.S. nationals, subparagraph (a) will obligate the United States to submit such cases to our competent authorities for the purpose of prosecution.

Since we would not have extraterritorial jurisdiction to prosecute such cases, to avoid an obligation to perform a pointless act, it is the Administration's intention to remedy the <u>Valentine</u> problem by seeking legislation to amend this class of treaties with an affirmative grant of discretion to surrender U.S. nationals. Unless this is done, we will be obligated under Article 4, paragraph 2(a)(ii) to establish extraterritorial jurisdiction to prosecute U.S. nationals here for Article 3(1) offenses committed abroad, in those situations in which we cannot extradite to a requesting country because of the <u>Valentine</u>

problem. In view of the general U.S. policy favoring extradition of nationals to the country where the greatest harm has been suffered because of the commission of criminal acts, and against creating "universal" jurisdiction, we believe it preferable to eliminate the situations in which we cannot extradite our nationals rather than create jurisdiction to prosecute them because we cannot extradite them.

Subparagraph (b) provides for a broader obligation to submit a case for prosecution when extradition is refused for any reason if the Party requested has established its jurisdiction to prosecute pursuant to the provisions of Article 4, paragraph 2, subparagraph (a). Thus if a Party has chosen to extend its jurisdiction to allow it to prosecute whenever the person who committed the offense is within its territory and extradition is refused for any reason, it is required to submit the case to its competent authorities for the purpose of prosecution. This provision does not apply to the United States because we do not recognize such a broad extension of our jurisdiction.

The obligations to submit a case to one's competent authorities for the purpose of prosecution contained in both subparagraphs (a) and (b) are qualified. Subparagraph (a) limits the obligation by the phrase "unless otherwise agreed to by the Parties". Subparagraph (b) limits the obligation by the phrase "unless otherwise requested by the requesting party for the purposes of preserving its legitimate jurisdiction." Both limiting clauses were included at the request of the United States negotiators in order to allow the requesting Party to have some say in whether or not prosecution would occur by the Requested Party. The requested party might prefer to retain the option of being able to extradite later from a third state, rather than having the offender prosecuted by the requested Party. The right of the requesting Party to block prosecution is more extensive in subparagraph (b) because the extension of jurisdiction in subparagraph (b) is more tenuously related to traditional concepts of criminal jurisdiction.

Paragraph 10 obligates parties whose domestic law so permits to enforce a foreign sentence when extradition is sought for the enforcement of that sentence and extradition is refused because the offender is a national of the requested country. United States law does not permit the enforcement of a foreign sentence when extradition is refused. Therefore this paragraph is not applicable to our domestic extradition practice.

Paragraph 11 calls upon Parties to seek to conclude other agreements to facilitate extradition. This provision is consistent with United States policy of continuing to negotiate modern extradition treaties.

Paragraph 12 is a permissive provision aimed at encouraging Parties to enter into prisoner transfer treaties. The United States has entered into a number of these treaties in the last ten years.

(Article 7 – MUTUAL LEGAL ASSISTANCE)

Comments:

Article 7 is a miniature mutual legal assistance treaty (or "MLAT"). The wide differences in the methods of developing admissible evidence in the varied legal systems of the states which participated in the negotiations of this article made it impossible to negotiate as detailed and comprehensive provisions as are often found in bilateral mutual legal assistance treaties. Therefore, the article focuses on key elements of mutual legal assistance relations but omits many detailed procedures for implementing those relations. Many details are left to the Parties involved to formulate on a case by case basis.

The most important aspect of Article 7 is that it establishes a treaty obligation upon a Party to provide mutual legal assistance to another Party in the investigation, prosecution or other judicial proceedings in relation to article 3 paragraph 1 offenses. Absent such a treaty obligation, mutual legal assistance between countries has been solely a matter of comity.

The article simplifies and codifies the procedures for mutual legal assistance between Parties which are not Parties to more detailed and comprehensive multilateral or bilateral treaties on mutual legal assistance. It also amends existing mutual legal assistance treaties to the extent necessary to include an obligation to provide assistance for all article 3, paragraph 1 offenses, thereby including money laundering in the context of illegal drug trafficking. Like the parallel provision in the article on extradition, the inclusion of drug-related money laundering with the offenses for which assistance is to be given is an important expansion of traditional mutual assistance relations.

There is a deliberate overlap between the provisions of Article 7 and of Article 9, titled "Other Forms of Cooperation and Training." Because of the wide variance among the different countries as to which forms of assistance can be provided directly by law enforcement officials and which forms require compulsory measures taken by a court or other judicial authority, the issue was left unresolved. For example, the United States permits the statement of a person who consents to be interviewed to be taken without a court order. Other countries require all statements be taken only upon order of their courts. A Party is obligated, however, to provide assistance requested pursuant to this article to the extent made possible by its legal system in the simplest fashion. It was understood that, except for the assistance identified in paragraph 2, Article 7 did not apply to existing or future agreements or arrangements concerning law enforcement assistance.

The Convention separates mutual legal assistance in forfeiture proceedings from such assistance in criminal investigations and prosecutions. Rather than including international assistance in forfeiture proceedings in Article 7, provision for such assistance is included in the article on confiscation, Article 5. Article 5, however, incorporates many of the procedural provisions of Article 7 by reference. The placement of mutual legal assistance for forfeiture proceedings outside the mutual legal assistance article was done solely to emphasize the importance of forfeiture assistance and not to change mutual assistance law.

Article 7 is consistent with United States law, codified in Title 28, United States Code, Section 1782, which grants broad power to United States courts to execute foreign requests for mutual legal assistance. No implementing U.S. legislation is necessary. The article is self-executing.

Paragraph 1 sets forth the general obligation of the Parties to provide legal assistance to one another. It was the intent of the negotiators that this obligation would be described as broadly as possible. The language used is taken from article 1(a) of the European Convention on Mutual Legal Assistance in Criminal Matters.[1] The reference to all"investigations, prosecutions and other judicial proceedings" is intended to include all criminal proceedings except forfeiture, including such proceedings as bail hearings, probation revocation hearings and grand jury investigations. The use of the term "investigations" is somewhat unclear. Some States, including in particular Austria, noted a reservation to an obligation to provide mutual legal assistance to purely police investigations.

Paragraph 2 contains an illustrative but not exhaustive list of the types of mutual legal assistance a Party may request pursuant to this article. These types of assistance are consistent with the types of assistance covered in United States bilateral treaties.[2]

----

1. European Treaty Series No. 130, entered into force June 12, 1962.

2. See, *e.g.*, Article 21, U.S.-Turkey Treaty on Extradition and Mutual Assistance in Criminal Matters, signed at Ankara on June 7, 1979, 32 UST 311, TIAS 9891 (entered into force Jan. 1, 1981); Article 1, U.S.-Italy Mutual Legal Assistance Treaty signed at Rome November 9, 1982, TIAS _____ (entered into force Nov. 13, 1985); Article 1, U.S.-Netherlands

Paragraph 3 provides that other forms of mutual legal assistance than those listed in paragraph 2 may be provided if permitted by the domestic law of a Party. This paragraph is an affirmative statement that the list in paragraph 2 is not intended to restrict a Party's domestic practice of providing additional assistance.

Paragraph 4 creates an obligation to facilitate or encourage the testimony of a witness from the requested Party in the territory of the requesting Party only to the extent permitted by a Party's domestic law and practice. Additionally, this obligation exists only when the witness consents to travel to and testify in the requesting Party's territory. The paragraph includes persons in custody. Not only is this paragraph intended to provide the legal basis for cooperation in these matters, but also to encourage Parties to simplify any obstacles to such travel as, for example, the witness's need for travel documents or permission to travel. The obligation is conditioned on the request of a Party. Therefore, there is no obligation on the requested Party to facilitate the travel of a person in custody in its territory, who demands permission to travel to another country to be present at a deposition being taken there in connection with his criminal case.

Paragraph 5 forbids a Party from refusing to execute a request for mutual legal assistance on the ground of its bank secrecy law. This provision was considered very important by the negotiators since it represents an affirmative statement that bank secrecy laws shall not be used as a ground for denying assistance. It is intended to apply not only to a request made according to the procedures set forth in the article, but also to modify any existing or future mutual legal assistance treaties. Thus, bank secrecy laws alone cannot be imposed to block assistance.

...Continued...

Treaty on Mutual Assistance in Criminal Matters, signed at the Hague June 12, 1981, TIAS 10734 (entered into force Sept. 15, 1943).

Paragraph 6 resolves the differences between this article and other mutual legal assistance treaties, many of which are more comprehensive than Article 7. The paragraph clearly states that Article 7 cannot be construed to lessen any existing or future obligation to provide mutual legal assistance pursuant to any bilateral or multilateral mutual legal assistance treaties between Parties. This paragraph does not, however, eliminate the obligation of a Party to provide assistance for Article 3(1) offenses even if there is a bilateral treaty between them. If the bilateral treaty does not include an obligation to provide assistance for Article 3(1) offenses, in particular the money laundering offense described in Article 3(1)(c), Article 7 amends that treaty to include an obligation to assist in the investigation, prosecution or other judicial proceedings in relation to that offense. In addition, paragraph 6 does not limit the obligation found in paragraph 5 not to impose bank secrecy laws to prevent the execution of a request.

Paragraph 7 is designed to ensure that the procedural paragraphs, paragraphs 8 to 19, only apply if either there is not a mutual legal assistance treaty between the Parties involved or if the Parties, although bound by a mutual assistance treaty, elect to use the procedural paragraphs of the Article. This paragraph reflects the consensus of the negotiators that treaties solely on mutual legal assistance, whether bilateral or multilateral, contain simpler, more effective procedural provisions than Article 7. This consensus was based on the realization by the negotiators that because of the number of countries participating in the negotiations, their widely varying legal systems, the differing levels of experience in providing mutual legal assistance of the countries, and insufficient time to negotiate a full mutual assistance treaty within the Convention, any bilateral and many multilateral mutual legal assistance treaties are likely to be more effective and comprehensive.

Paragraph 8 has two parts. First, it requires Parties to designate an authority or authorities with the power to execute requests and to notify the Secretary General of that authority.

United States negotiators wanted the paragraph to require each Party to designate a single authority rather than allow for more than one.[3] Unfortunately, a number of countries were adamant that it was politically impossible for them to designate a single authority. The paragraph therefore allows a party to designate more than one authority. A positive aspect of this provision is that it will allow countries which have dependent territories to designate a separate authority for that territory, thereby allowing communication directly with the territorial authority which will actually execute or supervise the execution of the request.

The second important aspect of this paragraph is that it encourages direct communication between authorities designated by the Parties. Unfortunately, it also permits a Party to require another Party to communicate through diplomatic channels, a much more time consuming and cumbersome procedure. The paragraph allows communication through INTERPOL channels if the Parties agree and the circumstances are urgent.

Paragraph 9 resolves the question of which Party chooses the language of the request by granting the choice to the requested Party. It also imposes a general obligation that the request be in writing but allows an exception when the Parties so agree, the circumstances are urgent, and the request is reduced to writing immediately thereafter. Finally, the paragraph provides for a notice provision through the Secretary General of what language or languages a Party will require requests to it to be in. This

----

3.   In the United States, the appropriate authority is the Attorney General as is the case in other mutual legal assistance treaties. The Attorney General has delegated his duties as Central Authority under mutual legal assistance treaties to the Assistant Attorney General in charge of the Criminal Division, pursuant to 28 C.F.R S 0.64-1. The Assistant Attorney General for the Criminal Division has in turn re-delegated his authority to the Deputy Assistant Attorney General and to Director of the Criminal Division's Office of International Affairs, in accordance with the regulation. Directive No. 81, 44 FR 18661, March 29, 1979, as amended at 45 FR 7541, January 29, 1980; 48 FR 54595, December 6, 1983.

Article is consistent, in general, with our mutual legal assistance treaties and allows the United States to require that any request to it be in English.

Paragraph 10 defines the basic contents of a request. The list is a practical list of information that the negotiators believed would be needed by the requested Party to be able to execute the request. Paragraph 11 clarifies that additional information may be requested by the requested Party if needed to execute the request or to facilitate such execution.

Paragraph 12 is critically important. It provides that all requests shall be executed in accordance with the domestic law of the requested Party. Thus this paragraph makes clear that the requested Party is not required to take any action pursuant to the request which would be prohibited under its law. The exception to this provision is provided by paragraph 5. Bank secrecy laws cannot be imposed to block execution of a request.

Paragraph 12 also allows the requested Party to follow procedures specified in the request, which although not required by the domestic law of the requested Party, are not contrary to that law. This provision is very important because of the wide differences among countries on procedures which must be followed to assure the admissibility of evidence at trial. For instance, United States law permits documentary evidence taken abroad to be admitted in evidence if it is fully certified and the defendant has been given a fair opportunity to test its authenticity.[4] Some countries' laws currently contain no similar provision. Thus, documents assembled in another country in strict conformity with its evidentiary procedures might not be admissible in United States courts. Similarly, United States courts frequently employ procedural techniques such as videotape depositions to enhance the reliability of evidence taken abroad. Some of these techniques, while not forbidden, are simply not used in other countries in connection with their investigations.

----

4.   Title 18, United States Code, Section 3505.

The negotiators agreed that the primary goal of Article 5, assisting in investigations and prosecutions in the requesting Party, could be frustrated if the requested Party were to insist on producing evidence in a manner which rendered the evidence inadmissible or less persuasive in the requesting Party's courts. For this reason, paragraph 12 requires the requested State to follow the procedure outlined in the request to the extent that it can, even if the procedure is not that usually employed in its own proceedings. However, if the procedure called for in the request is contrary to the law of the requested Party, as opposed to simply unfamiliar there, the procedures of the requested Party will be utilized. Paragraph 12 is consistent with U.S. law on the execution of foreign requests for mutual legal assistance. Section 1782 of Title 28, United States Code, confers a broad grant of authority to district courts to assist foreign tribunals and specifically provides that testimony may be taken and evidence produced according to the practice and procedure of the foreign country requesting the assistance.

Paragraph 10(f) requires the requested Party to state the purpose for which the evidence, information or action is sought in the request. Accordingly, paragraph 13 requires that the information or evidence provided under this article not be used for any purpose other than those stated in the request unless the requested Party gives its consent. Although U.S. authorities sometimes oppose use limits because they do not clearly exist under letters rogatory practice pursuant to 28 U.S.C. section 1782, most of our bilateral MLATs contain some such limitation. The language of Paragraph 13 is similar to that found in the U.S.-Canada MLAT. Because the Convention only covers certain crimes, i.e. those specified in Article 3, it is logical that the use of assistance provided under the Convention be limited to the investigation, prosecution or other proceedings pertaining to those crimes.

Paragraph 14 allows the requesting Party to require that the requested Party keep confidential the request except to the extent disclosure is necessary to execute it. This provision is important in that it protects sensitive investigative information from premature exposure. The paragraph includes, however, a recognition that it may be impossible to keep information confidential. In that case, the requested Party is required to so inform the requesting Party. The decision as to whether or not to proceed with the request then rests appropriately with the requesting Party.

Paragraph 15 specifies classes of requests in which assistance may be refused. Paragraph 15(a) states the obvious, that assistance may be refused if the request does not conform to the provisions of the article. Paragraph 15(b) permits refusal if the assistance would prejudice the sovereignty, security, ordre public or other essential interests of the requested Party. The United States has traditionally interpreted this type of provision sparingly and has viewed the terms "security" and "essential interests" as implicating national security. U.S. negotiators agreed to a somewhat broader listing of grounds for refusal than is usual in our bilateral mutual legal assistance treaties, including prejudice to sovereignty and ordre public, because the Convention is a multilateral agreement to which the United States has no say as to who its treaty partners might be. All negotiators agreed, however, that these grounds for refusal did not convert the article's mandatory provisions to discretionary ones. This provision, along with others, contains sufficient safeguards to permit the U.S. to refuse to execute, or to postpone execution of, a request in order to avoid being party to a miscarriage of justice.

Paragraph 15(c) and (d) allow a requested Party to refuse to grant the request if the request would violate its mutual legal assistance laws or if the domestic law of the requested Party would prohibit it from taking the same action in a domestic investigation or proceeding. Thus either ground could be asserted to refuse a request which would violate United States law or privilege. Section 1782 provides that a district court, in response to a foreign request, may not compel a person "to give his testimony or a statement or to produce a document or other thing in violation of a legally applicable privilege."

Paragraph 16 requires the requested Party to give its reasons for any refusal.

Paragraph 17 protects on-going proceedings in the requested Party which may be affected by the request by allowing assistance to be postponed as long as necessary. It imposes an obligation, however, to consult with the requesting Party to see if there is any way assistance can be given subject to whatever terms are necessary.

Paragraph 18 provides "safe conduct" for a person who consents to assist or give evidence pursuant to the Article when he is in the territory of the Requesting Party for acts that predate his departure from the requested Party. A time limit is suggested for this safe conduct of 15 days from the date he is notified officially that he is no longer needed in the territory. The Parties, however, may agree to a different time period. This provision does not protect a person from prosecution for perjury or for any other crime committed by him while he is in the territory of the requested Party.

Paragraph 19 attempts to answer the question of which Party must pay the costs associated with the execution of the request. The paragraph is flexible thereby allowing the Parties involved to reach different agreements. The ordinary costs are to be borne by the requested Party. If substantial or extraordinary costs are involved the Parties must consult concerning who shall bear them.

Paragraph 20 directs Parties to consider entering into bilateral or multilateral agreements or arrangements to enhance, or give effect to this article. This paragraph is intended to encourage Parties to build on the obligations included in the article by both formal and informal agreements.

(Article 9 - OTHER FORMS OF CO-OPERATION AND TRAINING)

Comments:

Article 9 provides for mutual assistance, cooperation and training between law enforcement (police-to-police) organizations, and should be distinguished from the more formal mutual legal assistance contained in Article 7. This article establishes a mechanism whereby law enforcement organizations may provide assistance, cooperation and training without the necessity of having to resort to the more formal and cumbersome procedures for mutual legal assistance contained in Article 7.

Paragraph 1 and its subparagraphs contain the provisions related to general law enforcement assistance. In the chapeau parties are obligated to cooperate closely with one another for the purpose of enhancing law enforcement effectiveness. The chapeau provides that this obligation is to be discharged consistent with the domestic legal and administrative systems of the Parties. After some discussion it was agreed that multilateral or bilateral agreements or arrangements would be essential in order to effectively carry out obligations contained in paragraph 1. Moreover, it was also agreed that multilateral or bilateral agreements or arrangements would be necessary for all the forms of assistance contemplated under the subparagraphs of paragraph 1. The reference to "agreements or arrangements" is intended to capture not only formal agreements (i.e. treaties or executive agreements) but also informal arrangements or practices between the Parties.

Subparagraph (a) requires the establishment of channels of communication and the exchange of information with respect to offenses contained in article 3, paragraph 1 of the Convention. Subparagraph (b) addresses the forms of investigatory assistance to be provided by the Parties. At the plenipotentiary conference the United States stated for the record that the text of paragraph 1(b) provided for the conduct of inquiries that involved offenses specified in Article 3(1) as well as the separate conduct of inquiries with respect to the items marked (i), (ii) and (iii). The U.S. did not want the placement of the word "concerning" by the Drafting Committee to be read as limiting inquiries regarding (i), (ii) and (iii) on the existence of an offense contrary to Article 3(1), which was not the intent of the Drafting Committee.

Subparagraph (c) relates to the establishment of joint law enforcement teams. It was agreed that the establishment of joint law enforcement teams could be a valuable tool in carrying out the provisions of paragraph 1. Nonetheless, it was also understood that the establishment of these teams would need to be done in a manner designed to ensure the sovereignty of the respective Parties. Subparagraph (d) deals with transferring samples of narcotic drugs and psychotropic substances for analytical and investigative purposes. Subparagraph (e) provides for the exchanges of expert personnel and the posting of liaison officers. It should be noted that under this subparagraph there is no requirement that the exchange of personnel or the posting of liaison officers be done on a reciprocal basis.

Paragraph 2 contains the provision related to international cooperation in the area of training. Several types of training programs are delineated in the subparagraphs to paragraph 2, which is simply a representative listing and not all-inclusive. The reference to "law enforcement and other personnel, including customs" was intended to address the fact that in some countries customs officers are not technically viewed as law enforcement personnel. Thus the reference ensures that all government organizations charged with policing offenses established under article 3, paragraph 1 were included within the coverage of this paragraph.

Paragraph 3 is a provision intended to address perceived special needs of transit States, which is more fully explained in the commentary to article 10.

DOCUMENT D

Political Declaration and Global Programme of Action adopted by the General Assembly at its 17th special session, devoted to the question of international co-operation against illicit production, supply, demand, trafficking and distribution of narcotic drugs and psychotropic substances

(extracts)

Source: General Assembly Resolution S-17/2, UN Doc. A/RES/s-17/2, 15 March 1990

The General Assembly

Adopts the Political Declaration and the Global Programme of Action on international co-operation against illicit production, supply, demand, trafficking and distribution of narcotic drugs and psychotropic substances annexed to the present resolution.

8th plenary meeting
23 February 1990

ANNEX

Political Declaration

We, the States Members of the United Nations,

Assembled at the seventeenth special session of the General Assembly to consider the question of international co-operation against illicit production, supply, demand, trafficking and distribution of narcotic drugs and psychotropic substances,

Deeply alarmed by the magnitude of the rising trend in the illicit demand, production, supply, trafficking and distribution of narcotic drugs and psychotropic substances, which are a grave and persistent threat to the health and well-being of mankind, the stability of nations, the political, economic, social and

cultural structures of all societies and the lives and dignity of
millions of human beings, most especially of young people,

<u>Aware</u> of the dangers posed for all countries alike by the
illicit cultivation, production, supply, demand, trafficking and
distribution of narcotic drugs and psychotropic substances, and
aware also of the need for a comprehensive approach in combating
them,

<u>Conscious</u> that the extraordinarily high levels of illicit
consumption, cultivation and production of narcotic drugs and of
illicit drug trafficking necessitate a more comprehensive approach to international co-operation in drug abuse control and
counter-offensives at the national, regional and international
levels,

<u>Reaffirming</u> our determination to combat the scourge of drug
abuse and illicit trafficking in narcotic drugs and psychotropic
substances in strict conformity with the principles of the Charter of the United Nations, the principles of international law,
in particular respect for the sovereignty and territorial integrity of States, the principle of non-interference in the internal
affairs of States and non-use of force or the threat of force in
international relations, and the provisions of the international
drug control conventions,

<u>Reaffirming</u> <u>also</u> the provisions set forth in the Single
Convention on Narcotic Drugs of 1961, and in that Convention as
amended by the 1972 Protocol Amending the Single Convention on
Narcotic Drugs of 1961, the Convention on Psychotropic Substances
of 1971 and the United Nations Convention against Illicit Traffic
in Narcotic Drugs and Psychotropic Substances adopted in 1988,

<u>Reaffirming</u> <u>further</u> the principle of shared responsibility
in combating drug abuse and illicit traffic in narcotic drugs and
psychotropic substances,

<u>Recognizing</u> the links between the illicit demand, consump-
tion, production, supply, trafficking and distribution of narcot-

ic drugs and psychotropic substances and the economic, social and cultural conditions in the countries affected by them,

Deeply concerned about the violence and corruption generated by the illicit demand, production, trafficking and distribution of narcotic drugs and psychotropic substances and the high human, political, economic and social costs of drug abuse and of the fight against the drug problem, entailing the diversion of scarce resources from other national priorities, which in the case of developing countries includes development activities,

Conscious that international co-operation for the development of the developing countries should be strengthened, allowing all countries to participate more fully in an effective fight against the drug problem,

Recognizing the links between drug abuse and a wide range of adverse health consequences, including the transmission of human immunodeficiency virus (HIV) infection and the spread of acquired immunodeficiency syndrome (AIDS),

Recognizing also that illicit trafficking in narcotic drugs and psychotropic substances is a criminal activity and that its suppression requires a higher priority and concerted action at the national, regional and international levels by all States, including rapid ratification of and accession to the United Nations Convention against Illicit Traffic in Narcotic Drugs and Psychotropic Substances,

Noting that the large financial profits derived from illicit drug trafficking and related criminal activities enable transnational criminal organizations to penetrate, contaminate and corrupt the structure of Governments, legitimate commercial activities and society at all levels, thereby vitiating economic and social development, distorting the process of law and undermining the foundations of States,

Recognizing that a growing number of countries, in particular developing countries, are affected by illicit transit traf-

ficking in narcotic drugs because of their geographical location
or economic situation, which imposes serious burdens on the drug
law enforcement machinery of those countries and forces
diversion of scarce resources from pressing developmental needs
and other national priorities,

Convinced that the fight against illicit trafficking in
narcotic drugs and psychotropic substances has to comprise effective measures aimed, inter alia, at eliminating illicit consumption, cultivation and production of narcotic drugs and psychotropic substances; preventing the diversion from legitimate uses
of precursor chemicals, specific substances, materials and equipment frequently used in the illicit manufacture of narcotic drugs
and psychotropic substances; and preventing the use of the banking system and other financial institutions for the laundering of
proceeds derived from illicit drug trafficking by making such
activities criminal offences,

Alarmed at the growing link between illicit trafficking in
narcotic drugs and terrorist activities, which is aggravated by
insufficient control of commerce in arms and by illicit or covert
arms transfers, as well as by illegal activities of mercenaries,

Mindful of the results already achieved by the United Na-
tions in the field of drug abuse control, including the Declara-
tion and the Comprehensive Multidisciplinary Outline of Future
Activities in Drug Abuse Control, adopted at the International
Conference on Drug Abuse and Illicit Trafficking, as well as the
United Nations Convention against Illicit Trafficking in Narcotic
Drugs and Psychotropic Substances,

Convinced that action against drug abuse and illicit production of and trafficking in narcotic drugs and psychotropic substances should, as a shared responsibility, be accorded a higher
priority by the international community and convinced also that
the United Nations should be the main focus for concerted action
and should play an enhanced role in that field,

Considering that the goals of intensified international co-operation and increased efforts of States in that direction would be served by the proclamation of a United Nations decade against drug abuse,

Agree on the following:

1. We resolve to protect mankind from the scourge of drug abuse and illicit trafficking in narcotic drugs and psychotropic substances;

2. We affirm that the fight against drug abuse and illicit trafficking in narcotic drugs and psychotropic substances should be accorded high priority by Governments and by all relevant regional and international organizations;

3. We are determined to take the necessary actions to combat the drug problem, taking into account the fundamental responsibility resting with each State in that regard;

4. We shall expand the scope and increase the effectiveness of international co-operation against illicit demand, production, supply, trafficking and distribution of narcotic drugs and psychotropic substances, with strict respect for the sovereignty and territorial integrity of States and the principle of non-inference in their internal affairs;

5. We shall increase our efforts and resources in order to intensify international co-operation and concerted action, based upon the principle of shared responsibility, including the necessary co-operation and assistance to affected States, when requested, in the economic, health, social, judicial and law enforcement sectors in order to strengthen the capabilities of States to deal with the problem in all its aspects;

6. We shall pursue strategies that are comprehensive and multidisciplinary in scope and that comprise measures to eliminate illicit demand for narcotic drugs and psychotropic substances, cultivation of illicit crops and illicit drug traffick-

ing, to prevent the misuse of the financial and banking systems and to promote effective treatment, rehabilitation and social reintegration;

16.   We urge the international community to strengthen international co-operation under mutually agreed conditions through bilateral, regional and multilateral mechanisms;

17.   We stress that all initiatives undertaken within the United Nations in the field of international drug abuse control shall take into consideration the competence of its organs as defined in the Charter of the United Nations;

18.   We shall further develop and utilize, to the maximum extent, existing bilateral and other international instruments or arrangements for enhancing international legal and law enforcement co-operation;

19.   We reaffirm the principles set forth in the Declaration of the International Conference on Drug Abuse and Illicit Trafficking and undertake to apply, as appropriate, the recommendations of the Comprehensive Multidisciplinary Outline of Future Activities in Drug Abuse Control;

20.   We urge States to ratify or accede to the United Nations conventions in the field of drug abuse control and illicit trafficking and, to the extent they are able to do so, to apply provisionally the terms of the United Nations Convention against Illicit Traffic in Narcotic Drugs and Psychotropic Substances;

28.   We attach high priority to the speedy and effective implementation of the Global Programme of Action;

29.   We proclaim the period from 1991 to 2000 the United Nations Decade against Drug Abuse, to be devoted to effective and sustained national, regional and international actions to promote the implementation of the Global Programme of Action, taking into account and paying due consideration to the guidelines for inter-

national decades recommended by the Economic and Social Council in its resolution 1988/63 of 27 July 1988;

30. We resolve to keep under constant review the activities set out in the present Declaration and in the Global Programme of Action.

Global Programme of Action

I. INTRODUCTION

1. The international community confronts a dramatic problem of drug abuse and the illicit cultivation, production, processing, distribution and trafficking of narcotic drugs and psychotropic substances, insufficiently effective controls over or monitoring of specific chemical substances and monitoring of the economic benefits of drug trafficking. States are not in a position to deal with this scourge individually. Therefore, international solidarity and the concerted, collective and simultaneous action of the international community are required.

2. An important aspect of the fight against drug abuse has been the elaboration of international legal instruments. The adoption of the Single Convention on Narcotic Drugs of 1961 and of that Convention as amended by the 1972 Protocol Amending the Single Convention on Narcotic Drugs of 1961 and of the Convention on Psychotropic Substances of 1971 were first important steps in that direction.

3. By its resolution 40/122 of 13 December 1985, the General Assembly decided to convene an International Conference on Drug Abuse and Illicit Trafficking. The Conference took place at Vienna from 17 to 26 June 1987 and adopted a Declaration and a Comprehensive Multidisciplinary Outline of Future Activities in Drug Abuse Control.

4. In order to reinforce and supplement the measures provided in existing legal instruments and to counter the new magnitude and extent of illicit drug trafficking and its grave conse-

quences, a United Nations plenipotentiary conference, held at Vienna from 25 November to 20 December 1988, adopted the United Nations Convention against Illicit Traffic in Narcotic Drugs and Psychotropic Substances.

5. The General Assembly, in its resolution 44/16 of 1 November 1989, decided to convene a special session of the Assembly to consider, as a matter of urgency, the question of international co-operation against illicit production, supply, demand, trafficking and distribution of narcotic drugs, with a view to expanding the scope and increasing the effectiveness of such co-operation.

6. Cognizant of the above, and following extensive deliberations at its seventeenth special session, the General Assembly, in order to achieve the goal of an international society free of illicit drugs and drug abuse, adopts the present Global Programme of Action and commits itself to its full and speedy implementation, where necessary following due consideration of the modalities by the competent technical bodies.

7. In adopting the Global Programme of Action, and without prejudice to the existing procedures, the General Assembly also decides to accord, within the United Nations system, a higher priority to the allocation of the necessary financial, personnel and other resources. There is a need for all parts of the United Nations system to galvanize efforts to improve international co-operation to stamp out the scourge of illicit drugs and drug abuse. The requirement for additional resources for that purpose is explicitly recognized, in the full expectation that that will be reflected as a high priority in the medium-term plan for the period 1992-1997 and in the programme budget for the biennium 1992-1993, as well as future medium-term plans and biennial budgets. The General Assembly also recognizes that the effective implementation of the Global Programme of Action will require examination of the structure of the existing drug control units based at the United Nations Office at Vienna with a view to enhancing their effectiveness and status in the system.

II.   ACTIVITIES OF THE GLOBAL PROGRAMME OF ACTION

8.   The Comprehensive Multidisciplinary Outline of Future Activities in Drug Abuse Control shall be used by national authorities and interested organizations as a basis for developing and translating into action, at the national, regional and international levels, to the widest extent possible, balanced strategies aimed at combating all aspects of drug abuse and illicit trafficking. Those strategies shall include, in particular, the aspects described below.

E.   Measures to be taken against the effects of money derived from, used in or intended for use in illicit drug trafficking, illegal financial flows and illegal use of the banking system

62.   Priority shall be accorded to the implementation of the United Nations Convention against Illicit Traffic in Narcotic Drugs and Psychotropic Substances, adopted in 1988, and the conclusion of bilateral, regional and multilateral agreements on tracing, freezing and seizure and forfeiture or confiscation of property and proceeds derived from, used in or intended for use in illicit drug trafficking.

63.   Mechanisms shall be developed to prevent the banking system and other financial institutions from being used for the processing and laundering of drug-related money. To this end, consideration should be given by States to entering into bilateral, regional and multilateral agreements and developing mechanisms to trace property and proceeds derived from, used in or intended for use in drug-related activities through the international banking system, facilitate access to banking records and provide for the exchange of information between law enforcement, regulatory or investigative agencies concerning the financial flow of property or proceeds related to illicit drug trafficking.

64.   The Division of Narcotic Drugs of the Secretariat, in co-operation with the Customs Co-operation Council and the International Criminal Police Organization (Interpol), should promote

bilateral or regional exchanges of information between governmental regulatory or investigative agencies concerning the financial flow of illicit drug proceeds.

65. The Division of Narcotic Drugs and Interpol shall be invited to develop a repository of laws and regulations on money laundering, currency reporting, bank secrecy and forfeiture of property and proceeds, as well as procedures and practices designed to prevent banking systems and other financial institutions from money laundering, and shall make this information available to States, at their request.

66. States shall consider enacting legislation to prevent the use of the banking system for the processing and laundering of drug-related money, inter alia, through declaring such activities criminal offences.

67. States shall consider enacting legislation to permit the seizure and forfeiture of property and proceeds derived from, used in or intended for use in illicit drug trafficking. To that end, consideration should be given by States to concluding bilateral and multilateral agreements to enhance the effectiveness of international co-operation, taking into particular account article 5, paragraph 5, of the United Nations Convention against Illicit Traffic in Narcotic Drugs and Psychotropic Substances.

68. States shall encourage international, regional and national financial associations to develop guidelines to assist their members in co-operating with government authorities in identifying, detecting, tracing, freezing and seizing proceeds and property related to illicit trafficking in narcotic drugs and psychotropic substances.

69. The elaboration of international agreements providing for stringent controls on money derived from, used in or intended for use in drug-related activities and penalizing the laundering of such money might be considered. Such instruments might also deal with the forfeiture or confiscation of funds, proceeds and

property acquired through revenues deriving from drug-related activities.

70. States shall consider measures on an international level, including the feasibility of a United Nations facility to strengthen the gathering, collation and exchange of information on the financial flow from drug-related funds, giving particular emphasis to principles, rules and national law concerning the protection of ongoing law enforcement investigations and of individuals with regard to automatic processing of personal data.

71. States should encourage international, regional and national financial institutions, within their respective areas of competence, to pay special attention, in their analyses of the economies of States, to the characteristics and magnitude of the conversion and transfer of drug-related monies in order to contribute to international efforts aimed at counteracting the negative economic and social consequences of the drug problem.

72. States shall consider the possibility of using forfeited property and proceeds for activities to combat drug abuse and illicit trafficking. In that context, the possible use of such proceeds and property or their equivalent value for United Nations drug-related activities shall also be taken into consideration.

73. All measures and proposals on possible action to prevent the use of the banking systems and financial institutions for money laundering, such as the conclusions arising from the study undertaken by the Financial Action Task Force, established at the Summit of seven major industrial nations, held in Paris from 14 to 16 July 1989, shall be made available to all States for information.

DOCUMENT E

Recommendations of the Intergovernmental Expert Group to Study the Economic & Social Consequences of Illicit Traffic in Drugs

(Extracts)

Source: UN Document E/CN.7/1991/25, 21 December 1990

INTRODUCTION

1.   The Intergovernmental Expert Group to Study the Economic and Social Consequences of Illicit Traffic in Drugs met at Vienna from 21 to 25 May and from
9 to 20 July 1990.   The Secretary-General had convened the meetings pursuant
to General Assembly resolution 44/142, in which he had been requested to undertake a study on the economic and social consequences of illicit traffic in
drugs.   The full report of the Expert Group, in English, is with the
Secretariat.

2.   At its forty-fifth session, the General Assembly had before it a report of
the Secretary-General (A/45/535) on action taken pursuant to General Assembly
resolution 44/142, section II (b) of which dealt with the work of the Expert
Group and set out the 18 recommendations it had adopted.

3.   In its resolution 45/149, entitled "International action to combat drug
abuse and illicit trafficking", the Assembly invited the Commission to study
the various recommendations and conclusions of the Expert Group, in particular
on the proposed framework for an in-depth study on the economic and social
consequences of illicit traffic in drugs and psychotropic substances, and to
report thereon to the General Assembly at its forty-sixth session through the
Economic and Social Council.

I.   RECOMMENDATIONS ADOPTED BY THE INTERGOVERNMENTAL EXPERT GROUP
TO STUDY THE ECONOMIC AND SOCIAL CONSEQUENCES OF ILLICIT
TRAFFIC IN DRUGS

4.   In order to allow the Commission to fulfil its mandate under these resolutions, the 18 recommendations of the Expert Group, and the proposed framework
for a future in-depth study on the economic and social consequences of illicit
traffic in drugs, are reproduced below.

B.   Recommendations adopted by the Expert Group following consideration
of General Assembly resolution 44/142, subparagraph 9 (b)

"5.   All States should implement such measures in order to counter
money laundering.

"6.   States should adopt:

"(a)   Measures to establish as criminal offences drug-related
money transfers and conversion, consistent with article 3, subparagraph 1 (b), of the United Nations Convention against Illicit Traffic
in Narcotic Drugs and Psychotropic Substances (E/CONF.82/15 and
Corr.2), adopted on 19 December 1988;

"(b)   Measures to make possible the identification, tracing,
freezing and seizure of proceeds, property or instrumentalities
derived from, used in or intended for use in illicit drug trafficking for the purpose of eventual confiscation, as set forth in
article 5 of the Convention;

"(c) Measures to ensure that bank and corporate secrecy laws, established professional practices and privilege laws do not inhibit criminal investigations into money laundering.

"7. States should increase their efforts to implement the provisions of the Global Programme of Action (General Assembly resolution S–17/2, annex), paragraphs 62–73, concerning measures to be taken against the effects of money derived from, used in or intended for use in illicit drug trafficking, illegal financial flows and illegal use of the banking system.

"8. States should examine the recommendations contained in the study undertaken by the Financial Action Task Force on money laundering of 7 February 1990 and, where appropriate, implement those recommendations to the widest extent possible.

"9. States should inform the Division of Narcotic Drugs of the United Nations Secretariat of specific problems encountered in implementing measures to prevent the use of their banking systems and the international financial system in money laundering, with a view to, <u>inter alia</u>, sharing experience and knowledge, devising ways of overcoming such problems and considering the advisability of adopting uniform procedures to this effect.

"10. All States should take steps to prevent the use of financial institutions, including non-bank financial institutions, for the purpose of processing and laundering drug-related money.

"11. States should encourage banks and other entities providing financial services, institutions and professional groups (attorneys, accountants, stockbrokers, trustees etc.) to co-operate fully with supervisory or law enforcement authorities in order to combat the processing and laundering of drug-related money and to ensure that such authorities are able to receive and, if necessary, to act upon reports of suspicious transactions.

"12. States, through their competent supervisory authorities, should encourage financial and other institutions to develop and implement self-regulatory processes to prevent the abuse of the financial system.

"13. Banks and other entities providing financial services, institutions and professional groups:

"(a) Should make certain that they have knowledge of the identity of their customers and clients when entering into business relations or conducting major business transactions on their behalf. If there is any doubt whether customers or clients are acting on their own behalf, reasonable measures should be taken to identify the persons on whose behalf they are acting;

"(b) Should scrutinize any unusual transaction or instruction concerning financial transfers without apparent economic rationality or legitimate purpose;

"(c) Should be required to report any suspicious transaction to the competent supervisory law enforcement authorities. The disclosure in good faith of such transactions should not constitute a breach of any restriction to disclose information and should not entail penal or civil liability for the individual or institution concerned.

"14.   The Expert Group recommends that:

"(a)   States should take steps to strengthen international co-operation in combating money laundering by preventive action, law enforcement activities and other measures such as the facilitation of mutual legal assistance and extradition procedures;

"(b)   States should foster mechanisms for the rapid and direct exchange of information between competent authorities at the international level.

"15.   The Secretary-General should be invited to convene an expert group comprising representatives drawn from the private and public sectors to define international minimal standards of professional conduct in financial and related professional activities to counter the processing and laundering of drug-related money.

"16.   The Division of Narcotic Drugs should act in liaison with the International Criminal Police Organization and the Customs Co-operation Council for the purpose of developing a unit with expertise to assist Member States, at their request, in developing and preparing laws and enforcement programmes to deal with matters relating to:

"(a)   Drug trafficking, money laundering and related criminal activities, including organized crime;

"(b)   The development and implementation of mechanisms to prevent banking and other financial institutions or systems from being used for processing or laundering money derived from, used in or intended for use in illicit drug trafficking;

"(c)   The corruption of law enforcement authorities, government officials and institutions;

"(d)   Methodologies for the investigation of money laundering and the tracing of assets.

"17.   Member States should give special consideration to contributing the value or a portion of the value of confiscated proceeds and assets to the United Nations for programmes related to the implementation of the United Nations Convention against Illicit Traffic in Narcotic Drugs and Psychotropic Substances (E/CONF.82/15 and Corr.2) and the development and maintenance of programmes related to illicit drug production, trafficking, processing and consumption and the laundering of drug-related money.

"18.   The Expert Group recommends to the General Assembly that the necessary funding for recommendations 1-17 above should be made available at the earliest opportunity so that they may be implemented as soon as possible and have the greatest impact and effectiveness."

DOCUMENT F

UN Model Treaty on Mutual Assistance in Criminal Matters, 1990
(Extracts)

Source: United Nations Document E/AC.57/1990/L.28

"1.   In this Protocol "proceeds of crime" means any property suspected, or found by a court, to be property directly or indirectly derived or realized as a result of the commission of an offence or to represent the value of property and other benefits derived from the commission of an offence.

"2.   The Requested State shall, upon request, endeavour to ascertain whether any proceeds of the crime alleged are located within its jurisdiction and shall notify the Requesting State of the results of its inquiries. In making the request, the Requesting State shall notify the Requested State of the basis of its belief that such proceeds may be located within its jurisdiction.

"3.   In pursuance of a request made under paragraph 2 of this Protocol, the Requested State shall endeavour to trace assets, investigate financial dealings, and obtain other information or evidence that may help to secure the recovery of proceeds of crime.

"4.   Where, pursuant to paragraph 2 of this Protocol, suspected proceeds of crime are found, the Requested State shall upon request take such measures as are permitted by its law to prevent any dealing in, transfer or disposal of, those suspected proceeds of crime, pending a final determination in respect of those proceeds by a court of the Requesting State.

"5.   The Requested State shall, to the extent permitted by its law, give effect to or permit enforcement of a final order forfeiting or confiscating the proceeds of crime made by a court of the Requesting State or take other appropriate action to secure the proceeds following a request by the Requesting State. b/

"6.   The Parties shall ensure that the rights of <u>bona fide</u> third parties shall be respected in the application of this Protocol.

---

a/ This Optional Protocol is included on the ground that questions of forfeiture are conceptually different from, although closely related to, matters generally accepted as falling within the description of mutual assistance. However, States may wish to include these provisions in the text because of their importance in dealing with organized crime. Moreover, assistance in forfeiting the proceeds of crime has now emerged as a new instrument in international co-operation. Provisions similar to those outlined in the Optional Protocol appear in many bilateral assistance treaties. Further details can be provided in bilateral arrangements. One matter that could be considered is the need for other provisions dealing with issues related to bank secrecy. An addition could, for example, be made to paragraph 4 providing that the Requested State shall, upon request, take such measures as are permitted by its law to require compliance with monitoring orders by financial institutions. Provision could be made for the sharing of the proceeds of crime between the Contracting States or for consideration of the disposal of the proceeds on a case-by-case basis.

b/ The Parties might consider widening the scope of the Optional Protocol by the inclusion of references to victims' restitution and the recovery of fines imposed as a sentence in a criminal prosecution.

CHAPTER III

COMMONWEALTH INITIATIVES

DOCUMENT A

Commonwealth Heads of Government Meeting
Kuala Lumpur, Malaysia, 18-24 October 1989
Communiqué (extracts)
Source: Commonwealth Secretariat, London

Countering Drug Abuse and Illicit Trafficking

56.   Heads of Government recalled their long-standing concern at the incidence of drug abuse and illicit trafficking, activities which had now grown to the extent that they posed an actual threat to the governance of some countries. They recognised that the drug problem was escalating at an alarming rate so as to represent both a serious obstacle to the processes of social and economic domestic development and a threat to the international community, to which small states were especially vulnerable. Heads of Government saw the need for an urgent strengthening of the capacity of the relevant international agencies so as to equip them more appropriately to address the problems. In particular, they welcomed initiatives to these ends being taken by the Governments of Jamaica and Trinidad and Tobago in the United Nations and believed that the Commonwealth should take the lead in promoting more effective national and international action on a number of key fronts. In this context they supported the enactment of appropriate legislation to attack drug trafficking and money-laundering, including provisions for the confiscation of the illicit assets of convicted drug traffickers. They agreed to support United Nations expert group studies on all the ways of using the United Nations system to fight the drugs menace. They also attached special importance to measures to promote crop substitution programmes and, in view of the connection between supply and consumption, to educational programmes among young people designed to reduce demand.

57. Heads of Government welcomed action in Commonwealth countries to implement the Commonwealth Scheme for Mutual Assistance
in Criminal Matters and looked forward to the early achievement
of effective, Commonwealth-wide arrangements. They acknowledged
that efficient arrangements for the extradition of fugitive
offenders are central to efforts to combat international crime,
and requested their Law Ministers to ensure that the requirements
for intra-Commonwealth extradition are no more onerous than those
for extradition as between Commonwealth and non-Commonwealth
countries.

58. Heads of Government expressed their pleasure at the successful conclusion of the United Nations Convention Against Illicit
Traffic in Narcotic Drugs and Psychotropic Substances, and urged
all members of the international community to accord priority to
its early ratification and implementation. Reference was also
made to the proposed London Conference on Demand Reduction and
Cocaine in April 1990 and the hope expressed that Commonwealth
governments would be represented.

59. Heads of Government expressed their strong support for the
Government of Colombia in its fight against the drugs problem,
and stood ready to provide what assistance they could.

DOCUMENT B

Commonwealth Law Ministers Meeting
Christchurch, New Zealand, 23-27 April 1990
Communiqué (extracts)
Source: Commonwealth Secretariat

<u>Mutual</u> <u>Assistance</u> <u>in</u> <u>Criminal</u> <u>Matters</u>

10. The Scheme relating to Mutual Assistance in Criminal Matters within the Commonwealth was one of the major achievements of the previous Meeting of Law Ministers in Harare in 1986. At Christchurch, Ministers noted with pleasure that, despite the relatively short time which had elapsed, considerable progress had been made towards the implementation of the Scheme. It was their firm hope that by the time of their next Meeting the legislative process would have been completed in many more Commonwealth countries, thus securing the broad geographical coverage important to the Scheme's success. Ministers invited the Commonwealth Secretariat to continue its work in monitoring progress and in facilitating the effective operation of the Scheme.

11. Ministers adopted a number of amendments to the Harare Scheme. In particular, they adopted substantial new provisions to strengthen and make more comprehensive the powers to trace, seize and confiscate the proceeds and instrumentalities of crime. They noted further that there were other proposals for amendments which required careful and early consideration by Senior Officials prior to the next Law Ministers' Meeting. They reviewed developing practice in this most important area. They agreed that ratifying and implementing the United Nations Convention against Illicit Traffic in Narcotic Drugs and Psychotropic Substances would make a valuable contribution and heard reports of progress to that end. They noted that the effective combating of drug trafficking and other serious crime required that attention be given to the part played by some bank secrecy laws and to the need for effective forfeiture legislation. The constitutional

difficulties to which forfeiture legislation could give rise in
some jurisdictions were also emphasised.

12. Ministers recognised, from experience in their own countries, the great benefits which could be derived from international co-operation between criminal investigation and prosecution agencies. For example, they heard of the criminal investigation following the Lockerbie aircraft disaster which had proved
to be the most complex international criminal investigation in
modern times. In the course of this investigation, assistance
has been sought from over fifty jurisdictions, many of them
Commonwealth countries, and the assistance which Commonwealth
countries had been able to give was acknowledged as having been
particularly prompt and valuable.

13. Ministers identified the need for the extension of mutual
assistance in the area of business regulation. The increasing
internationalisation of financial markets required effective
mutual assistance between national business regulatory agencies.
Voluntary co-operation needed to be reinforced by legislative
provisions to enable powers of compulsion to be exercised in the
fulfilment of requests in appropriate cases. Ministers agreed to
encourage their regulatory agencies to provide assistance to
corresponding agencies in other Commonwealth countries, and to
develop inter-agency agreements to that end. They invited the
Commonwealth Secretariat to report to their next Meeting on the
progress that had been made throughout the Commonwealth to develop this additional form of mutual assistance.

DOCUMENT C

Scheme Relating to Mutual Assistance in Criminal Matters Within the Commonwealth (Extracts)

(including amendments made by Law Ministers in April 1990)

Source: Commonwealth Secretariat, London

PURPOSE AND SCOPE

1 (1) The purpose of this Scheme is to increase the level and scope of assistance rendered between Commonwealth Governments in criminal matters. It augments, and in no way derogates from existing forms of cooperation, both formal and informal; nor does it preclude the development of enhanced arrangements in other fora.

(2) This Scheme provides for the giving of assistance by the competent authorities of one country (the requested country) in respect of criminal matters arising in another country (the requesting country).

(3) Assistance in criminal matters under this Scheme includes assistance in

  (a) identifying and locating persons;

  (b) serving documents;

  (c) examining witnesses;

  (d) search and seizure;

  (e) obtaining evidence;

  (f) facilitating the personal appearance of witnesses;

  (g) effecting a temporary transfer of persons in custody to appear as a witness;

  (h) obtaining production of judicial or official records; and

  (i) tracing, seizing and confiscating the proceeds or instrumentalities of crime.

CRIMINAL MATTER

3 (1) For the purposes of this Scheme, a criminal matter arises in a country if the Central Authority of that country certifies that criminal or forfeiture proceedings have been instituted in a court exercising jurisdiction in that country or that there is reasonable cause to believe that an offence has been committed in respect of which such criminal proceedings could be so instituted.

(2) "Offence", in the case of a federal country or a country having more than one legal system, includes an offence under the law of the country or any part thereof.

(3) "Forfeiture proceedings" means proceedings, whether civil or criminal, for an order -

    (a) restraining dealings with any property in respect of which there is reasonable cause to believe that it has been -

        (i)   derived or obtained, whether directly or indirectly, from; or

        (ii) used in, or in connection with,

    the commission of an offence;

    (b) confiscating any property derived or obtained as provided in paragraph (a)(i) or used as provided in paragraph (a)(ii); or

    (c) imposing a pecuniary penalty calculated by reference to the value of any property derived or obtained as provided in paragraph (a)(i) or used as provided in paragraph (a)(ii).

TRACING THE PROCEEDS OR INSTRUMENTALITIES OF CRIME

26 (1) A request under this Scheme may seek assistance in identifying, locating, and assessing the value of, property believed to have been derived or obtained, directly or indirectly, from, or to have been used in, or in connection with, the commission of an offence and believed to be within the requested country.

    (2) The request shall contain such information as is available to the Central Authority of the requesting country as to the nature and location of the property and as to any person in whose possession or control the property is believed to be.

SEIZING AND CONFISCATING THE PROCEEDS OR INSTRUMENTALITIES OF CRIME

27 (1) A request under this Scheme may seek assistance in securing

    (a) the making in the requested country of an order relating to the proceeds or instrumentalities of crime; or

    (b) the recognition or enforcement in that country of such an order made in the requesting country.

(2) For the purpose of this paragraph, "an order relating to the proceeds or instrumentalities of crime" means

(a) an order restraining dealings with any property in respect of which there is reasonable cause to believe that it has been derived or obtained, directly or indirectly, from, or used in, or in connection with, the commission of an offence;

(b) an order confiscating property derived or obt-ained, directly or indirectly, from, or used in or in connection with, the commission of an offence; and

(c) an order imposing a pecuniary penalty calcul-ated by reference to the value of any property so derived, obtained or used.

(3) Where the requested country cannot enforce an order made in the requesting country, the requesting country may request the making of any similar order available under the law of the requested country.

(4) The request shall be accompanied by a copy of any order made in the requesting country and shall contain, so far as reasonably practicable, all information available to the Central Authority of the requesting country which may be required in connection with the procedures to be followed in the requested country.

(5) The law of the requested country shall apply to determine the circumstances and manner in which an order may be made, recognised or enforced in response to the request.

DISPOSAL OR RELEASE OF PROPERTY

28 (1) The law of the requested country shall apply to determine the disposal of any property

(a) forfeited; or

(b) obtained as a result of the enforcement of a pecuniary penalty order

as a result of a request under this Scheme.

(2) The law of the requested country shall apply to determine the circumstances in which property made the subject of interim seizure as a result of a request under this Scheme may be released from the effects of such seizure.

DOCUMENT D

Commonwealth Heads of Government Meeting
Harare, Zimbabwe, 16–22 October 1991
Communiqué (extracts)

Source: Commonwealth Secretariat, London

Countering Drug Abuse and Illicit Trafficking

46.   Heads of Government expressed deep concern at the increasing menace of drug abuse and illicit trafficking which represents both a serious obstacle to the process of social and economic national development and a threat to the international community. They welcomed the restructuring of the United Nations drug control system, including the establishment of the United Nations International Drug Control Programme to enhance the international campaign against drug abuse and illicit trafficking, and affirmed their support for the Global Programme of Action adopted by the Seventeenth Special Session of the United Nations General Assembly in February 1990.

47.   They recognised that imaginative approaches were called for if effective responses were to be developed, particularly to reduce the demand for illicit drugs, and acknowledged that it was imperative for all countries to have appropriate legal frameworks to counter supply. In this regard they undertook to take such steps as might be necessary to become party to the 1988 United Nations Convention Against Illicit Traffic in Narcotic Drugs and Illicit Substances, and to implement the Commonwealth Scheme for Mutual Assistance in Criminal Matters. They also expressed their support for the Programme of Action adopted by the World Ministerial Summit on Demand Reduction held in London in April 1990.

CHAPTER IV

EUROPEAN DEVELOPMENTS

i. COUNCIL OF EUROPE

DOCUMENT A

Measures Against the Transfer and Safekeeping of Funds of Criminal Origin:

Recommendation No. R(80)10 Adopted by the Committee of Ministers of the Council of Europe on 27 June 1980 and Explanatory Memorandum

Source: Council of Europe, Strasbourg

The Committee of Ministers, under the terms of Article 15.*b* of the Statute of the Council of Europe;

Considering the large number of acts of criminal violence such as hold-ups and kidnappings which are becoming more and more frequent in many European countries and the anxiety felt by the public in this regard;

Considering that the transfer of funds of criminal origin from one country to another and the process by which they are laundered through insertion in the economic system give rise to serious problems, encourage the perpetration of further criminal acts and thus cause the phenomenon to spread nationally and internationally;

Intent on co-ordinating and strengthening action by member states to combat this phenomenon and wishing to define an overall policy, for which there is now a vital need;

Convinced that, within such an overall strategy, the banking system can play a highly effective preventive role, while the co-operation of the banks also assists in the repression of such criminal acts by the judicial authorities and the police;

Convinced of the importance that must be attached to the need for banks to know in effect the persons with whom they have dealings;

Convinced also that the recording of the serial numbers of bank notes entering into circulation as a result of a criminal act constitutes a useful if not indispensable means of detection,

---

1. When the recommendation was adopted, the Representative of *Ireland*, in application of Article 10.2.*c* of the Rules of Procedure for the meetings of the Ministers' Deputies, reserved the right of his Government to comply with it or not.

RECOMMENDATION No. R (80) 10

Recommends that the governments of member states:

a. arrange for the following measures to be taken by their banking system:

    i. identity checks on customers whenever:

       — an account or a securities deposit is opened;

       — safe-deposits are rented;

       — cash transactions involving sums of a certain magnitude are effected, bearing in mind the possibility of transactions in several parts;

       — inter-bank transfers involving sums of a certain magnitude are made, bearing in mind the possibility of transactions in several parts.

These checks must be made on the basis of an official document or, where the relationship with the customer has been established through correspondence or through a third party, by equivalent means;

    ii. rental of safe-deposits only to persons or firms with whom the bank has already had dealings over a certain period or whom the bank can regard as trustworthy on the strength of references;

    iii. constitution of reserve stocks of banknotes whose serial numbers are made known to the authorities if the banknotes have been used in connection with criminal offences;

    iv. suitable training for cashiers, particularly in checking identity papers and detecting criminal behaviour;

b. establish close national and international co-operation, *inter alia* with the help of Interpol, between banks and the appropriate authorities in exchanging information about the circulation of banknotes which have been used in connection with criminal offences and in following their movements;

c. set up machinery enabling banks, either by systematic comparison or by spot-checks, to refer to the list of banknotes used in connection with criminal offences when notes are paid in.

EXPLANATORY MEMORANDUM

General observations

1.   The European Committee on Crime Problems (CDPC) at its 26th Plenary Session in 1977 set up a Select Committee of Experts on Violence in Present-Day Society and gave it the task of studying, with a view to drafting recommendations, the general and specific problems raised by crimes of violence (e.g. hold-ups and kidnappings) in present-day European society. Politically motivated crime was excluded. However, in view of the scope and nature of the subject, the CDPC considered that it should be dealt with in stages each defined by ad hoc terms of reference. The first ad hoc terms of reference given to the Select Committee read as follows: "To examine the serious problems raised in many countries by the illicit transfer of funds of criminal origin frequently used for the perpetration of further crime".

The committee started its work in the first quarter of 1978 under the chairmanship of Mr G. Di Gennaro (Italy) who was later replaced by Mr V. Esposito (Italy).

The committee drew up a questionnaire on banking questions which was distributed to member states. On the basis of the replies thereto a report was produced by Mr L. Veneziani and Mr P. Klauser, consultant experts. This report was adopted by the committee.

2.   The motivation of the CDPC initiative is based on the assumption that modern forms of criminality in the majority of the European countries show an impressive increase in organised violent criminality supported by large financial resources and aimed at raising more and more gain. It is a vicious circle in which money is at the same time the target and tool of criminal groups and organisations. This type of criminality is usually related to the national or international practice of money laundering, *inter alia* by way of normal banking operations. Prevention and control to combat this behaviour cannot succeed if confined in a single national context. Therefore international collaboration is needed. Up to now this

problem has never been studied in the framework of the Council of Europe with a view to the elaboration of an international instrument.

3.   It emerges from the information collected on banking questions that authors of acts of criminal violence usually use banks in order to launder the money so obtained, and in order to hide it away.

The first object can best be achieved by cash operations such as exchange of banknotes or the purchase of either banknotes in a different currency, gold bars or bank drafts. These enable the criminal to put the banknotes he has acquired back into circulation and obtain in their place easily realisable assets without the need to have any lasting business dealings with the bank. His next step is to hide the money away, for example by renting a safe-deposit in which the now laundered assets can be placed.

These two objects can also be achieved by means of a single banking transaction which consists in handing the dirty money into the bank and asking for it to be paid into an account (current, savings or deposit account). The criminal thus exchanges his banknotes for a bank deposit which he can either retain or convert into clean banknotes as the need arises.

However, little use is apparently made of the second method. Laundering by a cash operation (purchase of bank drafts or securities) followed in some cases by use of a safe-deposit accounts for a larger proportion.

By carrying out several banking operations, usually with different banks, in order to separate the laundering process from the hiding-away process, the criminal can reduce the risk of discovery. In the first place, each individual bank sees only one part of the process and, in the second, banks pay less attention to cash transactions. That is the main reason why a cash operation is the preferred method of laundering the money.

4.   Banking practices in Council of Europe member states are astonishingly uniform, particularly as regards the formalities required to open an account or a securities deposit and to rent a safe-deposit. The identity of the client is checked in almost every state. This should be considered to be an extremely positive factor, the careful checking of a client's identity being of the utmost value when it comes to adequate enforcement of the bank's obligation to produce information and give evidence in criminal proceedings. It has now become particularly difficult to deposit money in a bank anonymously. There nevertheless ap-

EXPLANATORY MEMORANDUM

pears to be some slight differences in the degree of care taken by banks from one member state to another.

The practice in several countries of renting safe-deposits only to clients whose professional standing has been known to the bank for some time appears to be a most useful additional measure. In that case, the bank is in a position to determine the purpose or purposes for which the client is renting the safe-deposit (whether for keeping securities, jewellery, precious metals or works of art for instance).

The stricter regulations in some countries requiring banks to check not only the identity of any person opening an account but also that of the beneficial owner if the latter is a third party, is relatively widespread. It is, however, desirable that this practice extends to all Council of Europe member states even if its application still meets with some difficulties due to professional secrecy.

Banking practice in the sectors in which banks do not check the identity of persons with whom they have dealings is also largely similar everywhere. The operations in question are mainly those which do not involve any lasting relationship between bank and client, mainly cash operations, but also inter-bank transactions, that is when a cash sum is handed to one bank to be credited to an account in another bank which itself will also omit to check the identity of the person ordering such transfer.

These banking practices thus represent a weak spot in the system and one of which criminals are able to take advantage in order to launder money acquired through acts of criminal violence. The stricter the requirements regarding identity checks, the greater the chances of discovering the money obtained through criminal activities because it is through the banking system that money is usually laundered and hidden away.

The considerations above lead to the conclusion that co-ordination between the activities of banks and of the authorities competent in the prevention and control of criminal deeds is essential. To that effect it seems that particular obligations should be imposed on banks without, however, allowing them to replace the police or be assigned functions involving the exercise of a power of authority.

Comments on the recommendations

a. This paragraph sets out a list of measures which, as a minimum, should be taken by all private and public banks or other agencies per-

EXPLANATORY MEMORANDUM

forming similar activities. The ways and means by which governments may arrange for these measures to be taken are not specified. They may include, *inter alia,* statutory means and recommendations to, or agreements with, bankers' associations.

The basic idea underlying sub-paragraph i is that the identity of a customer must be known to and thus checked by the bank, when he wishes to open a current or a deposit account or to rent a safe-deposit; also if he wishes to make a cash operation or an inter-bank transfer involving sums of a certain magnitude.

"Customer" here means both the owner of the funds and the person who represents him in his relations with the bank.

By "sums of a certain magnitude" the experts who drew up this text in 1980 had in mind indicatively any sum above 10 000 European units of account (ECU). However, the expression may be understood, according to conditions prevailing in each member state, as any sum which is above the average flows ordinarily dealt with under similar circumstances. Breaking down the sum in several parts should not be allowed as a way out available to customers.

Customers presenting themselves personally at the counter should be requested to establish their identity by exhibiting a document issued or approved by an official authority and preferably containing a photograph of the holder. In this respect the Resolution (77) 26 on the establishment and harmonisation of national identity cards adopted by the Committee of Ministers of the Council of Europe on 28 September 1977 is recalled.

Customers who do not present themselves personally at the counter should also be asked to establish their identity by exhibiting an official document or else by means of a document which could not have been produced prior to an identity check performed by an authority or other trustworthy agent on the basis of an official document.

The rental of safe-deposits is the easiest and most immediate means of safeguarding almost any proceeds of crime. Therefore banks should not make them available to anyone regardless of personal considerations. Only customers well known to the bank and therefore regarded as trustworthy should be allowed to rent a safe. Two criteria are laid down in sub-paragraph ii, namely the experience enjoyed by the bank in dealing with the customer over a certain period of time and references. The latter includes the personal acquaintance of the banker.

EXPLANATORY MEMORANDUM

The committee of experts had also envisaged that banks should be bound to:

a. draw up a list of customers to whom safe-deposits were rented and to forward the list to the appropriate authorities;

b. forward this list to a judicial authority upon request;

c. keep an inventory of objects and funds placed in the safe.

This idea which would be given further examination did not, however, meet with the unanimous approval of the committee.

Sub-paragraph iii provides for banks to hold stocks of banknotes whose serial numbers are recorded. These stocks should be easily available for use in cases of, for example hold-ups and kidnappings, and when so used, banks should immediately make the serial numbers known to the authorities. In fact the only individual characteristic of any single banknote is its serial number. Hence the importance of recording the serial numbers of banknotes entered into circulation as the result of a criminal act (dirty money).

The effectiveness of most recommendations included in this document depends on the accuracy with which bank employees who deal with customers judge the person and the situation they have to face. Therefore, it should be part of their professional training to be given adequate knowledge in checking identity papers and in detecting criminal behaviour.

b.   This recommendation logically follows the recommendation contained in sub-paragraph iii. Banknotes which entered into circulation as a result of a criminal act and whose serial numbers are recorded, must be traced in order to prevent them from being laundered. To that effect, close co-operation is recommended between, on one side, the police and judicial or other appropriate authorities, and on the other side, banks. And this both at national and at international level, where the assistance of ICPO-Interpol is of great importance notably because of the technical means which it has or may acquire. These means should, in fact, include access by Interpol to the telecommunications system SWIFT (Society for World-wide Interbank Financial Telecommunications), which at present links the main banks in most European countries and should in the future be extended to every bank-counter. The possibility of implementing the European Conventions on Mutual Assistance in Criminal Matters and on the Transfer of Proceedings in Criminal Matters, and others, or bilateral conventions where applicable, is also recalled.

EXPLANATORY MEMORANDUM

c.   When notes are paid in, banks should be able to compare their serial numbers with the numbers which figure on the list of dirty money. For practical as well as technical reasons (absence of any widely used transnational electronic system) such comparison cannot be systematic at every single counter. Thus the recommendation provides for spot checks as an alternative solution. However, it is desirable that the use of such a system be extended to all Council of Europe member states.

DOCUMENT B

1990 Council of Europe Convention on Laundering, Search, Seizure and Confiscation of the Proceeds from Crime

Source: Council of Europe, Strasbourg

PREAMBLE

The member States of the Council of Europe and the other States signatory hereto,

Considering that the aim of the Council of Europe is to achieve a greater unity between its members;

Convinced of the need to pursue a common criminal policy aimed at the protection of society;

Considering that the fight against serious crime, which has become an increasingly international problem, calls for the use of modern and effective methods on an international scale;

Believing that one of these methods consists in depriving criminals of the proceeds from crime;

Considering that for the attainment of this aim a well-functioning system of international co-operation also must be established,

Have agreed as follows:

CHAPTER I

USE OF TERMS

Article 1

Use of terms

For the purposes of this Convention:

a.   "proceeds" means any economic advantage from criminal offences. It may consist of any property as defined in sub-paragraph *b* of this article;

b.   "property" includes property of any description, whether corporeal or incorporeal, movable or immovable, and legal documents or instruments evidencing title to, or interest in such property;

c.   "instrumentalities" means any property used or intended to be used, in any manner, wholly or in part, to commit a criminal offence or criminal offences;

d.   "confiscation" means a penalty or a measure, ordered by a court following proceedings in relation to a criminal offence or criminal offences resulting in the final deprivation of property;

e.   "predicate offence" means any criminal offence as a result of which proceeds were generated that may become the subject of an offence as defined in Article 6 of this Convention.

CHAPTER II

MEASURES TO BE TAKEN AT NATIONAL LEVEL

Article 2

Confiscation measures

1.   Each Party shall adopt such legislative and other measures as may be necessary to enable it to confiscate instrumentalities and proceeds or property the value of which corresponds to such proceeds.

2.   Each Party may, at the time of signature or when depositing its instrument of ratification, acceptance, approval or accession, by a declaration addressed to the Secretary General of the Council of Europe, declare that paragraph 1 of this article applies only to offences or categories of offences specified in such declaration.

Article 3

Investigative and provisional measures

Each Party shall adopt such legislative and other measures as may be necessary to enable it to identify and trace property which is liable to confiscation pursuant to Article 2, paragraph 1, and to prevent any dealing in, transfer or disposal of such property.

Article 4

Special investigative powers and techniques

1.   Each Party shall adopt such legislative and other measures as may be necessary to empower its courts or other competent authorities to order that bank, financial or commercial records be made available or be seized in order to carry out the actions referred to in Articles 2 and 3. A Party shall not decline to act under the provisions of this article on grounds of bank secrecy.

2.   Each Party shall consider adopting such legislative and other measures as may be necessary to enable it to use special investigative techniques facilitating the identification and tracing of proceeds and the gathering of evidence related thereto. Such techniques may include monitoring orders, observation, interception of telecommunications, access to computer systems and orders to produce specific documents.

Article 5

Legal remedies

Each Party shall adopt such legislative and other measures as may be necessary to ensure that interested parties affected by measures under Articles 2 and 3 shall have effective legal remedies in order to preserve their rights.

Article 6

Laundering offences

1.   Each Party shall adopt such legislative and other measures as may be necessary to establish as offences under its domestic law, when committed intentionally:

a. the conversion or transfer of property, knowing that such property is proceeds, for the purpose of concealing or disguising the illicit origin of the property or of assisting any person who is involved in the commission of the predicate offence to evade the legal consequences of his actions;

b. the concealment or disguise of the true nature, source, location, disposition, movement, rights with respect to, or ownership of, property, knowing that such property is proceeds;

and, subject to its constitutional principles and the basic concepts of its legal system:

c. the acquisition, possession or use of property, knowing, at the time of receipt, that such property was proceeds;

d. participation in, association or conspiracy to commit, attempts to commit and aiding, abetting, facilitating and counselling the commission of any of the offences established in accordance with this article.

2.   For the purposes of implementing or applying paragraph 1 of this article:

a. it shall not matter whether the predicate offence was subject to the criminal jurisdiction of the Party;

b. it may be provided that the offences set forth in that paragraph do not apply to the persons who committed the predicate offence;

c. knowledge, intent or purpose required as an element of an offence set forth in that paragraph may be inferred from objective, factual circumstances.

3.   Each Party may adopt such measures as it considers necessary to establish also as offences under its domestic law all or some of the acts referred to in paragraph 1 of this article, in any or all of the following cases where the offender:

a. ought to have assumed that the property was proceeds;

b. acted for the purpose of making profit;

c. acted for the purpose of promoting the carrying on of further criminal activity.

4.   Each Party may, at the time of signature or when depositing its instrument of ratification, acceptance, approval or accession, by declaration addressed to the Secretary General of the Council of Europe declare that paragraph 1 of this article applies only to predicate offences or categories of such offences specified in such declaration.

CHAPTER III

INTERNATIONAL CO-OPERATION

Section 1

Principles of international co-operation

Article 7

General principles and measures for international co-operation

1.   The Parties shall co-operate with each other to the widest extent possible for the purposes of investigations and proceedings aiming at the confiscation of instrumentalities and proceeds.

2.   Each Party shall adopt such legislative or other measures as may be necessary to enable it to comply, under the conditions provided for in this chapter, with requests:

a. for confiscation of specific items of property representing proceeds or instrumentalities, as well as for confiscation of proceeds consisting in a requirement to pay a sum of money corresponding to the value of proceeds;

b. for investigative assistance and provisional measures with a view to either form of confiscation referred to under *a* above.

Section 2

Investigative assistance

Article 8

Obligation to assist

The Parties shall afford each other, upon request, the widest possible measure of assistance in the identification and tracing of instrumentalities, proceeds and other property liable to confiscation. Such assistance shall include any measure providing and securing evidence as to the existence, location or movement, nature, legal status or value of the aforementioned property.

Article 9

Execution of assistance

The assistance pursuant to Article 8 shall be carried out as permitted by and in accordance with the domestic law of the requested Party and, to the extent not incompatible with such law, in accordance with the procedures specified in the request.

Article 10

Spontaneous information

Without prejudice to its own investigations or proceedings, a Party may without prior request forward to another Party information on instrumentalities and proceeds, when it considers that the disclosure of such information might assist the receiving Party in initiating or carrying out investigations or proceedings or might lead to a request by that Party under this chapter.

Section 3

Provisional measures

Article 11

Obligation to take provisional measures

1.   At the request of another Party which has instituted criminal proceedings or proceedings for the purpose of confiscation, a Party shall take the necessary provisional measures, such as freezing or seizing, to prevent any dealing in, transfer or disposal of property which, at a later stage, may be the subject of a request for confiscation or which might be such as to satisfy the request.

2.   A Party which has received a request for confiscation pursuant to Article 13 shall, if so requested, take the measures mentioned in paragraph 1 of this article in respect of any property which is the subject of the request or which might be such as to satisfy the request.

Article 12

Execution of provisional measures

1.   The provisional measures mentioned in Article 11 shall be carried out as permitted by and in accordance with the domestic law of the requested Party and, to the extent not incompatible with such law, in accordance with the procedures specified in the request.

2.   Before lifting any provisional measure taken pursuant to this article, the requested Party shall, wherever possible, give the requesting Party an opportunity to present its reasons in favour of continuing the measure.

Section 4

Confiscation

Article 13

Obligation to confiscate

1.   A Party, which has received a request made by another Party for confiscation concerning instrumentalities or proceeds, situated in its territory, shall:

   a. enforce a confiscation order made by a court of a requesting Party in relation to such instrumentalities or proceeds; or

   b. submit the request to its competent authorities for the purpose of obtaining an order of confiscation and, if such order is granted, enforce it.

2.   For the purposes of applying paragraph 1.*b* of this article, any Party shall whenever necessary have competence to institute confiscation proceedings under its own law.

3.   The provisions of paragraph 1 of this article shall also apply to confiscation consisting in a requirement to pay a sum of money corresponding to the value of proceeds, if property on which the confiscation can be enforced is located in the requested Party. In such cases, when enforcing confiscation pursuant to paragraph 1, the requested Party shall, if payment is not obtained, realise the claim on any property available for that purpose.

4.   If a request for confiscation concerns a specific item of property, the Parties may agree that the requested Party may enforce the confiscation in the form of a requirement to pay a sum of money corresponding to the value of the property.

Article 14

Execution of confiscation

1.   The procedures for obtaining and enforcing the confiscation under Article 13 shall be governed by the law of the requested Party.

2.   The requested Party shall be bound by the findings as to the facts in so far as they are stated in a conviction or judicial decision of the requesting Party or in so far as such conviction or judicial decision is implicitly based on them.

3.   Each Party may, at the time of signature or when depositing its instrument of ratification, acceptance, approval or accession, by a declaration addressed to the Secretary General of the Council of Europe, declare that paragraph 2 of this article applies only subject to its constitutional principles and the basic concepts of its legal system.

4.   If the confiscation consists in the requirement to pay a sum of money, the competent authority of the requested Party shall convert the amount thereof into the currency of that Party at the rate of exchange ruling at the time when the decision to enforce the confiscation is taken.

5.   In the case of Article 13, paragraph 1.*a*, the requesting Party alone shall have the right to decide on any application for review of the confiscation order.

Article 15

Confiscated property

Any property confiscated by the requested Party shall be disposed of by that Party in accordance with its domestic law, unless otherwise agreed by the Parties concerned.

Article 16

Right of enforcement and maximum amount of confiscation

1.   A request for confiscation made under Article 13 does not affect the right of the requesting Party to enforce itself the confiscation order.

2.   Nothing in this Convention shall be so interpreted as to permit the total value of the confiscation to exceed the amount of the sum of money specified in the confiscation order. If a Party finds that this might occur, the Parties concerned shall enter into consultations to avoid such an effect.

Article 17

Imprisonment in default

The requested Party shall not impose imprisonment in default or any other measure restricting the liberty of a person as a result of a request under Article 13, if the requesting Party has so specified in the request.

Section 5

Refusal and postponement of co-operation

Article 18

Grounds for refusal

1.   Co-operation under this chapter may be refused if:

   a. the action sought would be contrary to the fundamental principles of the legal system of the requested Party; or

   b. the execution of the request is likely to prejudice the sovereignty, security, *ordre public* or other essential interests of the requested Party; or

   c. in the opinion of the requested Party, the importance of the case to which the request relates does not justify the taking of the action sought; or

   d. the offence to which the request relates is a political or fiscal offence; or

   e. the requested Party considers that compliance with the action sought would be contrary to the principle of *ne bis in idem*; or

   f. the offence to which the request relates would not be an offence under the law of the requested Party if committed within its jurisdiction. However, this ground for refusal applies to co-operation under Section 2 only in so far as the assistance sought involves coercive action.

2.   Co-operation under Section 2, in so far as the assistance sought involves coercive action, and under Section 3 of this chapter, may also be refused if the measures sought could not be taken under the domestic law of the requested Party for the purposes of investigations or proceedings, had it been a similar domestic case.

3.   Where the law of the requested Party so requires, co-operation under Section 2, in so far as the assistance sought involves coercive action, and under Section 3 of this chapter may also be refused if the measures sought or any other measures having similar effects would not be permitted under the law of the requesting Party, or, as regards the competent authorities of the requesting Party, if the request is not authorised by either a judge or another judicial authority, including public prosecutors, any of these authorities acting in relation to criminal offences.

4.   Co-operation under Section 4 of this chapter may also be refused if:

   a. under the law of the requested Party confiscation is not provided for in respect of the type of offence to which the request relates; or

   b. without prejudice to the obligation pursuant to Article 13, paragraph 3, it would be contrary to the principles of the domestic laws of the requested Party concerning the limits of confiscation in respect of the relationship between an offence and:

i.   an economic advantage that might be qualified as its proceeds; or

ii.   property that might be qualified as its instrumentalities; or

   c. under the law of the requested Party confiscation may no longer be imposed or enforced because of the lapse of time; or

   d. the request does not relate to a previous conviction, or a decision of a judicial nature or a statement in such a decision that an offence or several offences have been committed, on the basis of which the confiscation has been ordered or is sought; or

   e. confiscation is either not enforceable in the requesting Party, or it is still subject to ordinary means of appeal; or

   f. the request relates to a confiscation order resulting from a decision rendered *in absentia* of the person against whom the order was issued and, in the opinion of the requested Party, the proceedings conducted by the requesting Party leading to such decision did not satisfy the minimum rights of defence recognised as due to everyone against whom a criminal charge is made.

5.   For the purposes of paragraph 4.*f* of this article a decision is not considered to have been rendered *in absentia* if:

    a. it has been confirmed or pronounced after opposition by the person concerned; or

    b. it has been rendered on appeal, provided that the appeal was lodged by the person concerned.

6.   When considering, for the purposes of paragraph 4.*f* of this article, if the minimum rights of defence have been satisfied, the requested Party shall take into account the fact that the person concerned has deliberately sought to evade justice or the fact that that person, having had the possibility of lodging a legal remedy against the decision made *in absentia*, elected not to do so. The same will apply when the person concerned, having been duly served with the summons to appear, elected not to do so nor to ask for adjournment.

7.   A Party shall not invoke bank secrecy as a ground to refuse any co-operation under this chapter. Where its domestic law so requires, a Party may require that a request for co-operation which would involve the lifting of bank secrecy be authorised by either a judge or another judicial authority, including public prosecutors, any of these authorities acting in relation to criminal offences.

8.   Without prejudice to the ground for refusal provided for in paragraph 1.*a* of this article:

    a. the fact that the person under investigation or subjected to a confiscation order by the authorities of the requesting Party is a legal person shall not be invoked by the requested Party as an obstacle to affording any co-operation under this chapter;

    b. the fact that the natural person against whom an order of confiscation of proceeds has been issued has subsequently died or the fact that a legal person against whom an order of confiscation of proceeds has been issued has subsequently been dissolved shall not be invoked as an obstacle to render assistance in accordance with Article 13, paragraph 1.*a.*

Article 19

Postponement

The requested Party may postpone action on a request if such action would prejudice investigations or proceedings by its authorities.

Article 20

Partial or conditional granting of a request

Before refusing or postponing co-operation under this chapter, the requested Party shall, where appropriate after having consulted the requesting Party, consider whether the request may be granted partially or subject to such conditions as it deems necessary.

Section 6

Notification and protection of third parties' rights

Article 21

Notification of documents

1.   The Parties shall afford each other the widest measure of mutual assistance in the serving of judicial documents to persons affected by provisional measures and confiscation.

2.   Nothing in this article is intended to interfere with:

    a. the possibility of sending judicial documents, by postal channels, directly to persons abroad;

b. the possibility for judicial officers, officials or other competent authorities of the Party of origin to effect service of judicial documents directly through the consular authorities of that Party or through judicial officers, officials or other competent authorities of the Party of destination,

unless the Party of destination makes a declaration to the contrary to the Secretary General of the Council of Europe at the time of signature or when depositing its instrument of ratification, acceptance, approval or accession.

3.   When serving judicial documents to persons abroad affected by provisional measures or confiscation orders issued in the sending Party, this Party shall indicate what legal remedies are available under its law to such persons.

Article 22

Recognition of foreign decisions

1.   When dealing with a request for co-operation under Sections 3 and 4, the requested Party shall recognise any judicial decision taken in the requesting Party regarding rights claimed by third parties.

2.   Recognition may be refused if:

a. third parties did not have adequate opportunity to assert their rights; or

b. the decision is incompatible with a decision already taken in the requested Party on the same matter; or

c. it is incompatible with the *ordre public* of the requested Party; or

d. the decision was taken contrary to provisions on exclusive jurisdiction provided for by the law of the requested Party.

Section 7

Procedural and other general rules

Article 23

Central authority

1.   The Parties shall designate a central authority or, if necessary, authorities, which shall be responsible for sending and answering requests made under this chapter, the execution of such requests or the transmission of them to the authorities competent for their execution.

2.   Each Party shall, at the time of signature or when depositing its instrument of ratification, acceptance, approval or accession, communicate to the Secretary General of the Council of Europe the names and addresses of the authorities designated in pursuance of paragraph 1 of this article.

Article 24

Direct communication

1.   The central authorities shall communicate directly with one another.

2.   In the event of urgency, requests or communications under this chapter may be sent directly by the judicial authorities, including public prosecutors, of the requesting Party to such authorities of the requested Party. In such cases a copy shall be sent at the same time to the central authority of the requested Party through the central authority of the requesting Party.

3.   Any request or communication under paragraphs 1 and 2 of this article may be made through the International Criminal Police Organisation (Interpol).

4.   Where a request is made pursuant to paragraph 2 of this article and the authority is not competent to deal with the request, it shall refer the request to the competent national authority and inform directly the requesting Party that it has done so.

5.   Requests or communications under Section 2 of this chapter, which do not involve coercive action, may be directly transmitted by the competent authorities of the requesting Party to the competent authorities of the requested Party.

Article 25

Form of request and languages

1.   All requests under this chapter shall be made in writing. Modern means of telecommunications, such as telefax, may be used.

2.   Subject to the provisions of paragraph 3 of this article, translations of the requests or supporting documents shall not be required.

3.   At the time of signature or when depositing its instrument of ratification, acceptance, approval or accession, any Party may communicate to the Secretary General of the Council of Europe a declaration that it reserves the right to require that requests made to it and documents supporting such requests be accompanied by a translation into its own language or into one of the official languages of the Council of Europe or into such one of these languages as it shall indicate. It may on that occasion declare its readiness to accept translations in any other language as it may specify. The other Parties may apply the reciprocity rule.

Article 26

Legalisation

Documents transmitted in application of this chapter shall be exempt from all legalisation formalities.

Article 27

Content of request

1.   Any request for co-operation under this chapter shall specify :

a. the authority making the request and the authority carrying out the investigations or proceedings ;

b. the object of and the reason for the request ;

c. the matters, including the relevant facts (such as date, place and circumstances of the offence) to which the investigations or proceedings relate, except in the case of a request for notification ;

d. in so far as the co-operation involves coercive action :

i.   the text of the statutory provisions or, where this is not possible, a statement of the relevant law applicable ; and

ii.   an indication that the measure sought or any other measures having similar effects could be taken in the territory of the requesting Party under its own law ;

e. where necessary and in so far as possible :

i.   details of the person or persons concerned, including name, date and place of birth, nationality and location, and, in the case of a legal person, its seat ; and

ii.   the property in relation to which co-operation is sought, its location, its connection with the person or persons concerned, any connection with the offence, as well as any available information about other persons' interests in the property ; and *f.* any particular procedure the requesting Party wishes to be followed.

2.   A request for provisional measures under Section 3 in relation to seizure of property on which a confiscation order consisting in the requirement to pay a sum of money may be realised shall also indicate a maximum amount for which recovery is sought in that property.

3.   In addition to the indications mentioned in paragraph 1, any request under Section 4 shall contain:

a. in the case of Article 13, paragraph 1.*a*:

i.   a certified true copy of the confiscation order made by the court in the requesting Party and a statement of the grounds on the basis of which the order was made, if they are not indicated in the order itself;

ii.   an attestation by the competent authority of the requesting Party that the confiscation order is enforceable and not subject to ordinary means of appeal;

iii.   information as to the extent to which the enforcement of the order is requested; and

iv.   information as to the necessity of taking any provisional measures;

b. in the case of Article 13, paragraph 1.*b*, a statement of the facts relied upon by the requesting Party sufficient to enable the requested Party to seek the order under its domestic law;

c. when third parties have had the opportunity to claim rights, documents demonstrating that this has been the case.

Article 28

Defective requests

1.   If a request does not comply with the provisions of this chapter or the information supplied is not sufficient to enable the requested Party to deal with the request, that Party may ask the requesting Party to amend the request or to complete it with additional information.

2.   The requested Party may set a time-limit for the receipt of such amendments or information.

3.   Pending receipt of the requested amendments or information in relation to a request under Section 4 of this chapter, the requested Party may take any of the measures referred to in Sections 2 or 3 of this chapter.

Article 29

Plurality of requests

1.   Where the requested Party receives more than one request under Sections 3 or 4 of this chapter in respect of the same person or property, the plurality of requests shall not prevent that Party from dealing with the requests involving the taking of provisional measures.

2.   In the case of plurality of requests under Section 4 of this chapter, the requested Party shall consider consulting the requesting Parties.

Article 30

Obligation to give reasons

The requested Party shall give reasons for any decision to refuse, postpone or make conditional any co-operation under this chapter.

Article 31

Information

1.   The requested Party shall promptly inform the requesting Party of:

a. the action initiated on a request under this chapter;

b. the final result of the action carried out on the basis of the request;

c. a decision to refuse, postpone or make conditional, in whole or in part, any co-operation under this chapter;

d. any circumstances which render impossible the carrying out of the action sought or are likely to delay it significantly; and

e. in the event of provisional measures taken pursuant to a request under Sections 2 or 3 of this chapter, such provisions of its domestic law as would automatically lead to the lifting of the provisional measure.

2.   The requesting Party shall promptly inform the requested Party of:

a. any review, decision or any other fact by reason of which the confiscation order ceases to be wholly or partially enforceable; and

b. any development, factual or legal, by reason of which any action under this chapter is no longer justified.

3.   Where a Party, on the basis of the same confiscation order, requests confiscation in more than one Party, it shall inform all Parties which are affected by an enforcement of the order about the request.

Article 32

Restriction of use

1.   The requested Party may make the execution of a request dependent on the condition that the information or evidence obtained will not, without its prior consent, be used or transmitted by the authorities of the requesting Party for investigations or proceedings other than those specified in the request.

2.   Each Party may, at the time of signature or when depositing its instrument of ratification, acceptance, approval or accession, by declaration addressed to the Secretary General of the Council of Europe, declare that, without its prior consent, information or evidence provided by it under this chapter may not be used or transmitted by the authorities of the requesting Party in investigations or proceedings other than those specified in the request.

Article 33

Confidentiality

1.   The requesting Party may require that the requested Party keep confidential the facts and substance of the request, except to the extent necessary to execute the request. If the requested Party cannot comply with the requirement of confidentiality, it shall promptly inform the requesting Party.

2.   The requesting Party shall, if not contrary to basic principles of its national law and if so requested, keep confidential any evidence and information provided by the requested Party, except to the extent that its disclosure is necessary for the investigations or proceedings described in the request.

3.   Subject to the provisions of its domestic law, a Party which has received spontaneous information under Article 10 shall comply with any requirement of confidentiality as required by the Party which supplies the information. If the other Party cannot comply with such requirement, it shall promptly inform the transmitting Party.

Article 34

Costs

The ordinary costs of complying with a request shall be borne by the requested Party. Where costs of a substantial or extraordinary nature are necessary to comply with a request, the Parties shall consult in order to agree the conditions on which the request is to be executed and how the costs shall be borne.

Article 35

Damages

1.   When legal action on liability for damages resulting from an act or omission in relation to co-operation under this chapter has been initiated by a person, the Parties concerned shall consider consulting each other, where appropriate, to determine how to apportion any sum of damages due.

2.   A Party which has become subject of a litigation for damages shall endeavour to inform the other Party of such litigation if that Party might have an interest in the case.

CHAPTER IV

FINAL PROVISIONS

Article 36

Signature and entry into force

1.   This Convention shall be open for signature by the member States of the Council of Europe and non-member States which have participated in its elaboration. Such States may express their consent to be bound by:

a. signature without reservation as to ratification, acceptance or approval; or

b. signature subject to ratification, acceptance or approval, followed by ratification, acceptance or approval.

2.   Instruments of ratification, acceptance or approval shall be deposited with the Secretary General of the Council of Europe.

3.   This Convention shall enter into force on the first day of the month following the expiration of a period of three months after the date on which three States, of which at least two are member States of the Council of Europe, have expressed their consent to be bound by the Convention in accordance with the provisions of paragraph 1.

4.   In respect of any signatory State which subsequently expresses its consent to be bound by it, the Convention shall enter into force on the first day of the month following the expiration of a period of three months after the date of the expression of its consent to be bound by the Convention in accordance with the provisions of paragraph 1.

Article 37

Accession to the Convention

1.   After the entry into force of this Convention, the Committee of Ministers of the Council of Europe, after consulting the Contracting States to the Convention, may invite any State not a member of the Council and not having participated in its elaboration to accede to this Convention, by a decision taken by the majority provided for in Article 20.*d* of the Statute of the Council of Europe and by the unanimous vote of the representatives of the Contracting States entitled to sit on the Committee.

2.   In respect of any acceding State the Convention shall enter into force on the first day of the month following the expiration of a period of three months after the date of deposit of the instrument of accession with the Secretary General of the Council of Europe.

Article 38

Territorial application

1.   Any State may, at the time of signature or when depositing its instrument of ratification, acceptance, approval or accession, specify the territory or territories to which this Convention shall apply.

2.   Any State may, at any later date, by a declaration addressed to the Secretary General of the Council of Europe, extend the application of this Convention to any other territory specified in the declaration. In respect of such territory the Convention shall enter into force on the first day of the month following the expiration of a period of three months after the date of receipt of such declaration by the Secretary General.

3.   Any declaration made under the two preceding paragraphs may, in respect of any territory specified in such declaration, be withdrawn by a notification addressed to the Secretary General. The withdrawal shall become effective on the first day of the month following the expiration of a period of three months after the date of receipt of such notification by the Secretary General.

Article 39

Relationship to other conventions and agreements

1.   This Convention does not affect the rights and undertakings derived from international multilateral conventions concerning special matters.

2.   The Parties to the Convention may conclude bilateral or multilateral agreements with one another on the matters dealt with in this Convention, for purposes of supplementing or strengthening its provisions or facilitating the application of the principles embodied in it.

3.   If two or more Parties have already concluded an agreement or treaty in respect of a subject which is dealt with in this Convention or otherwise have established their relations in respect of that subject, they shall be entitled to apply that agreement or treaty or to regulate those relations accordingly, in lieu of the present Convention, if it facilitates international co-operation.

Article 40

Reservations

1.   Any State may, at the time of signature or when depositing its instrument of ratification, acceptance, approval or accession, declare that it avails itself of one or more of the reservations provided for in Article 2, paragraph 2, Article 6, paragraph 4, Article 14, paragraph 3, Article 21, paragraph 2, Article 25, paragraph 3 and Article 32, paragraph 2. No other reservation may be made.

2.   Any State which has made a reservation under the preceding paragraph may wholly or partly withdraw it by means of a notification addressed to the Secretary General of the Council of Europe. The withdrawal shall take effect on the date of receipt of such notification by the Secretary General.

3.   A Party which has made a reservation in respect of a provision of this Convention may not claim the application of that provision by any other Party; it may, however, if its reservation is partial or conditional, claim the application of that provision in so far as it has itself accepted it.

Article 41

Amendments

1.   Amendments to this Convention may be proposed by any Party, and shall be communicated by the Secretary General of the Council of Europe to the member States of the Council of Europe and to every non-member State which has acceded to or has been invited to accede to this Convention in accordance with the provisions of Article 37.

2.   Any amendment proposed by a Party shall be communicated to the European Committee on Crime Problems which shall submit to the Committee of Ministers its opinion on that proposed amendment.

3.   The Committee of Ministers shall consider the proposed amendment and the opinion submitted by the European Committee on Crime Problems and may adopt the amendment.

4.   The text of any amendment adopted by the Committee of Ministers in accordance with paragraph 3 of this article shall be forwarded to the Parties for acceptance.

5.   Any amendment adopted in accordance with paragraph 3 of this article shall come into force on the thirtieth day after all Parties have informed the Secretary General of their acceptance thereof.

Article 42

Settlement of disputes

1.   The European Committee on Crime Problems of the Council of Europe shall be kept informed regarding the interpretation and application of this Convention.

2.   In case of a dispute between Parties as to the interpretation or application of this Convention, they shall seek a settlement of the dispute through negotiation or any other peaceful means of their choice, including submission of the dispute to the European Committee on Crime Problems, to an arbitral tribunal whose decisions shall be binding upon the Parties, or to the International Court of Justice, as agreed upon by the Parties concerned.

Article 43

Denunciation

1.   Any Party may, at any time, denounce this Convention by means of a notification addressed to the Secretary General of the Council of Europe.

2.   Such denunciation shall become effective on the first day of the month following the expiration of a period of three months after the date of receipt of the notification by the Secretary General.

3.   The present Convention shall, however, continue to apply to the enforcement under Article 14 of confiscation for which a request has been made in conformity with the provisions of this Convention before the date on which such a denunciation takes effect.

Article 44

Notifications

The Secretary General of the Council of Europe shall notify the member States of the Council and any State which has acceded to this Convention of:

   a. any signature;

   b. the deposit of any instrument of ratification, acceptance, approval or accession;

   c. any date of entry into force of this Convention in accordance with Articles 36 and 37;

   d. any reservation made under Article 40, paragraph 1;

   e. any other act, notification or communication relating to this Convention.

In witness whereof the undersigned, being duly authorised thereto, have signed this Convention.

Done at Strasbourg, this 8th day of November 1990, in English and in French, both texts being equally authentic, in a single copy which shall be deposited in the archives of the Council of Europe. The Secretary General of the Council of Europe shall transmit certified copies to each member State of the Council of Europe, to the non-member States which have participated in the elaboration of this Convention, and to any State invited to accede to it.

DOCUMENT C

Explanatory Report on the Convention on Laundering, Search, Seizure and Confiscation of the Proceeds from Crime

Source: Council of Europe, Strasbourg

Introduction

1.   At their 15th Conference (Oslo, 17-19 June 1986), the European Ministers of Justice discussed the penal aspects of drug abuse and drug trafficking, including the need to combat drug abuse by smashing the drugs market, which was often linked with organised crime and even terrorism, for example by freezing and confiscating the proceeds from drug trafficking. The discussion resulted in the adoption of Resolution No. 1, in which the Ministers recommend that the European Committee on Crime Problems (CDPC) should examine "the formulation, in the light *inter alia* of the work of the United Nations, of international norms and standards to guarantee effective international co-operation between judicial (and where necessary police) authorities as regards the detection, freezing and forfeiture of the proceeds of illicit drug trafficking".

2.   Following this initiative and the substantial work which had already been carried out by the Pompidou Group, *inter alia*, at two *ad hoc* technical conferences in Strasbourg in November 1983 and March 1985, the creation of a Select Committee of Experts on international co-operation as regards search, seizure and confiscation of the proceeds from crime (PC-R-SC) was proposed by the CDPC at its 36th Plenary Session in June 1987 and authorised by the Committee of Ministers in September 1987.

3.   The PC-R-SC's terms of reference were to examine the applicability of the European penal law conventions to the search, seizure and confiscation of the proceeds from crime — and consider this question, in the light of the ongoing work of the Pompidou Group and the United Nations, in particular as regards the financial assets of drug traffickers. The PC-R-SC should prepare, if need be, an appropriate European legal instrument in this field.

It should already be noted here that it follows from the terms of reference that the work of the PC-R-SC did not only concern proceeds from drug-trafficking.

4. The PC-R-SC was initially composed of experts from sixteen Council of Europe member states (Belgium, Denmark, Finland, France, the Federal Republic of Germany, Greece, Italy, Liechtenstein, Luxembourg, the Netherlands, Portugal, Spain, Sweden, Switzerland, Turkey and the United Kingdom). Austria, Ireland and the European Community joined the committee at a later stage in its work. Australia, Canada and the United States of America as well as Interpol, the United Nations, the International Association of Penal Law, the International Penal and Penitentiary Foundation and the International Society of Social Defence were represented by observers. Mr G. Polimeni (Italy) was elected Chairman of the Select Committee. The secretariat was provided by the Directorate of Legal Affairs of the Council of Europe.

5. At the extraordinary Conference of the Pompidou Group in London in May 1989, the ministers urged the Council of Europe to expedite the work of the committee. Following that meeting, steps were taken to considerably speed up the work on the convention.

The draft convention was prepared at nine meetings of the Select Committee between October 1987 and April 1990. (The last meeting was enlarged to enable experts from all member states to participate.)

6. The draft convention was finalised by the CDPC at its 39th Plenary Session in June 1990 and forwarded to the Committee of Ministers.

7. At the 443rd meeting of their Deputies in September 1990, the Committee of Ministers approved the text of the convention and decided to open it for signature on 8 November 1990.

General considerations

8. One of the purposes of the Convention is to facilitate international co-operation as regards investigative assistance, search, seizure and confiscation of the proceeds from all types of criminality, especially serious crimes, and in particular drug offences, arms dealing, terrorist offences, trafficking in children and young women (see Resolution No. 3 of the 16th Conference of the European Ministers of Justice, 1988) and other offences which generate large profits.

The committee noted, when studying answers to a questionnaire which was distributed to the experts at the beginning of its deliberations, that not all states possessed domestic laws which would enable them to combat serious criminality efficiently. Investigations, searches, seizures and other measures were often carried out on the basis of codes of criminal procedure which were drafted a number of years ago. In respect of confiscation, the member states' legislation differed widely, in respect of both substantive and procedural rules.

As a result of these differences, it was felt that international co-operation which traditionally depends on shared concepts and principles of law might be seriously impaired. The Convention should therefore devise ways and means to overcome such differences, which may necessitate a need for substantial amendments to the domestic legislation of states that wish to become bound by it.

9.   Another main purpose of the new Convention is to complement already existing instruments, drawn up within the framework of the Council of Europe. The committee noted in respect of the European Convention on Mutual Assistance in Criminal Matters that Article 3, paragraph 1, of that convention, which concerns the execution of letters rogatory "relating to a criminal matter ... for the purpose of procuring evidence or transmitting articles to be produced in evidence", does not apply to search and seizure of property with a view to its subsequent confiscation. The wording of Article 1, paragraph 1, of that convention would however not exclude for example investigative assistance which could be considered "judicial" between judicial authorities in the field of simply tracing the whereabouts of criminally acquired assets. Co-operation between police authorities for the same purpose would normally not be covered by the terms of that convention.

The European Convention on the International Validity of Criminal Judgments provides for the possibility of enforcing a "sanction", including measures to confiscate objects. The sanctions must be applied to individuals in respect of an offence and expressly ordered in the criminal judgment. Provisional seizure is provided for, but only following a request for the enforcement of a confiscation order which has already been made in the requesting state, and not prior to that moment. The Validity Convention has so far been ratified by a limited number of states.

The European Convention on the Transfer of Proceedings in Criminal Matters provides that a state which has received a request for proceedings has jurisdiction to apply such provisional measures as could be applied under its own law if the offence in respect of which proceedings are requested had been committed in the territory of the requested state (Article 28). This convention has also so far been ratified by only a limited number of states.

10. In order to overcome these and other difficulties related to the European penal law conventions, the Convention seeks to provide a complete set of rules, covering all the stages of the procedure from the first investigations to the imposition and enforcement of confiscation sentences and to allow for flexible but effective mechanisms of international co-operation to the widest extent possible in order to deprive criminals of the instruments and fruits of their illegal activities. Section 1 of Chapter III provides for this general principle of international co-operation.

This goal is attained in the Convention through the adoption of several types of measures. It is important that states give each other assistance in order to secure evidence about instrumentalities and proceeds. States are also called upon to co-operate, even without a request, when they learn about events in relation to criminal activity which might be of interest to another state. This and other kinds of investigative assistance are provided for in Section 2 of Chapter III of the Convention.

Where the law enforcement agencies and judicial authorities have gathered information through investigations, there should also be efficient means available to ensure that the offender does not remove the instruments and proceeds of his criminal activities. "Freezing" of bank accounts, seizure of property or other measures of conservancy need to be taken to ensure this. Section 3 of Chapter III provides for international co-operation in respect of provisional measures.

In order to secure the confiscation of the instruments and proceeds from crime, the Convention provides in Section 4 of Chapter III principally two forms of international co-operation, namely the execution by the requested state of a confiscation order made abroad and, secondly, the institution, under its own law, of national proceedings leading to a confiscation by the requested state at the request of another state. In respect of the first alternative, the Convention follows the pattern of the European Convention on the International Validity of Criminal

Judgments. The second method of international co-operation could be compared to the one which is provided for in the European Convention on the Transfer of Proceedings in Criminal Matters.

11.   International co-operation need not only be effective, it must also be flexible. The Convention provides therefore, in Section 5 of Chapter III, for the possibility of refusal and postponement of co-operation. Flexibility is also shown in the distinction between the grounds for refusal, only some of which are valid for all kinds of international co-operation. Moreover, the grounds for refusal are all optional at the international level. Only a limited number of the grounds will be mandatory at national level. The Convention provides also that the Parties shall, before refusing or postponing co-operation, consult each other and consider whether the request may be granted partially or subject to conditions.

12.   In order to protect the legitimate interests of third parties, the Convention provides in Section 6 of Chapter III for certain notification requirements and for situations where it may not be possible to recognise decisions concerning third parties. Moreover, the Convention imposes an obligation on each Party to provide in its domestic legislation for effective legal remedies available to third parties to have their rights (which may be affected by provisional or confiscation measures) preserved.

13.   Another of the main purposes of the Convention is to provide an instrument obliging states to adopt efficient measures in their national laws to combat serious crime and to deprive criminals of the fruits of their illicit activities. The committee noted, when studying answers to the previously mentioned questionnaire, that the national law of the member states differs widely and sometimes does not contain the necessary powers for law enforcement agencies to achieve these goals at domestic level. This situation is sometimes exploited by criminals to avoid detection and punishment.

The need for efficient national legal remedies was basically considered by the committee from the point of view of international co-operation. Differences in legislation may in fact impede the successful fight against serious criminality which is tending to become better organised, more international and increasingly dangerous to society. The Select Committee considered that it was necessary for member states to make their respective legislations come nearer to each other and to adopt efficient measures to investigate offences, to take provisional measures and to confiscate the instruments and fruits of illegal activity. This is imperative because, in order to be able to co-operate at international level, states should possess at least a comparable level of efficiency. This does not mean that the states' legislation need necessarily be harmonised but that they should at least find ways and means to enable them to co-operate more effectively.

14. The United Nations Convention against Illicit Traffic in Narcotic Drugs and Psychotropic Substances (hereinafter referred to as the United Nations Convention), concluded in Vienna in December 1988, played an important role in the deliberations of the experts. The relevant provisions of the United Nations Convention were constantly taken into consideration: on the one hand, the experts tried as far as possible to use the terminology and the systematic approach of that convention unless changes were felt necessary for improving different solutions; on the other hand, the experts also explored the possibilities of introducing in the Council of Europe instrument stricter obligations than those of the United Nations Convention on the understanding that the new Convention — in spite of the fact that it is open to other states than the member states of the Council of Europe — will operate in the context of a smaller community of like-minded states. For instance, in the field of international co-operation for the purposes of confiscation, the combination of the obligation to confiscate provided for in Article 13 and the grounds for refusal in Article 18 represents a more binding system than that created by Article 5 of the United Nations Convention. Moreover, the Convention addresses many questions and issues about which the United Nations Convention is either completely silent or which it has left to be resolved or worked out in further bilateral or multilateral arrangements between Parties.

15. The experts were able to identify considerable differences with regard to the basic systems of confiscation at national level in the member states of the Council of Europe. All states have a system of so-called property confiscation, that is, the confiscation of specific property, with respect to the instrumentalities used in the commission of offences, including items or substances whose uncontrolled possession is in itself illegal. Some states also know property confiscation for the proceeds, directly or indirectly derived from offences, or their substitutes. As a result of property confiscation, the ownership rights in the specific property concerned are transferred to the state.

With regard to the proceeds from offences, another system of confiscation is widely used in some of the member states of the Council of Europe: so-called value confiscation, which consists of the requirement to pay a sum of money based on an assessment of the value of the proceeds directly or indirectly derived from offences, or their substitutes. As a result of a value confiscation, the state can exert a financial claim against the person against whom the order is made, which, if not paid, may be realised in any property (no matter whether legally or illegally acquired) belonging to that person. The order is thus executed in a similar way to fines or court orders in civil cases.

Some states have, as far as the confiscation of proceeds is concerned, the two systems (both property and value confiscation) available under their domestic law.

The experts were also able to identify considerable differences in respect of the procedural organisation of the taking of decisions to confiscate (decisions taken by criminal courts, administrative courts, separate judicial authorities, in civil or criminal proceedings totally separate from those in which the guilt of the offender is determined (these proceedings are referred to in the text of the Convention as "proceedings for the purpose of confiscation" and in the explanatory report sometimes as "*in rem* proceedings"), etc.). It was also possible to distinguish differences in respect of the procedural framework of such decisions (presumptions of licitly/illicitly acquired property, time-limits, etc.).

The experts agreed that it would be impossible to devise an efficient instrument of international co-operation without taking into account these basic differences in national legislation. On the other hand, effective co-operation must recognise that the systems may not be alike but that they aim to achieve the same goals. This is why the committee agreed to put the two systems (value and property confiscation) of confiscation on an equal footing and to make the text unambiguous on this point.

16. The Select Committee also stressed that the successful fight against serious criminality required the introduction of a laundering offence in states which had not already introduced such an offence. The United Nations Convention requires the Parties to that convention to adopt such measures as may be necessary to establish laundering in respect of drug offences as criminal offences under domestic law. The Select Committee

considered it possible to go further in the framework of mainly European co-operation, but recognised that full harmonisation of national laws would not be feasible. It therefore, on the one hand, subjected the implementation of some of the provisions to the constitutional and other basic principles of the legal system of the Parties and, on the other hand, allowed Parties to limit the range of predicate offences by making a reservation to this effect.

17. International co-operation as regards the proceeds of crime requires that efficient instruments be put at the disposal of law enforcement agencies. Since property (aircraft, vessels, money, etc.) might be moved from one country to another in a matter of days, hours and sometimes minutes, it is necessary that rapid measures may be taken in order to "freeze" a current situation to enable the authorities to take the necessary steps.

18. Unlike most other conventions on international co-operation in criminal matters prepared within the framework of the Council of Europe, the present Convention does not carry the word "European" in its title. This reflects the drafters' opinion that the instrument should from the outset be open also to like-minded states outside the framework of the Council of Europe. Three such states — Australia, Canada and the United States of America — were, in fact, represented on the Select Committee by observers and actively associated with the drafting of the text.

Commentary on the articles of the Convention

CHAPTER I

Use of terms

Article 1 — Use of terms

19. Article 1 defines certain terms which form the basis of the mechanism of international co-operation provided for in the Convention and the scope of application of Chapter II. Following practice from other conventions elaborated within the framework of the Council of Europe, the number of terms requiring a definition has been limited to what is absolutely necessary for the correct application of the Convention. Several of the definitions are drafted in a broad manner in order to ensure that particular features of national legislation are not excluded from the application of the Convention.

20. It was the opinion of the experts that the terminology used in the Convention did not, as a rule, refer to a specific legal system or a particular law. Rather they intended to create an autonomous terminology which, in the light of the national laws involved, should be so interpreted as to ensure the most efficient and faithful application of the Convention. If, as an example, a foreign confiscation order referred to a "forfeiture" instead of a "confiscation", this should not prevent the authorities of the requested state from applying the Convention. Likewise, if the "freezing" of a bank account has been requested, the requested state should not refuse to co-operate merely on the ground that the national law only provided for "seizure" in the case under question. The Select Committee recognised that national procedural laws could sometimes differ widely but the end result would often be the same despite formal differences. In addition, the Select Committee thought it wise that all definitions should, as far as possible, be in harmony with the aforementioned United Nations Convention. This was justified since a number of cases that were to be dealt with under the Convention would concern drug offences.

21. The definition of "proceeds" was intended to be as broad as possible since the experts agreed that it was important to deprive the offender of any economic advantage from his criminal activity. By adopting a broad definition, this ultimate goal would be made possible. Also, the experts felt that by adopting this approach they could avoid a discussion as to whether, for example, substitutes or indirectly derived proceeds would in principle be subject to international co-operation. If a Party could not, in a particular case, accept international co-operation because of the remote relationship between the confiscated property and the offence, that Party could instead invoke Article 18, paragraph 4.*b*, which provides for the possibility of refusing co-operation in such a case.

The committee discussed whether the words "economic advantage" implied that the cost of making the profit (for instance the purchase price of narcotic drugs) should be deducted from the gross profit. It discovered that national legislation varied considerably on this point; there were even differences within the same legal system depending on the categories of offences. The experts also considered that differences in national legislation or legal practice in this respect between Parties should not be invoked as an obstacle to international co-operation. As regards drug offences, the experts agreed that the value of drugs initially purchased would always be subsumed within the definition of proceeds.

The committee deliberately chose to speak of "criminal offences" to make it clear that the scope of application of the Convention is limited to criminal activity. It was therefore not necessary to define the term "offence".

The wording of the definition of "proceeds" does not rule out the inclusion of property and assets that may have been transferred to third parties.

In the broad definition of property, the experts deleted the initially proposed terms "tangible or intangible" since it was found that those terms could be subsumed under the definition. The experts also considered adding the term "assets" but decided against it for the same reasons.

In respect of "instrumentalities", the experts discussed whether instrumentalities that were used to facilitate the commission of an offence or intended to be used to commit an offence were covered by the definition. In respect of instrumentalities that were used in the preparatory acts leading to the commission of an offence or to hinder the detection of an offence, the experts agreed that such questions should be resolved according to the national law of the requested Party while taking account of the differences in national law and the need for efficient international co-operation. The term "instrumentalities" should, for the purposes of international co-operation, be interpreted as broadly as possible. Property which facilitates the commission of the offence, for instance, could in some cases be included in the definition.

22. The experts discussed whether it was necessary to include "objects of offences" under the scope of application of the Convention but decided against it. The terms "proceeds" and "instrumentalities" are sufficiently broadly defined to include objects of offences whenever necessary. The broad definition of "proceeds" could include in the scope of application, for instance, stolen property such as works of art or trading in endangered species.

23. The committee discussed whether it was necessary to define "confiscation" or "confiscation order" under the Convention. Such a definition exists in the United Nations Convention where "confiscation", which includes forfeiture where applicable, means the permanent deprivation of property by order of a court or other competent authority. The European Convention on the International Validity of Criminal Judgments defines a "European criminal judgment" as any final decision delivered by a criminal court of a contracting state as a result of criminal proceedings and a "sanction" as any punishment or other measure expressly imposed on a person, in respect of an offence, in a European criminal judgment or in an *ordonnance pénale*.

The definition of "confiscation" was drafted in order to make it clear that, on the one hand, the Convention only deals with criminal activities or acts connected therewith, such as acts related to civil *in rem* actions and, on the other hand, that differences in the organisation of the judicial systems and the rules of procedure do not exclude the application of the Convention. For instance, the fact that confiscation in some states is not considered as a penal sanction but as a security or other measure is irrelevant to the extent that the confiscation is related to criminal activity. It is also irrelevant that confiscation might sometimes be ordered by a judge who is, strictly speaking, not a criminal judge, as long as the decision was taken by a judge. The term "court" has the same meaning as in Article 6 of the European Convention on Human Rights. The experts agreed that purely administrative confiscation was not included in the scope of application of the Convention.

The use of the word "confiscation" includes also, where applicable, "forfeiture".

"Predicate offence" refers to the offence which is at the origin of a laundering offence, that is, the offence which generated the proceeds. The expression is found in Article 6, paragraphs 1, 2 and 4.

CHAPTER II

Measures at national level

24. The reasons for and the aim of this chapter are described above under "General considerations". The wording of the articles in the chapter makes it clear that if states already possess the necessary measures, it is not necessary to take further legislative steps.

Article 2 — Confiscation measures

25. Paragraph 1 was drafted because several states do not yet possess sufficiently broad and effective legal provisions in respect of confiscation. It seeks to create an effective scheme for confiscation. It should be seen as a positive obligation for states to enact legislation which would enable them to confiscate instrumentalities and proceeds. This would also enable states to co-operate in accordance with the terms of the Convention, see Article 7, paragraph 2.

26. The expression "property the value of which corresponds to such proceeds" refers to the obligation to introduce measures which enable Parties to execute value confiscation orders by satisfying the claims on any property, including such property which is legally acquired. Value confiscation is, of course, still based on an assessment of the value of illegally acquired proceeds. The expression is also found in the United Nations Convention.

27. The committee discussed whether it was possible to define certain offences to which the Convention should always be applicable. The experts agreed that Parties should not limit themselves to offences as defined by the United Nations Convention. The offences would include drug trafficking, terrorist offences, organised crime, violent crimes, offences involving the sexual exploitation of children and young persons, extortion, kidnapping, environmental offences, economic fraud, insider trading and other serious offences. Offences which generate huge profits could also be included in such a list. The experts thought however that the scope of application of the Convention should in principle be made as wide as possible. For that purpose, the committee created an obligation to introduce measures of confiscation in relation to all kinds of offences. At the same time, they felt that this approach required a possibility for states to restrict co-operation under the Convention to certain offences or categories of offences. The possibility of entering a reservation was therefore introduced. The mere fact that a Party may enter a reservation as regards a specific offence does not necessarily mean that it must refuse a request made by a Party which has not made a similar reservation. Article 18 of the Convention states only optional grounds for refusal.

Without the possibility of entering a reservation, states would be obliged to adopt measures which would enable them to confiscate the proceeds of all kinds of offences. Even if this were regarded as desirable, for the criminal should never gain from his criminal activities, the experts considered it premature to require this. It could in fact be counter-productive to the aim of the Convention to require such a condition, since this would prevent several states from ratifying the Convention as quickly as possible in order to enact the necessary domestic legislation. The experts agreed, however, that such states should review their legislation periodically and expand the applicability of confiscation measures, in order to be able to restrict the reservations subsequently as much as possible. They also agreed that such measures should at least be made applicable to serious criminality and to offences which generate huge profits.

Article 3 — Investigative and provisional measures

28. This article was drafted with the same object in mind as the previous one. It concerns the categories of measures indicated in Articles 8 and 11,

in so far as they do not relate to the special investigative techniques referred to in Article 4, paragraph 2. As in the case of Article 2, the present paragraph should be seen as an obligation for ratifying states to take legislative action. This would also enable them to co-operate in accordance with the terms of the Convention (see Article 7, paragraph 2).

This article does not allow for declarations. Thus, while a Party may declare what offences or categories of offences it wishes to include within the obligation in Article 2, it must none the less enact possibilities of taking investigative and provisional measures concerning all offences or categories of offences. In so far as the relation between this article and Chapter III is concerned, a Party should not have the possibility of refusing measures under Section 2 or 3 simply because it has made a declaration under Article 2, paragraph 2, in respect of a certain offence. The faculty of using Article 18, paragraph 1.*f*, will of course still remain open. Article 7 requires Parties to adopt measures to enable them to comply with requests for investigative assistance and the taking of provisional measures, under the conditions provided for in Chapter III.

Article 4 — Special investigative powers and techniques

29. Article 4, paragraph 1, was drafted with the same object in mind as Articles 2 and 3. In general, bank secrecy does not constitute an obstacle to domestic criminal investigations or the taking of provisional measures in the member states of the Council of Europe, in particular when the lifting of bank secrecy is ordered by a judge, a grand jury, an investigating judge or a prosecutor. The second sentence of the paragraph is also found in the United Nations Convention. The sentence should, for the purposes of international co-operation, be read in conjunction with Article 18, paragraph 7.

30. Paragraph 2 of the article was drafted to make states aware of new investigative techniques which are common practice in some states but which are not yet implemented in other states. The paragraph imposes an obligation on states at least to consider the introduction of new techniques which in some states, while safeguarding fundamental human rights, have proved successful in combating serious crime. Such techniques could then also be used for the purposes of international co-operation. In such cases, Chapter III, Section 2, would apply. The enumeration of the techniques is not exhaustive.

Monitoring orders means, in the sense used by the committee, judicial orders to a financial institution to give information about transactions conducted through an account held by a particular person with the institution. Such an order is usually valid for a specific period.

Observation is an investigative technique, employed by the law enforcement agencies, consisting in covertly watching the movements of persons, without hearing them.

Interception of telecommunications includes interception of telephone conversations, telex and telefax communications. Recommendation No. R (85) 10 concerning the practical application of the European Convention on Mutual Assistance in Criminal Matters in respect of letters rogatory for the interception of telecommunications deals with this question.

Access to computer systems is discussed in the report on computer-related crime, elaborated by a committee of experts under the CDPC (see Recommendation No. R (89) 9 on computer-related crime). Such access creates special difficulties both at national and international level because of the possibilities of transfrontier transmission of data.

Production orders instruct individuals to produce specific records, documents or other items of property in their possession. Failure to comply with such an order may result in an order for search and seizure. The order might require that records or documents be produced in a specific form, as when the order concerns computer-generated material (see also the report on computer-related crime).

Article 5 — Legal remedies

31. Interested parties are basically all persons who claim that their rights with respect to property subject to provisional measures and confiscation are unjustifiably affected. These claims should in principle be honoured in cases where the innocence or *bona fides* of the party concerned is likely or beyond reasonable doubt. As long as no final confiscation order has been made against him, the accused may also qualify as an interested party. The legal provisions required by this article should guarantee "effective" legal remedies for interested third parties. This implies that there should be a system where such parties, if known, are duly informed by the authorities of the possibilities to challenge decisions or

measures taken, that such challenges may be made even if a confiscation order has already become enforceable, if the party had no earlier opportunity to do so, that such remedies should allow for a hearing in court, that the interested party has the right to be assisted or represented by a lawyer and to present witnesses and other evidence, and that the party has a right to have the court decision reviewed.

This article does not bestow upon private citizens any right beyond those normally permitted by the domestic law of the Party. In any case, minimum rights of the defence are safeguarded by the Convention for the Protection of Human Rights and Fundamental Freedoms.

Article 6 — Laundering offences

32. The first paragraph of the article is based on the United Nations Convention. However, the wording differs slightly from that convention in respect of the element of "participation" which is found in the United Nations Convention, and also as regards the predicate offences to which the proceeds relate. Participation has not been included in paragraph 1, sub-paragraphs *a*, *b* and *c*, of the article since, because of the different approach taken by the committee, it appeared to be redundant. The present Convention is not limited to proceeds from drug offences. The experts considered that it was not necessary to provide that states could not limit the scope of application *vis-à-vis* the United Nations Convention, which had become a universally recognised instrument in the fight against drugs.

The first part of paragraph 1 establishes an obligation to criminalise laundering. The second part makes this obligation in respect of certain categories of laundering offences dependent on the constitutional principles and the basic concepts of the legal system of the ratifying state. To the extent that criminalisation of the act is not contrary to such principles or concepts, the state is under an obligation to criminalise the acts which are described in the paragraph. A further explanation of what is meant by basic concepts of the legal system is found in the explanatory report in respect of Article 18, paragraph 1.*a*.

Paragraphs 2 and 3, with the exception of paragraph 2.*c*, are not found in the United Nations Convention. The experts thought it useful to make it clear that the present Convention is intended to cover extra-territorial predicate offences. Paragraph 2.*b* takes into account that in some states the person who committed the predicate offence will not, according to basic principles of domestic penal law, commit a further offence when laundering the proceeds. On the other hand, in other states laws to such effect have already been enacted.

Paragraph 3 criminalises acts other than those designated in the United Nations Convention. It is, however, not mandatory for Parties to enact any or all of the offences described in the paragraph. Paragraph 3.*a* suggests the criminalisation of negligent behaviour whereas the following sub-paragraph concerns a person who lawfully trades with a criminal, knowing that the payment is proceeds from crime but who does not see this fact as an obstacle to a business relationship. The case mentioned in paragraph 3.*c* concerns a person who promotes criminal activity.

33. The question has been raised, in relation to the United Nations Convention, whether it would be illegal for a lawyer's fees to be paid out of funds related to a laundering offence. Some lawyers have even suggested that the United Nations Convention would, by its wording, make it criminal to hire a lawyer or to accept a fee. In the view of the experts, the wording of the present Convention cannot be misinterpreted to that effect.

34. In respect of paragraph 4 of the present article, reference is made to the commentary on Article 2, paragraph 2. The offences or categories of offences referred to therein are however not necessarily the same as the ones referred to in the present article.

CHAPTER III

INTERNATIONAL CO-OPERATION

Section 1

Principles of international co-operation

Article 7 — General principles and measures for international co-operation

35. Paragraph 1 of this introductory article was drafted to indicate the scope and the aims of the international co-operation which is detailed in the following sections. Those sections should, in principle, exclusively define the scope of international co-operation, but Section 1 will affect the interpretation of the other sections. Where co-operation concerns

investigations or proceedings which aim at confiscation, Parties should co-operate with each other to the widest extent possible.

Paragraph 2 of this provision should also be considered in connection with the obligation provided for under Article 13. If a state has only the system of value confiscation of proceeds, it would be necessary for it to take legislative measures which would enable it to grant a request from a state which applies property confiscation. The converse would be true, since the two systems are equal under the Convention.

So-called "fishing expeditions" (general and not determined investigations which are carried out sometimes even without the existence of a suspicion that an offence has been committed) lie outside the scope of application of the Convention. If the requesting Party has no indication of where the property might be found, the requested Party is not obliged to search, for instance, all banks in a country (see Article 27, paragraph 1, sub-paragraph e.ii).

Section 2

Investigative assistance

Article 8 — Obligation to assist

36. This article should be interpreted in a broad manner since the committee refers to the "widest possible measure of assistance". Such assistance could relate to criminal proceedings, but it could also be proceedings for the purpose of confiscation which are related to a criminal activity.

The latter part of the paragraph should only be seen as giving examples of assistance and does not limit its application. For example, if monitoring or telephone tapping orders may be made under the law of the requested Party, they should also be granted in international co-operation.

The paragraph relates to "identification and tracing" of property. In that respect, the wording should also be interpreted broadly so that, for instance, notifications relating to investigations as well as evaluation of property are included in the scope of application. To the extent that the scope of application of the present Convention and the European

Convention on Mutual Assistance in Criminal Matters converge, Parties should, if no reasons to the contrary exist, endeavour to use the latter convention.

The words "other property liable to confiscation" have been added to make it clear that investigative assistance should also be rendered when the requesting Party applies value confiscation and the assistance relates to property which might be of licit origin.

The assistance also includes seizure for evidentiary purposes.

The wording of the Convention does not exclude the possibility of the investigative assistance referred to in this paragraph also being rendered to authorities other than judicial ones, such as police or customs authorities, in so far as such assistance does not involve coercive action (see Article 24, paragraph 5).

Article 9 — Execution of assistance

37. Paragraph 1 of this article describes the general principle that the carrying out of investigative measures is governed by the law of the requested Party. However, the requesting Party may in its request ask that special procedures be used in relation to the measure. Such procedures could for example consist of special notifications to third parties, preserving the chain of custody of seized items of evidence or the allowing of a policeman, prosecutor or judge of the requesting Party to be present during an investigation. The question of compatibility will necessarily be determined in the requested Party in accordance with its own legal system.

The words "as permitted by" indicate that the decision concerning the assistance should also be taken according to the law of the requested Party. That law must, under Article 7, provide for the possibility of taking the investigative measures so that the requested Party can comply with its obligations under the Convention. The aforementioned words also make reference to the use of discretionary powers that some authorities might have.

The words "in accordance with" also define the procedural rules governing requests for assistance.

In carrying out requests under this article, the requested Party should endeavour not to prejudice investigations or proceedings in the requesting Party.

Article 10 — Spontaneous information

38. This article introduces a novelty in the field of legal assistance in criminal matters: a possibility for states to forward without prior request information about investigations or proceedings or which might become relevant in relation to co-operation under the Convention. Such information must of course not be transmitted if it might harm or endanger investigations or proceedings in the sending Party. As regards confidentiality, see Article 33, paragraph 3.

Section 3

Provisional measures

Article 11 — Obligation to take provisional measures

39. Paragraph 1 of the article concerns cases where a confiscation order has not yet been rendered by the requesting Party but where proceedings have been instituted. The experts agreed that, in respect of this paragraph, an obligation to take the provisional measures exists, subject of course to the provisions on grounds for refusal and postponement. Freezing and seizing are only examples of provisional measures. They do not refer to any specific legal instrument as defined by national law. The words "to prevent any dealing in, transfer or disposal..." are the same as those used in the United Nations draft model treaty on mutual assistance in criminal matters. They indicate the aim of the provisional measures. The wording "which, at a later stage, may be the subject of a request... or which might be such as to satisfy the request" makes it clear that both systems of confiscation are subject to the provision. Any property, including legally acquired property, in cases of value confiscation is envisaged. Of course, such property should be made subject to provisional measures only in cases where this is explicitly requested by the requesting Party.

40. Paragraph 2 deals with the case where a Party has already received a request for confiscation pursuant to Article 13. The requested Party shall then, when requested, take the necessary provisional measures so

that the request for confiscation can be executed. The requesting Party should indicate necessary provisional measures in accordance with Article 27, paragraph 3, sub-paragraph a.iv. Since the words "pursuant to Article 13" are used, it follows that both systems of international co-operation apply.

The "measures" under paragraph 2 of the article are the same as those mentioned in the previous paragraph. As to the term "property", the same considerations apply as to paragraph 1 of the article.

Article 12 — Execution of provisional measures

41. Paragraph 1 of·this article describes the general principle which is found in most instruments of international legal co-operation, that the carrying out of provisional measures is governed by the law of the requested Party.

The words "as permitted by... the domestic law" indicates that decisions should also be taken according to the law of the requested Party. That law must, under Article 7, provide for the possibilities of taking provisional measures so that the requested state can comply with its obligations under the Convention. The Convention does not, however, oblige Parties, in all cases where confiscation is possible, to provide at the same time for the right to apply provisional measures. Parties may, if they deem this appropriate, restrict the applicability of provisional measures to certain conditions, such as the seriousness of the offence or the value of the property to be seized (see Article 18, paragraph 1.c). Therefore, a Party may be in a position where it can comply with a request for confiscation, but not with a request for provisional measures prior to the requested confiscation. This situation is also reflected in Article 18, paragraph 2.

The requesting Party might in its request ask that special procedures be taken in relation to the measure. Such requests should be granted to the extent that they are not incompatible with the law of the requested Party. The question of compatibility will necessarily be determined in the requested Party in accordance with its own legal system.

42. The national law of the requested Party governs when the provisional measures may or must be lifted. Paragraph 2 of the article institutes an obligation for the requested Party to give the requesting

Party an opportunity to present its reasons in favour of continuing the provisional measure. This could be done either directly to the court, for example, as an intervention *amicus curiae*, if permitted by national law, or as a notification through official channels. Unless the requesting Party has had the opportunity of presenting its views, the provisional measure may not be lifted if special reasons do not exist. Such reasons may be that the property concerned has been the subject of a bankruptcy, in which case the property comes into the custody of the receiver, or that the measure must automatically be lifted because an event has or has not occurred. In the latter case, the requesting state will know in advance that the measure might be lifted since the requested state is obliged to inform it of the provisions of the national law. Reference is made to Article 31, paragraph 1.*e*, which obliges the requested Party to inform the requesting Party about such provisions of its domestic law as would automatically lead to the lifting of the provisional measure. Such laws could for instance require that a provisional measure be lifted if a prosecutor has not applied for a renewal of the measure within a specified time-limit.

Section 4

Confiscation

Article 13 — Obligation to confiscate

43. Article 13, paragraph 1, describes the two forms of international co-operation regarding confiscation. Paragraph 1.*a* concerns the enforcement of an order made by a judicial authority in the requesting state; paragraph 1.*b* creates an obligation for a state to institute confiscation proceedings in accordance with the domestic law of the requested Party, if requested to do so, and to execute an order pursuant to such proceedings. This dual scheme of international co-operation follows the United Nations Convention, Article 5, paragraph 4.

From the wording of the article, it follows that the request must concern instrumentalities or proceeds from offences. In respect of value confiscation, see the commentary on Article 13, paragraph 3.

It also follows from the article that the request concerns a confiscation which by its very nature is criminal and thus excludes a request which is not connected with an offence, for example administrative confiscation. However, the decision of a court to confiscate need not be taken by a court of criminal jurisdiction following criminal proceedings.

Any type of proceedings, independently of their relationship with criminal proceedings and of applicable procedural rules, might qualify in so far as they may result in a confiscation order, provided that they are carried out by judicial authorities and that they are criminal in nature, that is, that they concern instrumentalities or proceeds. Such types of proceedings (which include, for instance, the so called "*in rem* proceedings") are, as indicated under "General considerations" above, referred to in the text of the Convention as "proceedings for the purpose of confiscation".

44. Paragraph 1.*a* speaks of "courts" whereas paragraph 1.*b* refers to "competent authorities". This means that a limit is set to the scope of application of the Convention. The term "competent authorities" in paragraph 1.*b* may include authorities responsible for prosecution, who in their turn are to bring the case before their judicial authorities (courts). It has not been considered necessary to restrict the Convention with respect to the procedure under Article 13, paragraph 1.*b*, since such confiscation entirely follows national law.

The obligation to co-operate for the purpose of confiscation under Article 13, paragraph 1, is fulfilled when the requested Party acts in accordance with at least one of the two methods of co-operation specified in the paragraph. The requested Party has the possibility, in general or in relation to a specific case, of excluding the use of one of the two methods. However, the simultaneous use of both methods is admissible. Nothing in the Convention prevents Parties from providing for the possibility of applying both systems under their law. Exceptional cases may occur when a state requests co-operation under paragraph 1.*a* in respect of a certain type of property and under paragraph 1.*b* for some other property, irrespective of the fact that the underlying offence might be the same. This may be the case where property has been substituted, where third party interests are involved or where the request concerns indirectly derived proceeds or intermingled property (licitly acquired property intermingled with illicitly acquired property). Moreover, the competent authorities of the requested Party should in such a case ensure that the scope of a confiscation order to be obtained does not go beyond the objectives specified in the request of the requesting Party.

If a state requests co-operation under paragraph 1.*a*, nothing prevents the requested state from granting co-operation under paragraph 1.*b* instead, since the choice of the form of co-operation rests with the requested Party. In such cases, the foreign order of confiscation might serve as proof or presumption, depending on the legal practices under the domestic law of the requested Party. Article 14, paragraph 2, is however still valid in such cases.

45. The way paragraph 1.*b* is drafted implies an obligation for the requested state always to submit the request to its competent authorities for the purpose of obtaining an order of confiscation. The question arises as to whether the government of the requested state has to submit the request in a case where it intends to invoke one of the grounds for refusal under Article 18. This is not, however, the intention of the experts. An obligation to submit the request to the competent authorities should only exist if the competent authority of the requested Party, after a summary test, considers that there are no immediate obstacles to granting the request. This does not prevent the competent authority, if it subsequently finds obstacles, from deciding not to pursue the matter, provided of course that the conditions of the Convention are met.

46. Paragraph 2 is modelled on Article 2 of the European Convention on the Transfer of Proceedings in Criminal Matters. If the requested state already has competence under its own law to institute confiscation proceedings, the provisions of the paragraph are superfluous. If, however, no such jurisdiction exists, the necessary competence follows, on the basis of this paragraph, directly from the request of the requesting Party made under paragraph 1. Such jurisdiction need not have been expressly established by the domestic law of the requested Party. It goes without saying that this paragraph can only be applicable to the procedure envisaged in paragraph 1.*b*.

It follows necessarily that the requested Party has competence to render investigative assistance and to take provisional measures also in cases where it may be foreseen that assistance under Article 13 will be rendered in accordance with paragraph 1.*b*. Articles 8 and 11 contain an obligation to take measures without making a distinction between the two systems of international co-operation.

47. The application of the procedure under paragraph 1.*b* presupposes that the requested state, at least for international cases, is equipped to

undertake proceedings for the purposes of confiscation (independently of the trial of the offender).

48. The committee drafted paragraph 3 of the article in order to make it clear that value confiscation, consisting of a requirement to pay a sum of money to the state corresponding to the value of the proceeds, is covered by the Convention. The requested Party, acting under paragraph 1, sub-paragraph *a* or *b*, will ask for payment of the sum due and, if payment is not obtained, then realise the claim on any property available. The wording "any property available" shows that the claim might be realised on either legally or illegally acquired property. It also indicates that property which is in the possession of third parties, such as ostensible persons or in cases where a so-called *Actio Pauliana* might be invoked under national law, is affected. The expression "if payment is not obtained" also includes part-payments.

According to this paragraph, Parties must, for purposes of international co-operation in the confiscation of proceeds, be able to apply both the system of property confiscation and the system of value confiscation. This is made clear by Article 7, paragraph 2.*a*. It may imply that Parties which have only a system of property confiscation in domestic cases have to introduce legislation providing for a system of value confiscation of proceeds, including the taking of provisional measures on any realisable property, in order to be able to comply with requests to that effect from value confiscation countries. On the other hand, Parties which have only a system of value confiscation of proceeds in domestic cases must introduce legislation providing for a system of property confiscation of proceeds in order to be able to comply with requests to that effect from property confiscation countries.

49. Paragraph 4 plays only a subsidiary role in that, failing agreement, paragraph 1 of the article applies. If a request for confiscation of a specific property has been made, a country which applies value confiscation must also enforce the decision on that particular property.

Article 14 — Execution of confiscation

50. Article 14, paragraph 1, states the fundamental rule that, once the authorities of a state have accepted a request for enforcement or a request under Article 13, paragraph 1.*b*, everything relating to the request must be done in accordance with that state's law and through

its authorities. This rule of *lex fori* is normally interpreted to the effect that the law of the forum governs matters of procedure, mode of confiscation proceedings, matters relating to evidence and also limitation of actions based on time bars (see, however, Article 18, paragraph 4.*e*). In the case of remedies in respect of cases relating to Article 13, paragraph 1.*a*, a special rule is provided for in Article 14, paragraph 5, which preserves the right to deal with applications for review of confiscation orders, originally issued by the requesting Party, for that Party alone.

As one of the consequences of the interpretation of paragraph 1, the experts agreed that, if the law of the requested Party requires notification of a confiscation order and such notification was not given, the requested Party would not be in a position to execute the order since the execution is governed by the law of the requested Party. In addition, the paragraph covers possible interventions by the requested Party which might lead to the mitigation of confiscation orders which have already been issued.

51. The question of limitation of actions is particularly complicated in respect of confiscation. Some countries may not provide for any rules in this respect, whereas others may have provided for a set of rules relating to the original offence, the service of summons, the enforcement of the confiscation order, etc. In the view of the experts, such limitations, where they exist, should always be interpreted under the law of the requested state in conformity with what is provided under Article 14. If a confiscation order is statute-barred under the law of the requesting state, this would normally mean that it is not enforceable in the requesting Party. Confiscation may then be refused under Article 18. There should therefore be no room for doubt. Under Article 27, paragraph 3.*a*.ii, the competent authority of the requesting Party should certify that the confiscation order is enforceable and not subject to ordinary means of appeal. In addition, the requesting Party is obliged to inform the requested Party of any development by reason of which the confiscation order ceases to be wholly or partially enforceable (see Article 31, paragraph 2.*a*).

52. Paragraph 2 was inspired by Article 42 of the European Convention on the International Validity of Criminal Judgments. Similar wording is found also in Article 11, paragraph 1.*a*, of the Convention on the Transfer of Sentenced Persons. The experts considered this provision to be of crucial importance in the field of co-operation in penal matters, but

provided a possibility of making a reservation in paragraph 3 to assure a sufficient degree of flexibility to the Convention. Such possibility is however limited only to those few states which, for constitutional or similar reasons, would otherwise have had difficulties in ratifying the Convention.

Without prejudice to the principle of review of a confiscation order provided for in Article 14, paragraph 5, the following could be stated in order to clarify the meaning of paragraph 2.

Paragraph 2 is in principle only applicable to a request for enforcement of a confiscation order under Article 13, paragraph 1.*a*. If, for instance, the requested state chooses to initiate its own proceedings under Article 13, paragraph 1.*b*, despite the fact that an enforceable confiscation order by the requesting state exists, the present paragraph applies equally to those proceedings. The purpose of the paragraph is that, if a factual situation has already been tried by the competent authorities of one state, then the competent authorities should not once again try those facts. It should place confidence in the foreign authorities' decision. Regarding the additional protection provided for innocent third parties, see also Article 22.

It is another matter if a party invokes new facts which, since they occurred later, were not tried by the authorities of the requesting Party (*factum superveniens*) or facts that existed but, for a valid reason (for example they were not known), were not brought before the authorities of the requesting Party. In such cases, the authorities of the requested Party are, of course, free to decide on such facts.

The requested state is bound by the "findings as to the facts". It is not immediately apparent what may constitute facts and what may constitute legal consequences of such facts. An example would be the case where the courts of the requesting state have found a person guilty of illegal trafficking of 100 kg of cocaine. In consequence, property equal to the proceeds of trafficking 100 kg was confiscated. The offender cannot, in such a case, in proceedings before the authorities of the requested state argue that he had only trafficked 10 kg since the authorities of the requested state are bound by the findings of the authorities of the requesting state.

Legal consequence, on the other hand, is not binding upon the requested state. If, for instance, mental deficiency does not constitute a ground for non-confiscation in the requesting state, the requested state might still examine the confiscation order and take into account the mental deficiency. The requested state may even examine whether the facts relating to the mental deficiency, as stated in the decision by the court in the requesting state, amount to mental deficiency under the law of the requested state.

If there is a difference between the legal systems to the effect that a certain fact constitutes a legitimate defence in the requested but not in the requesting state, the requested state would in some circumstances be in a position to refuse enforcement if it finds such a fact to be present. Such refusal would then be based on Article 18, paragraph 1.*f*. Thus, it may be necessary for the court or authority in the requested state to conduct a supplementary investigation into facts not determined by the decision in the requesting state. However, the court of the requested state is not allowed to proceed to the hearing of new evidence in respect of facts contained in the decision of the requesting state, unless such evidence was not produced for valid reasons, for instance because the evidence was not known.

It follows from the above that the court of the requested state cannot make any independent assessment of evidence bearing upon the guilt of the person convicted and contained in the decision of the requesting state.

53. The rate of exchange in paragraph 4 refers to the official middle rate of exchange. Paragraph 5 is inspired by Article 10, paragraph 2, of the Validity Convention. Since the requesting state took the decision to confiscate, it seems logical that it should also have the right to review its decision. This implies of course a review of the conviction as well as the judicial decision on the basis of which the confiscation was made. The term "review" also covers extraordinary proceedings which in some states may result in a new examination of the legal aspects of a case and not only of the facts.

54. When elaborating Article 14, the committee discussed whether it was necessary to draft a ground for refusal in respect of the case where the confiscation order had been the subject of amnesty or pardon. This question, which is of little significance, might be covered by other

grounds for refusal and need not be treated expressly in the Convention. Under Article 31, paragraph 2.*a*, the requesting Party is obliged to inform the requested Party of any decision by reason of which the confiscation ceases to be enforceable.

Article 15 — Confiscated property

55. The agreements referred to in the article may be included in multilateral or bilateral agreements already concluded or in *ad hoc* agreements for the purpose of the disposal of the property. When elaborating the Convention, several experts considered that such *ad hoc* agreements should take into account the work of international funds or organisations engaged in the fight against serious criminality as well as individuals who might be the victims of offences on which the confiscation is based. Parties were also encouraged to enter into agreements whereby the confiscated property is shared among the co-operating Parties in such a manner as to generally reflect their participation in the case. Such international sharing should be designed to further the co-operative spirit embodied in this Convention.

Article 16 — Right of enforcement and maximum amount of confiscation

56. Paragraph 1 of this article states the general principle that the requesting state maintains its right to enforce the confiscation, whereas paragraph 2 seeks to avoid adverse effects of a value confiscation which is enforced simultaneously in two or more states, including the requesting state. This solution departs from the one adopted in Article 11 of the Validity Convention.

Article 17 — Imprisonment in default

57. In some states it is possible to imprison persons who have not complied with an order of confiscation of a sum of money or where the confiscated property is out of reach of the law enforcement agencies of the state. Also, other measures restricting the liberty of the affected person exist in some states. Imprisonment or such measures may in other states have been declared unconstitutional.

Section 5

Refusal and postponement of co-operation

Article 18 — Grounds for refusal

58. In order to set up an efficient but at the same time flexible system, the committee chose not to elaborate a system of conditions coupled with mandatory grounds for refusal. It considered instead that the Convention should provide for a system which would, to the fullest extent possible, place states wishing to co-operate in a position to do so. No grounds for refusal are therefore mandatory in the relationship between states. However, this does not exclude states from providing that some of the grounds for refusal will be mandatory at the domestic level. This is especially true for the two first grounds listed in paragraph 1, sub-paragraphs *a* and *b*.

There are two sides to Article 18. On the one hand, the requested state may always claim that a ground for refusal exists and the requesting state will usually not be in a position to contest that assessment. On the other hand, the requested state may not claim any other grounds for refusal than those enumerated in the article. If no grounds for refusal exist or if it is not possible to postpone action in accordance with Article 19, the requested state is bound to comply with the request for co-operation. Moreover, the requested Party is obliged to consider, before refusing co-operation, whether the request may be granted partially or subject to conditions.

It goes without saying that the requested state is not obliged to invoke a ground for refusal even if it has the power to do so. On the contrary, several of the grounds for refusal are drafted in such a way that it will be a matter of discretion for the competent authorities of the requested state to decide whether to refuse co-operation.

59. Paragraph 1 is valid for all kinds of international co-operation under Chapter III of the Convention. Paragraphs 2 and 3 concern only measures involving coercive action, whereas paragraph 4 only concerns confiscation. Paragraphs 5 and 6 concern proceedings *in absentia*, paragraph 7 contains a special rule for bank secrecy and paragraph 8 limits the possibility of invoking the ground for refusal in paragraph 1.*a* in two particular situations.

60. The ground for refusal contained in paragraph 1, sub-paragraph *a*, is also found in Article 11, paragraph *j*, of the European Convention on the Transfer of Proceedings in Criminal Matters and Article 6, paragraph *a*, of the European Convention on the International Validity of Criminal Judgments. As stated in the explanatory reports to those conventions, it is impossible to conceive of an obligation to enforce a foreign judgment (the Validity Convention) or to make prosecution compulsory (the Transfer Convention) if it contravenes the constitutional or other fundamental laws of the requested state. Observance of these fundamental principles underlying domestic legislation constitutes for each state an overriding obligation which it may not evade; it is therefore the duty of the organs of the requested state to see that this condition is fulfilled in practice. This ground for refusal takes account of particular cases of incompatibility by means of a reference to the distinctive characteristics of each state's legislation, for it is impossible, in general regulations, to enumerate individual cases.

The committee of experts on several occasions discussed possible cases when this ground might come into play. During these discussions, the following examples were mentioned:

— where the proceedings on which the request are based do not meet basic procedural requirements for the protection of human rights such as the ones contained in Articles 5 and 6 of the Convention for the Protection of Human Rights and Fundamental Freedoms;

— where there are serious reasons for believing that the life of a person would be endangered;

— where in particular cases it is forbidden under the domestic law of the requested Party to confiscate certain types of property;

— cases of exorbitant jurisdictional claims asserted by the requesting Party;

— where the confiscation order is determined on the basis of an assumption that certain property represents proceeds, whereas the burden of proof as to its legitimate origin was incumbent upon the convicted person, and such a determination would, under the law of the requested Party, be contrary to the fundamental principles of its legal system. It follows from this that, if a state recognises this principle in respect of one category of offence, it cannot apply this ground for refusal for another category of offences;

— where interests of the requested state's own nationals could be jeopardised. One example is when a request for enforcement concerns property which is already subject to a restraint order for the benefit of a privileged creditor in a bankruptcy or concerns property which is subject to litigation in a fiscal matter. Such priority problems should be solved according to the requested state's own legislation.

The scope of application of sub-paragraph *a* is limited by Article 18, paragraphs 5 and 6.

61. The ground for refusal in sub-paragraph *b* is also found in Article 2, paragraph *b*, of the European Convention on Mutual Assistance in Criminal Matters. It is however slightly reworded in the present Convention to indicate that the criterion is judged objectively.

The phrase "essential interests" refers to the interests of the state, not of individuals. Economic interests may, however, be covered by this concept.

62. Sub-paragraph *c* is intended to cover three different cases of grounds for refusal. This is why the committee deliberately chose the general term "importance". The first concerns cases when there an apparent disproportion between the action sought and the offence to which it relates. If, for example, a state is requested to confiscate a large sum of money when the offence to which it relates is of a minor nature, international co-operation could in most cases be refused on the basis of the principle of proportionality. In addition, if the costs of confiscation outweigh the law enforcement benefit at which the confiscation action is directed, the requested Party may refuse co-operation, unless an agreement to share costs is reached.

The second case relates to requests where the sum in itself is minor. It is clear that the often expensive system of international co-operation should not be burdened with such requests.

The third case concerns offences which are inherently minor (see Recommendation No. R (87) 18 on the simplification of criminal justice). The system of international co-operation provided under this Convention should not be used for such cases.

Where the request gives rise to extraordinary costs, Article 34 will apply. It is clear that the present paragraph can be applied if no such agreement as is envisaged under Article 34 can be reached.

63. In respect of sub-paragraph *d*, the committee agreed that the terms "political" and "fiscal" should be interpreted in conformity with other European penal law conventions elaborated under the auspices of the Council of Europe. The experts agreed that no offence defined as a drug offence or a laundering offence under the United Nations Convention should be considered a political or fiscal offence.

64. The principle of *ne bis in idem* is generally recognised in domestic cases. It also plays an important role in cases with a foreign element, but its application may vary from country to country. Sub-paragraph *e* refers only to the principle as such without defining its content. The principle and its limits must be interpreted in the light of the domestic law of the requested Party.

Ne bis in idem will usually be interpreted in relation to the facts in a specific case. If, in a given case, other facts were involved than the ones relied upon in the request, it would be possible to postpone co-operation on the basis of Article 19.

65. The ground for refusal contained in sub-paragraph *f* indicates the requirement of double criminality. It is not, however, a requirement which is valid for all kinds of assistance under the Convention. In respect of assistance under Section 2, the requirement is only valid when coercive action is implied.

In the field of international co-operation in criminal matters, the principle of double criminality may be *in abstracto* or *in concreto*. It was agreed, for the purpose of requests under Section 4 of Chapter III of the present Convention, to consider the principle *in concreto*, as in the case of the Validity Convention and the European Convention on the Transfer of Proceedings in Criminal Matters. In cases where double criminality is required for assistance to be afforded under Section 2, it is sufficient to consider the principle *in abstracto*. For requests under Section 3, it may depend on whether the request is one covered by paragraph 1 of Article 11, or by paragraph 2 of that article. For requests under Article 11, paragraph 2, double criminality *in concreto* would be necessary.

This condition is fulfilled if an offence which is punishable in a given state would have been punishable if committed in the jurisdiction of the requested state and if the perpetrator of that offence had been liable to a sanction under the legislation of the requested state.

This rule means that the *nomen juris* need not necessarily be identical, since the laws of two or more states cannot be expected to coincide to the extent that certain facts should invariably be considered as constituting the same offence. Besides, the general character of the wording of the clause indicates that such identity is not, in fact, necessary, which implies that differences in the legal classification of an offence are unimportant where the condition considered here is concerned. The requirement of double criminality should thus be applied flexibly to ensure that co-operation under the Convention stresses substance over form. The technical title of the offence or the penalty carried by that offence should not be a basis for refusal if the actions criminalised in both states are approximately the same or seek to redress the same injury.

It is for the authorities of the requested state to establish whether or not there is double criminality *in concreto*. Article 28 gives the requested state the possibility of asking for additional information if the information supplied is not sufficient to deal with the request.

66. When coercive action is sought, the requesting state might not be in a position to give a full account of the facts on which the request is based simply because that state does not yet possess information in respect of all relevant elements. This implies that the requested state must consider such a request liberally in respect of the requirement of double criminality.

"Coercive action" must be defined by the requested Party. It is in the interest of that Party that the requirement of double criminality is upheld.

67. Paragraph 2 concerns only provisional measures and investigative assistance involving coercive action. The paragraph should be read in conjunction with Articles 9 and 12, paragraph 1. It affords to the requested Party the possibility of refusing co-operation if the measure could not be taken under its law if the case had been a purely domestic one. By mentioning a "similar" domestic case, it becomes clear that not all objective elements need to be the same. The requested Party must also take account of the urgency of the measures requested. It will be obliged sometimes to consider a request liberally in respect of the requirement in this paragraph.

68. During the elaboration of the Convention, the experts discussed whether it was necessary to draft similar grounds for refusal for these

measures to the ones contained in Article 18, paragraph 4, sub-paragraphs *a* to *c*. It was agreed however that the wording of Article 18, paragraph 2, would also cover such situations.

69. Paragraph 3 provides for the possibility of refusing co-operation where a Party requests another Party to take measures which would not have been permitted under the law of the requesting Party. Not all the experts considered that it was necessary to draft a ground for refusal for this situation. The latter part of the paragraph refers to the competence of the authorities in the requesting Party. The experts thought that a request for measures involving coercive action should always be authorised by a judicial authority, including public prosecutors, competent in criminal matters. This would exclude administrative courts or judges or courts competent in civil cases only.

70. With regard to Article 18, paragraph 4, sub-paragraph *a*, the expression "type of offence" is meant to cover cases where confiscation is not at all provided for in respect of a certain offence in the requested Party. The sub-paragraph applies to those offences or categories of offences which are excluded from the scope of application of Article 2, paragraph 1, pursuant to a declaration under Article 2, paragraph 2.

71. Sub-paragraph *b* refers to laws other than those relating to fundamental principles of the legal system (paragraph 1.*a* of Article 18). Such laws may restrict the possibility of confiscation on the basis of the relationship between the offence and the economic advantage of it, for example by excluding or permitting confiscation through a reference to concepts such as "direct/indirect proceeds", "substitute property" for instrumentalities or proceeds, "fruits of licit activities financed by illicit proceeds", etc. When a request for confiscation relates to a case that, had it been a domestic case, would not result in a confiscation because of those laws, the requested Party should have the possibility of refusing co-operation.

The committee discussed the interaction between this paragraph and the obligation under Article 13, paragraph 3. In this connection, the experts agreed: on the one hand, that the paragraph will apply only when a request emanates from states which apply property confiscation or when it concerns a request from a value confiscation country to a value confiscation country; on the other hand, if, at the stage of realising the claim, there is no relationship between an offence and the property, which can be the case in the system of value confiscation, that that alone is no ground for refusal since the expression "advantage that might be qualified as proceeds" refers to the assessment stage. Another way of expressing this would be to state that co-operation may be refused when the assessment of the proceeds made by the requesting Party would run counter to the principles of the domestic law of the requested Party, because of the remote relationship between the offence and the proceeds.

Experts from states which mainly use the system of value confiscation expressed misgivings, during the elaboration of this provision, that it might be misinterpreted in a way which would exclude the application of value confiscation orders. In order to remedy this, the beginning of the sub-paragraph was added to make it clear that the application of the provision should be without prejudice to the value confiscation system. Experts were also reminded of the general principle embodied in the Convention that the two systems were equal under the Convention.

The committee also concluded that, where the confiscation is not at all based on an assessment of proceeds but only of the capital of the convicted person, such cases were outside the scope of application of the Convention. It was noted that, besides confiscation of instrumentalities, Articles 2 and 3 refer to confiscation procedures essentially based on an assessment of the existence and quantity of illicit proceeds. This is valid both for property confiscation (when the property assessed as proceeds is usually also the object of the enforcement of the confiscation) and for value confiscation (where the confiscation order may ultimately be satisfied by realising the claim on property which does not constitute proceeds, but where in any case the "value" to be confiscated is determined by assessing the proceeds from offences).

72. Sub-paragraph *c* need not be commented on in great detail. In respect of the enforcement of a foreign confiscation order (Article 13, paragraph 1.*a*), it is obvious that the requested Party must make an assessment as if the confiscation had been a similar national case. In cases where confiscation procedures are initiated in accordance with Article 13, paragraph 1.*b*, the requested Party may wish to recognise any acts performed by the requesting Party which may have had the effect of interrupting running periods of time-limitations under its law.

73. Sub-paragraph *d* was discussed at great length by the experts. It is probable that most requests for co-operation under Chapter III, Section 4, will concern cases where a previous conviction exists already. However, it is also possible in some states to confiscate proceeds without a formal conviction of the offender, sometimes because the offender is a fugitive or because he is deceased. In certain other states, the legislation makes it possible to take into account, when confiscating, offences other than the one which is adjudicated without a formal charge being made. The latter possibility concerns in particular certain states' drug legislation. The experts agreed that international co-operation should not be excluded in such cases, provided however that a decision of a judicial nature exists or that a statement to the effect that an offence has or several offences have been committed is included in such a decision. The expression "decision of a judicial nature" is meant to exclude purely administrative decisions. Decisions by administrative courts are however included. The statements referred to in this article do not concern decisions of a provisional nature.

74. Sub-paragraph *e* describes the case where confiscation is not possible because of the rules relating to the enforceability of a decision or because the decision might not be final. Although in most cases a decision is enforceable if it is final, recourse to an extraordinary remedy may preclude enforcement. On the other hand, an enforceable decision may not be final, for instance in cases where the decision has been rendered *in absentia*. The lodging of an opposition or appeal against such a decision may have an interruptive effect as to its enforceability, but need not affect the part of the decision which may already have been enforced, nor necessarily imply the lifting of any seizure of realisable property. Thus, enforceability cannot be completely identified with finality and for this reason it was held essential to differentiate between the two possibilities. Under Article 27, paragraph 3.a.ii, the competent authority of the requesting Party should certify that the confiscation order is enforceable and not subject to ordinary means of appeal.

75. Sub-paragraph *f* concerns *in absentia* proceedings. The paragraph is inspired by the Second Additional Protocol to the European Convention on Extradition. The committee had in mind, when drafting the provision, Resolution (75) 11 of the Committee of Ministers on the criteria governing proceedings held in the absence of the accused as well as Article 6 of the European Convention on Human Rights.

76. Paragraphs 5 and 6 were drafted to limit the possibility of criminals escaping justice by simply refusing to answer the summons to appear in court. Paragraph 6 is, however, not compulsory. It is a matter for the authorities of the requested state to assess the fact that the decision was taken *in absentia* and the weight of the circumstances mentioned in the paragraph in the light of the domestic law of the requested Party.

77. Paragraph 7 deals with bank secrecy in the framework of international co-operation. As regards the national level, see Article 4, paragraph 1, and the explanatory report on that article.

In most states, the lifting of bank secrecy requires the decision of a judge, an investigating judge, a prosecutor or a grand jury. The experts considered it natural that a Party may require that international co-operation should be limited to instances where the decision to lift bank secrecy had been ordered or authorised by such authority.

Under the United Nations Convention, bank secrecy may never be invoked to refuse co-operation in respect of proceeds from drug or laundering offences. The present Convention is not intended to restrict international co-operation for such offences.

Article 19 — Postponement

78. A decision to postpone will usually indicate a time-limit. The requested Party may therefore postpone action on a request several times. According to Article 20, the requested Party must also consider whether the request may be granted partially or subject to conditions before taking a decision to postpone. It is normal that any such decision be taken in consultation with the requesting Party. If the requested Party decides to postpone action, Articles 30 and 31, paragraph 1.c, will apply.

Article 20 — Partial or conditional granting of a request

79. Reference is made to the commentary under Article 19 above. The words "where appropriate" indicate that consultation should be the rule; immediate decisions should be the exception unless they are purely based on questions of law, because it is usually appropriate to seek consultations with the Party that requests international co-operation. The Convention does not prescribe any form for such consultations. They may also be informal, via a simple telephone call for instance between the competent authorities.

Conditions can be laid down either by the central authorities of the requested Party or, where applicable, by any other authority which decides upon the request. Such conditions may for instance concern the rights of third parties or they may require that a question of ownership of a certain property be resolved before a final decision as to the disposal of the property is taken.

The paragraph also covers partial refusal which could take the form of admitting only confiscation of certain property or enforcing only part of the sum of a value confiscation order.

Section 6

Notification and protection of third parties' rights

Article 21 — Notification of documents

80. This article has been drafted on the basis of the Hague Convention on the serving of legal documents in civil or commercial matters but differs slightly from that convention. Notification requirements are in particular relevant to rights of third parties. The article has therefore been placed in this section to stress this fact.

As to the relationship between this article and other conventions, see Article 39.

The Convention provides the legal basis, if such does not exist on the basis of other instruments, for international co-operation in the fulfilment of notification requirements. Among the notifications that might be required, depending on domestic law, can be mentioned a court order to seize property, the execution of such an order, seizure of property in which third party rights are vested, seizure of registered property, etc. The type of judicial documents that might be served must always be determined under the national law.

In cases where it is important to act quickly or in respect of notifications of judicial documents which are of a less important nature, the law of the notifying state might permit the sending of such documents directly or the use of direct, official channels. Provided that a Party to the Convention does not object to this procedure, by entering a reservation under Article 21, paragraph 2, states should have the possibility of using such direct means of communication.

In respect of the indication of legal remedies, the experts agreed that it is sufficient to indicate the court of the sending state to which the person served has direct access and the time-limits, if any, within which such court has to be accessed. It should also be indicated whether this has to be done by the person himself or whether he may be represented by a lawyer for this purpose. No indication of further possibilities of appeal is necessary.

Article 22 — Recognition of foreign decisions

81. Article 22 describes how third party rights should be considered under the Convention. Practice has shown that criminals often use ostensible "buyers" to acquire property. Relatives, wives, children or friends might be used as decoys. Nevertheless, the third parties might be persons who have a legitimate claim on property which has been subject to a confiscation order or a seizure. Article 5 obliges the Parties to the Convention to protect the rights of third parties.

By third party the committee understood any person affected by the enforcement of a confiscation order or involved in confiscation proceedings under Article 13, paragraph 1.*b*, but who is not the offender. This could also include, depending on national law, persons against whom the confiscation order could be directed. See also the commentary under Article 5.

The rights of third parties could either have been considered in the requesting state or not considered in that state. In the latter case, the affected third party will always have the right to put forward his claim in the requested state according to its law. In fact, this could often happen since, in some states such as the United Kingdom, third party rights are safeguarded at the stage of the execution of the confiscation order and not at the stage of decision. A consequence of this is that states cannot in this case invoke any of the grounds for refusal, such as Article 18, paragraph 1.*a*, on the grounds that third party rights had not been examined.

In the case where third party rights had already been dealt with in the requesting state, the Convention is based on the principle that the foreign decision should be recognised. However, when any of the situations enumerated in paragraph 2 exist, recognition may be refused. In particular, when the third parties did not have adequate opportunity to assert their rights, recognition may be refused. This does not however mean that the request for co-operation must be refused. It might be appropriate to remedy the situation in the requested Party, in which case refusal does not seem necessary. Article 20 could also be used in so far as the requested Party may make co-operation conditional on the protection of the rights of third parties.

It follows that Article 14, paragraph 2, does not concern the adjudication of rights in respect of third parties. The present article deals exclusively with the rights of third parties. Nothing in the Convention shall be construed as prejudicing the rights of *bona fide* third parties.

Section 7

Procedural and other general rules

Most provisions of this section are evident and need no further comments. The following should however be explained.

82. Article 23 gives the Parties a right to designate several central authorities where necessary. This possibility should be used restrictively so as not to create unnecessary confusion and to promote close co-operation between states. Even if not expressly stated in the Convention, the Parties should, depending on internal organisational matters, have the right to change central authorities when appropriate. The powers of the central authorities are determined by national law.

83. Article 24 describes the communication channels. Normally, the central authority should be used. The application of paragraph 2 is optional. However, the judicial authority is obliged to send a copy of the request to its own central authority which must forward it to the central authority of the requested Party. For the purposes of this Convention, the term "judicial authority" also includes public prosecutors. Requests or communications referred to in paragraph 5 of the article are mostly intended for simple requests for information, for instance information from a land register.

84. Article 25 permits an evolution if techniques change. The term "telecommunications" should therefore be interpreted broadly.

In the event of urgency, states might prefer to make the first contact by telephone. Requests for co-operation must however in any case be confirmed in writing. States should pay attention to the security aspects of using public networks, for instance by protecting the communication through encryption. Article 27, paragraph 3.*a*, requires that a certified true copy be sent. It should be possible to send a copy of the certificate by telefax but confirm such certification by sending the original certificate at a later stage.

85. Article 27 states the important rules pertaining to the contents of the request for co-operation. If the rules are not strictly followed, it is clear that international co-operation will be difficult. In particular, it is absolutely necessary that the requesting Party follow conscientiously the provisions of paragraph 1, sub-paragraphs *c* and *e*. In particular, with regard to banks, it is necessary to indicate in detail the relevant branch office and its address. It is however not the intention of the committee that the article should be interpreted as implying a requirement on a requesting Party to furnish *prima facie* evidence.

Paragraph 1.*f* refers to Articles 9 and 12.

Paragraph 2 requires an indication of a maximum amount for which recovery is sought. It concerns, in particular, requests for provisional measures with a view to the eventual enforcement of value confiscation orders.

Paragraph 3, sub-paragraph *a*.iii, may in particular be relevant to the enforcement of a value confiscation order which has already been partly enforced. It may also be relevant when requests for enforcement are made in several states or when the requesting state seeks to execute part of the order.

Paragraph 3, sub-paragraph *a*.iv, might in some states amount to a request for the taking of provisional measures.

Paragraph 3.*b* is of a general nature. In order to fully understand its implications in a specific case, the Parties should read this paragraph in conjunction with the preceding paragraphs of the article.

86. Article 28 makes it possible for a Party to ask for additional information. It may do so but, at the same time, it may take necessary provisional measures if the request for co-operation would cease to have any purpose if the provisional measures were not taken.

87. Article 29 seeks to avoid any adverse effects of requests concerning the same property or person. It may happen, particularly when the system of value confiscation is used, that the same property is subject to confiscation. In cases concerning requests for confiscation, Article 29 obliges the requested Party to consider consulting the other Parties.

88. Article 31, paragraph 1.*a*, requires the requested Party to promptly inform the requesting Party of the action initiated. Such obligation to inform concerns in particular cases where a Party undertakes measures which might continue for some time and where the requesting Party has a legitimate interest in being kept informed that action is taken and of its continued results, for instance in respect of telephone tapping, monitoring orders, etc. Paragraph 1.*b* might include communications relating to events affecting the final result of the co-operation. Paragraph 2 deals with the obligation for the requesting Party to inform the requested Party of any development by reason of which any action under the Convention is not justified, for instance a decision by the requesting Party on amnesty or pardon. When such an event occurs, the requested Party is obliged to discontinue the procedures. This is usually the case under the law of the requested Party (see Article 14, paragraph 1). The requesting Party always has the possibility of withdrawing its request for co-operation.

89. Article 32 indicates the rule of speciality which is contained in several other European conventions. The committee did not wish, however, to make the rule compulsory in all the cases to which the Convention applies. It provided therefore, in paragraph 1, for the possibility that the requested Party may make the execution of a request dependent upon the rule of speciality. Certain Parties would always use this possibility. The experts provided therefore, in paragraph 2, for the possibility of declaring that the rule of speciality would always be applied in relation to other Parties to the Convention.

90. Article 33 deals with confidentiality both in the requesting Party and the requested Party. It is important that national law be adapted so that, for instance, financial institutions are not able to warn their clients that criminal investigations or proceedings are being carried out. Disclosure of such facts is a criminal offence in certain states. The degree of confidentiality in international co-operation coincides with the degree

of confidentiality in national cases. The term "confidential" might have different legal connotations under the law of some states.

91. Article 34 refers only to "costs" of the action sought. The experts discussed whether Article 34 should also refer to "expenses", but decided against it.

92. Article 35, paragraph 1, requires Parties, in principle, to enter into consultations in the case of any liability for damages. Such consultations shall be without prejudice to any obligation of a Party to promptly pay the damages due to the injured person pursuant to a judicial decision to that effect. Consultations are however not always necessary when a question has arisen on how such damages should be paid. If a Party decides to pay damages to a victim because of an error made by that Party, no obligation to consult the other Party exists.

If another Party might have an interest in a case, it is normal that that Party should have an opportunity to be able to take care of its interests. The Party against whom legal action has been taken should therefore, whenever possible, endeavour to inform the other Party of the matter.

CHAPTER IV

FINAL PROVISIONS

93. With some exceptions, the provisions contained in this chapter are, for the most part, based on the "Model final clauses for conventions and agreements concluded within the Council of Europe" which were approved by the Committee of Ministers of the Council of Europe at the 315th meeting of their Deputies in February 1980. Most of these articles do not therefore call for specific comments, but the following points require some explanation.

94. Articles 36 and 37 have been drafted on several precedents established in other conventions elaborated within the framework of the Council of Europe, for instance the Convention on the Transfer of Sentenced Persons, which allow for signature, before the convention's entry into force, not only by the member states of the Council of Europe,

but also by non-member states which have participated in the elaboration of the convention. These provisions are intended to enable the maximum number of interested states, not necessarily members of the Council of Europe, to become Parties as soon as possible. The provision in Article 36 is intended to apply to three non-member states, Australia, Canada and the United States of America, which were represented on the Select Committee by observers and were actively associated with the elaboration of the Convention.

95. Article 39 is intended to ensure the coexistence of the Convention with other treaties — multilateral or bilateral — dealing with matters which are also dealt.with in the present Convention.

Paragraph 1 concerns, *inter alia*, the United Nations Convention. It is possible that a request made under the present Convention might be dealt with under either of the two conventions. The same is valid for requests which might fall within the scope of application of both the present Convention and the Mutual Assistance Convention or the Validity Convention. Paragraph 2 expresses in a positive way that Parties may, for certain purposes, conclude bilateral or multilateral agreements relating to matters dealt with in the Convention. The drafting permits the *a contrario* deduction that Parties may not conclude agreements which derogate from the Convention. Paragraph 3 safeguards the continued application of agreements, treaties or relations relating to subjects which are dealt with in the present Convention, for instance in the Nordic co-operation.

96. Article 41 is an innovation in respect of the penal law conventions elaborated within the framework of the Council of Europe. The amendment procedure is mostly thought to be for minor changes of a procedural character. The experts considered that major changes to the Convention should be made in the form of additional protocols. It was noted that, in accordance with paragraph 5, any amendment adopted would come into force only when all Parties had informed the Secretary General of their acceptance.

97. The Committee of Ministers, which adopted the original text of this Convention, is also competent to adopt any amendments.

98. Article 42, paragraph 1, is slightly redrafted in comparison with other penal law conventions elaborated within the framework of the

Council of Europe, without there being, however, any intention to change the substance of the paragraph. The experts thought it appropriate to clarify that the CDPC should also be kept informed about the interpretation of the provisions of the Convention.

Paragraph 2 imposes an obligation on the Parties to seek a peaceful settlement of any dispute concerning the interpretation or the application of the Convention. Any procedure for solving disputes should be agreed upon by the Parties concerned.

DOCUMENT D

Recommendation No. R (91) 12 of the Committee of Ministers of the Council of Europe to Member States Concerning the Setting Up and Functioning of Arbitral Tribunals under Article 42, Paragraph 2, of the Convention of 8 November 1990 on Laundering, Search, Seizure and Confiscation of the Proceeds from Crime

(Adopted by the Committee of Ministers on 9 September 1991 at the 461st meeting of the Ministers' Deputies)

Source: Council of Europe, Strasbourg

The Committee of Ministers, under the terms of Article 15.*b* of the Statute of the Council of Europe,

Having regard to the Convention on Laundering, Search, Seizure and Confiscation of the Proceeds from Crime, concluded at Strasbourg on 8 November 1990 (European Treaty Series, No. 141);

Considering that Article 42, paragraph 2, of that convention dealing with the settlement of disputes between Parties as to its interpretation or application, envisages, as an alternative to negotiation, submission of the dispute to the European Committee on Crime Problems or to the International Court of Justice, the setting up and functioning of arbitral tribunals whose decisions shall be binding upon the Parties to such disputes;

Considering the absence in the convention of any provisions as to the specific procedures to be followed by Parties concerned for the establishment of such arbitral tribunals, or any rules of procedure to be observed in the course of such arbitration;

Considering that such provisions might appropriately be reflected in a recommendation of the Committee of Ministers of the Council of Europe to the governments of the states signatories or parties to the convention;

Considering that reference to the European Convention for the Peaceful Settlement of Disputes of 29 April 1957 (European Treaty Series, No. 23) would not be appropriate for this purpose, in view of its limited number of Contracting Parties and the fact that it does not apply to states which are not members of the Council;

Desirous to present a single set of recommendations for the governments of all states, whether member states of the Council of Europe or not, which may be or become bound by the Convention on Laundering, Search, Seizure and Confiscation of the Proceeds from Crime,

Recommends the governments of such states to be guided, when seeking arbitration in accordance with Article 42, paragraph 2, of the aforementioned convention, by the following rules:

1. The Party to the convention requesting arbitration pursuant to Article 42, paragraph 2, shall inform the other Party in writing of the claim and of the grounds on which its claim is based.

2.   Upon acceptance of the request for arbitration, the two Parties concerned shall establish an arbitral tribunal.

3.   The arbitral tribunal shall consist of three members. Each Party shall nominate an arbitrator. Both Parties shall, by common accord, appoint the presiding arbitrator.

4.   Failing such nomination or such appointment by common accord within four months from the date on which the arbitration was requested, the necessary nomination or appointment shall be entrusted to the Secretary General of the Permanent Court of Arbitration.

5.   The Parties shall draw up a special agreement determining the subject of the dispute and the details of the procedure. Failing the conclusion of a special agreement within a period of six months from the date on which arbitration was requested, the dispute may be brought before the arbitral tribunal upon application of either Party. In the latter case, the tribunal shall establish its own procedure.

6.   Unless otherwise agreed between the Parties, the tribunal shall decide on the basis of the applicable rules of international law; in the absence of such rules, it shall decide *ex aequo et bono*.

7.   If the dispute concerns the amount of compensation due to one Party as a result of its being held liable for damages in accordance with Article 35, paragraph 1, of the convention, the tribunal may establish the sum of such compensation or the apportionment of such sum.

8.   Any third state which considers that its legitimate interests are involved in the dispute, may submit to the arbitral tribunal a request to intervene as a third party. It is for the tribunal to decide on this request.

ii. THE EUROPEAN COMMUNITIES

DOCUMENT E

Commission of the European Communities: Proposal for a Council Directive on Prevention of Use of the Financial System for the Purpose of Money Laundering

and Explanatory Memorandum, 23 March 1990

*Source: House of Lords Select Committee on the European Communities, **Money Laundering**, HL Paper 6, 1990-91*

Explanatory Memorandum

I. GENERAL CONSIDERATIONS

1. Laundering of proceeds from criminal activities (in short "money laundering") is a phenomenon which concerns national and international authorities. Indeed, it is an activity becoming more and more widespread every day and it has an evident influence on the rise of organised crime in general and drug trafficking in particular. Internationalisation of economies and financial services are opportunities which are seized by money launderers to carry out their criminal activities, since the origin of funds can be better disguised in an international context.

2. Nowadays, several events and initiatives at various levels show the increase of international awareness of the necessity to combat money laundering especially in the field of drugs, although the phenomenon is far from being controlled. At a national level, some Community and non-Community countries have adopted criminal legislation against laundering of proceeds from drug related offences or terrorism and some others have started the discussion of bills of laws in this sense.

3. Concerning the international instruments focused on a repressive approach towards money laundering, reference should be made to the United Nations Convention against Illicit Traffic in Narcotic Drugs and Psychotropic Substances adopted the 19 December 1988 in Vienna (hereinafter the Vienna Convention).

This Convention—in the discussions of which the Commission has participated, and of which the EEC is one of the signing parties—provides, among other points, that the states adhering to it shall criminalise a series of conducts related to drugs as well as money laundering related to such offences. In addition, it contains a set of provisions which afford important help to combat money laundering such as those concerning confiscation and seizure of criminal proceeds, international judicial assistance and prohibition of invoking banking secrecy in order to avoid investigations in the scope covered by the Convention.

4. With respect to the international developments focused on a preventive approach, mention should be made of the Recommendation of the Council of Europe of the 27 June 1980 and of the Declaration of Principles adopted in December 1988 in Basle by the banking supervisory authorities of the Group of Ten, both of which constitute major steps towards preventing the use of the financial system for purposes of money laundering.

Most recently, the Financial Action Task Force against Money Laundering established in July 1989 by the Paris Summit of the Seven Most Developed Countries, in which the Commission has actively participated, together with 15 Community and non-Community countries, has carried out important work in this area, particularly in the aspects of laundering methods and statistics, judicial assistance, and administrative and financial co-operation. The final report of the Task Force, which incorporates up-to-date information about the existing situation concerning these points, as well as a list of recommendations, was completed in February 1990 and submitted to the Governments for approval.

II. NECESSITY OF COMMUNITY ACTION IN THIS FIELD

1. Money laundering must mainly be combated by penal means (criminal legislation), and in the framework of international co-operation among law enforcement agencies and judicial authorities. This has been the approach, for example, in the above mentioned Vienna Convention.

2. However, a penal approach should not be the only strategy to combat money laundering since, as credit and financial institutions are frequently used to carry out these kinds of activities, the soundness and stability of the particular institutions involved as well as the prestige of the financial system as a whole could be seriously jeopardised, thereby losing the confidence of the public. The Community, which is responsible for adopting the necessary measures to ensure the

soundness and stability of the European financial system, cannot be indifferent to the involvement of credit and financial institutions in money laundering.

In a similar way to that in which the Community Directives in the financial sector try to guarantee that persons who effectively direct the business of credit institutions have "good repute" (Article 3, paragraph 2 of the First Banking Co-ordination Directive) as well as the "suitability" of the Shareholders (Article 5 and Article 11, paragraph 1 of the Second Banking Co-ordination Directive), Community legislation must ensure the integrity and cleanliness of the financial system.

3. Moreover, the financial system itself can play a highly effective preventive role in the struggle against money laundering.

4. At the same time, the Community has the responsibility to impede launderers from taking advantage of the single financial market, and of the freedoms of capital movements and supplying of financial services which this financial area involves to facilitate their criminal activities. Lack of Community action against money laundering could lead Member States, with the purpose to protect their financial system, to adopt measures which could be inconsistent with the completion of the Single Market.

5. Finally, it is important to consider the public demand throughout the Community for measures which can help to reduce the scourge of drugs. The resolutions of the European Parliament of the 18 January 1989, which requested the Commission to establish a global Community program to combat drug trafficking, including provisions on prevention of money laundering, are relevant in this respect.

III.   CONTENT OF THE DIRECTIVE

The content of the Directive is as follows.

(1) *General Coverage of the Whole Financial System* (Article 1, first and second indents, and Article 8)

Since a partial coverage of the financial system could provoke a shift in money laundering from one to another kind of financial institutions, the Directive covers not only banks but all kinds of credit and financial institutions.

Credit institutions are defined according to the Community banking legislation (Article 1 of the First Banking Co-ordination Directive). The concept of financial institutions is defined in a very broad meaning as an undertaking other than a credit institution whose principal activity is to carry out one or more of the activities included in the Annex of the Second Banking Co-ordination Directive. This annex contains a list of virtually all kinds of financial services. Since insurance, however, is not included in this annex, a special reference has been made in the definition of financial institutions to insurance companies so that this important part of the financial sector is covered by the Directive.

"Non-formal financial institutions" are not directly covered by the Directive due to the difficulty of establishing who these are and to the fact that they do not usually have any supervisory authorities. Nevertheless Article 8 provides that Member States shall extend its provisions, where applicable, to professions and undertakings which "because of their involvement with cash transaction business, may be particularly susceptible to being used for money laundering purposes". These would include casinos, money changers, etc.

(2) *Definition of Money Laundering including Proceeds from All Serious Criminal Offences* (Article 1, third indent)

The definition of money laundering is literally taken from Article 3(1)(b) of the Vienna Convention. The only difference is that instead of being limited to drugs related offences, as in the Convention, it covers laundering of proceeds from drugs related offences, terrorism and any other serious crimes (including particularly organised crime), as defined by Member States. Indeed, in spite of the importance that laundering of proceeds from drug trafficking has in the context of money laundering in general it would not have been appropriate to exclude laundering of other serious crimes from the scope of the Directive. The soundness of the financial system is also jeopardised in these cases. Moreover, even if financial institutions have reasons to suspect that certain funds come from criminal activities, it is practically impossible for them to know from what kind of crime the money to be laundered proceeds.

(3) *Criminalising Money Laundering by Member States* (Article 2)

Criminalising money laundering by Member States is not only a necessary repressive means of combating money laundering, but also a previous prerequisite for co-operation between financial institutions and judicial or law enforcement authorities.

According to legal principles existing in most Member States bank secrecy must be lifted in cases of Criminal Law. Criminalisation therefore becomes a precondition for such a co-operation.

In this respect, the Directive requires that Member States make laundering of proceeds from serious crimes, regardless whether they are related to drugs or not, a criminal offence.

(4) *Identification of Customers and Beneficial Owners* (Article 3)

Prevention of use of the financial system for money laundering, as well as effectiveness in any eventual criminal enquiry, demand as an essential measure, that credit and financial institutions require identification of their customers when entering into business relations. Besides this general obligation, credit and financial institutions must take reasonable measures to establish the real identity of the persons on whose behalf an operation is carried out or an account is opened (beneficial owner) in the case of doubts whether customers are acting on their own behalf. Because of the difficulties which this identification of beneficial owners could involve in some circumstances, credit and financial institutions are exhorted to take "reasonable measures".

The obligation of keeping records of the identity for an established period is a necessary condition for the effectiveness of the identification requirement.

(5) *Due Diligence of Credit and Financial Institutions* (Article 4)

This principle encompasses two related obligations for credit and financial institutions: careful examination of any unusual transaction and refraining from entering into any suspected operation.

This provision is a consequence, expressed in a negative way, of the principle of co-operation which will be dealt with in the following paragraph, as well as an exigency of the financial institutions' responsibility in order to preserve their own soundness and integrity.

(6) *Co-operation between Credit and Financial Institutions and Judicial or Law Enforcement Authorities Competent for Criminal Matters* (Article 5)

This co-operation encompasses two different obligations for credit and financial institutions and their directors and employees:

— to inform the judicial or law enforcement authorities competent for criminal matters on their own initiative, of any facts they discover which could be related to a money laundering offence;

— to furnish these authorities all information, documents or records requested on this subject.

Both obligations lie on the principle, already mentioned, that bank secrecy must be lifted in cases of Criminal Law.

The first of the above mentioned indents establishes a mandatory system of reporting suspicious transactions, involving an active co-operation of financial institutions and their directors and employees on preventing money laundering.

A special clause has been forseen in Article 5, paragraph 2 of the Directive to exempt employees and directors from responsibility by breaching restrictions on disclosure of information. This is an important provision to encourage personnel of credit and financial institutions to co-operate with the judicial authorities.

(7) *Co-operation between Financial Supervisors and Judicial or Law Enforcement Authorities Competent for Criminal Matters* (Article 6)

The supervisor's obligation to inform the judicial authorities of any facts that they discover which could constitute a criminal offence is completely coherent with the supervisor's duties of preserving the soundness and stability of the financial system.

(8) *Establishing Procedures of Internal Control and Training Programs by Credit and Financial institutions* (Article 7)

These complementary measures should play an important role, however. Since they must be according to the particular circumstances of the different institutions the Directive only enunciates them, without providing for the details. Member States shall establish the necessary guidelines in this respect.

Proposal for a

Council Directive

**on prevention of use of the financial system for
the purpose of money laundering**

THE COUNCIL OF THE EUROPEAN COMMUNITIES,

Having regard to the Treaty establishing the European Economic Community, and in particular Article 57(2), third sentence, thereof,

Having regard to the proposal from the Commission,

In co-operation with the European Parliament,

Whereas when credit and financial institutions are used to launder proceeds from criminal activities (hereinafter money laundering), the soundness and stability of the particular institution concerned and confidence in the financial system as a whole could be seriously jeopardised, thereby losing the trust of the public;

Whereas lack of Community action against money laundering could lead Member States, with the purpose of protecting their financial system, to adopt measures which could be inconsistent with the completion of the Single Market; whereas, in order to facilitate their criminal activities, launderers could try to take advantage of the freedom of capital movements and freedom to supply financial services which the integrated financial area involves, if certain co-ordinating measures are not adopted at Community level;

Whereas money laundering has an evident influence on the rise of organised crime in general and drug trafficking in particular; whereas there is more and more awareness that combating money laundering is one of the most effective means of opposing this form of criminal activity, which constitutes a particular threat to Member States' societies;

Whereas money laundering must be mainly combated by penal means and within the framework of international co-operation among judicial and law enforcement authorities, as has been undertaken, in the field of drugs, by the United Nations Convention Against Illicit Traffic in Narcotic Drugs and Psychotropic Substances, adopted on 19 December 1988 in Vienna (hereinafter the Vienna Convention);

Whereas a penal approach should, however, not be the only way to combat money laundering, since the financial system can play a highly effective role; whereas reference must be made in this context to the Recommendation of the Council of Europe of 27 June 1980 and to the Declaration of Principles adopted in December 1988 in Basle by the banking supervisory authorities of the Group of Ten, both of which constitute major steps in order to prevent the use of the financial system for purposes of money laundering;

Whereas money laundering is usually carried out in an international context so that the criminal origin of the funds can be better disguised; whereas measures exclusively adopted at a national level, without taking account of international co-ordination and co-operation, would have very limited effects;

Whereas any measures adopted by the Commission in this field should be consistent with other action undertaken in other international fora; whereas the Commission, to this end, has participated, together with fifteen Community and non-Community countries, in the important work carried out by the Financial Action Task Force on money laundering, established in July 1989 by the Paris Summit of the Seven Most Developed Countries;

Whereas the European Parliament has requested the Commission, in several resolutions, to establish a global Community programme to combat drug trafficking, including provisions on prevention of money laundering;

Whereas, in order to avoid the difficulties of establishing a generally accepted definition of money laundering it is appropriate to follow the definition adopted by the Vienna Convention; whereas, however, since the phenomenon of money laundering not only affects proceeds from drug offences, but also those from any serious crimes, this definition should be extended to include laundering of proceeds of serious criminal offences, as defined by the Member States;

Whereas making money laundering a criminal offence in the Member States, although it goes beyond the scope of the financial system, constitutes a necessary condition for any action to combat this phenomenon and in particular to permit co-operation between financial institutions or banking supervisors and judicial authorities; whereas, in this context, ratification and implementation by the Member States of the Vienna Convention is an essential measure to oppose money laundering in the field of drugs;

Whereas ensuring that credit and financial institutions require identification of their customers when entering into business relations or conducting transactions, and that they keep records of the identity documents required, are necessary to avoid launderers' taking advantage of anonymity to carry out their criminal activities; whereas such provisions must also be extended, as far as possible, to any beneficial owners;

Whereas ensuring that credit and financial institutions examine with special attention any unusual operation not having an apparent economic or lawful purpose and that they refrain from entering into any suspected money laundering transaction is necessary in order to preserve the soundness and integrity of the financial system as well as to contribute to combating this phenomenon;

Whereas preserving the financial system from money laundering is a task which can not be carried out by the judicial and law enforcement authorities without the co-operation of credit and financial institutions and their supervisory authorities; whereas banking secrecy must be lifted in criminal cases; whereas a mandatory system of reporting suspicious transactions is the most effective way to accomplish such co-operation; whereas a special protection clause is necessary to exempt employees and directors from responsibility by breaching restrictions on disclosure of information;

Whereas establishment by credit and financial institutions of procedures of internal control and training programs in this field are complementary provisions without which the other measures contained in this Directive could become ineffective;

Whereas, since money laundering can be carried out not only through credit and financial institutions but also through other types of professions and undertakings involving cash transaction business, Member States must extend, where applicable, this Directive to include these professions and undertakings;

HAS ADOPTED THIS DIRECTIVE:

Article 1

For the purpose of this Directive:

— "credit institution" is defined in accordance with the first indent of Article 1 of Council Directive 77/780/EEC;[1]

— "financial institution" means an undertaking other than a credit institution whose principal activity is to carry out one or more of the operations included in numbers 2 to 12 and 14 of the list annexed to Council Directive 89/646/EEC,[2] as well as an insurance company duly authorised according to Council Directives 73/239/EEC[3] and 79/267/EEC;[4]

— "money laundering" means:

the conversion or transfer of property, knowing that such property is derived from a serious crime, for the purpose of concealing or disguising the illicit origin of the property or of assisting any person who is involved in committing such an offence or offences to evade the legal consequences of his action, and

the concealment or disguise of the true nature, source, location, disposition, movement, rights with respect to, or ownership of property, knowing that such property is derived from a serious crime;

[1] OJ No. L322, 17.12.1977, p 30.
[2] OJ No. L386, 30.12.1989, p 1.
[3] OJ No. L228, 16.8.1973, p 3.
[4] OJ No. L63, 13.3.1979, p 1.

— "property" means assets of every kind, whether corporeal or incorporeal, movable or immovable, tangible or intangible, and legal documents or instruments evidencing title to or interest in such assets;

— "serious crime" means a crime specified in Article 3, paragraph 1(a) and (c), of the Vienna Convention, terrorism and any other serious criminal offence (including in particular organised crime), whether or not connected with drugs, as defined by the Member States;

— "competent authorities" means the national authorities empowered by law or regulation to supervise credit or financial institutions.

Article 2

Member States shall ensure that money laundering of proceeds from any serious crime is treated as a criminal offence according to their national legislation.

Article 3

Member States shall ensure that credit and financial institutions require identification of their customers when entering into business relations or conducting transactions, and in the case of doubt whether customers are acting on their own behalf, that these institutions take reasonable measures to establish the real identity of the persons on whose behalf a transaction is carried out or an account is opened. Credit and financial institutions shall keep records of the identity documents required until at least five years after relations with their clients have ended.

Article 4

Member States shall ensure that credit and financial institutions examine with special attention any unusual transaction not having an apparent economic or visible lawful purpose, and that such institutions refrain from entering into any transaction which they have reason to suspect may have any relation to money laundering.

Article 5

Member States shall ensure:

1. That credit and financial institutions and their directors and employees co-operate fully with the relevant judicial or law enforcement authorities competent for criminal matters:

— by informing these authorities, on their own initiative, of any facts they discover which could be related to a money laundering offence;

— by furnishing these authorities with all information requested in the case of any criminal inquiry or rogatory commission on money laundering carried out according to the applicable legislation.

2. That the disclosure in good faith to the relevant judicial or law enforcement authorities competent for criminal matters by any employee or director of a credit or financial institution of any suspicion or belief that an operation is aimed at or connected to money laundering, shall not constitute a breach of any restriction on disclosure of information imposed by contract or by any legislative, regulatory or administrative provision, and shall not involve for such employees and directors any civil or penal responsibility of any kind.

Article 6

Member States shall ensure that if, in the course of inspections carried out in credit or financial institutions by the competent authorities, or in any other way, these authorities discover facts that could constitute evidence of money laundering, they inform the relevant judicial or law enforcement authorities competent for criminal matters.

Article 7

Member States shall ensure:

1. That credit and financial institutions establish adequate procedures of internal control in order to prevent, detect and impede their engaging in operations related with money laundering.

2. That credit and financial institutions take the appropriate measures so that their employees are aware of the provisions contained in this Directive, and that they also establish special training programs for their employees, to help them detect operations which may be related with money laundering as well as to instruct them as to how to proceed in such cases.

Article 8

Member States shall extend the provisions of this Directive, where applicable, to professions and undertakings, other than credit and financial institutions, which because of their involvement with cash transaction business, may be particularly susceptible to being used for money laundering purposes.

Article 9

1. Member States shall take the measures necessary to comply with this Directive by 1 January 1992 at the latest.

The provisions adopted pursuant to the first subparagraph shall make express reference to this Directive.

2. Member States shall communicate to the Commission the text of the main provisions of national law which they adopt in the field governed by this Directive.

Article 10

This Directive is addressed to the Member States.

Done at Brussels   For the Council

Financial Sheet

The proposal will not give rise to any costs in the budget of the European Communities.

DOCUMENT F

Council Directive of 10 June 1991 on Prevention of the Use of the Financial System for the Purpose of Money Laundering

Source: H M Treasury, London

COUNCIL DIRECTIVE

of **1 0. VI. 1991**

[COUNCIL DIRECTIVE 91/308/EEC]

on prevention of the use of the

financial system for the purpose of money laundering

THE COUNCIL OF THE EUROPEAN COMMUNITIES,

Having regard to the Treaty establishing the European Economic Community, and in particular Article 57(2), first and third sentences, and Article 100a thereof,

Having regard to the proposal from the Commission [1],

In co-operation with the European Parliament [2],

Having regard to the Opinion of the Economic and Social Committee [3],

---

(1) OJ No C 106, 28. 4.1990, p. 6 and
    OJ No C 319, 19.12.1990, p. 9.
(2) OJ No C 324, 24.12.1990, p. 264 and Decision of 17 April 1991 (not yet
    published in the Official Journal).
(3) OJ No C 332, 31.12.1990, p. 86.

Whereas when credit and financial institutions are used to launder proceeds from criminal activities (hereinafter referred to as "money laundering"), the soundness and stability of the institution concerned and confidence in the financial system as a whole could be seriously jeopardized, thereby losing the trust of the public;

Whereas lack of Community action against money laundering could lead Member States, for the purpose of protecting their financial systems, to adopt measures which could be inconsistent with completion of the single market; whereas, in order to facilitate their criminal activities, launderers could try to take advantage of the freedom of capital movement and freedom to supply financial services which the integrated financial area involves, if certain co-ordinating measures are not adopted at Community level;

Whereas money laundering has an evident influence on the rise of organized crime in general and drug trafficking in particular; whereas there is more and more awareness that combating money laundering is one of the most effective means of opposing this form of criminal activity, which constitutes a particular threat to Member States' societies;

Whereas money laundering must be combated mainly by penal means and within the framework of international co-operation among judicial and law enforcement authorities, as has been undertaken, in the field of drugs, by the United Nations Convention Against Illicit Traffic in Narcotic Drugs and Psychotropic Substances, adopted on 19 December 1988 in Vienna (hereinafter referred to as the "Vienna Convention") and more generally in relation to all criminal activities, by the Council of Europe Convention on laundering, tracing, seizure and confiscation of proceeds of crime, opened for signature on 8 November 1990 in Strasbourg;

Whereas a penal approach should, however, not be the only way to combat money laundering, since the financial system can play a highly effective role; whereas reference must be made in this context to the Recommendation of the Council of Europe of 27 June 1980 and to the Declaration of Principles adopted in December 1988 in Basle by the banking supervisory authorities of the Group of Ten, both of which constitute major steps towards preventing the use of the financial system for money laundering;

Whereas money laundering is usually carried out in an international context so
that the criminal origin of the funds can be better disguised; whereas measures
exclusively adopted at a national level, without taking account of international
co-ordination and co-operation, would have very limited effects;

Whereas any measures adopted by the Community in this field should be consistent
with other action undertaken in other international fora; whereas in this respect
any Community action should take particular account of the recommendations
adopted by the Financial Action Task Force on money laundering, set up in
July 1989 by the Paris Summit of the Seven Most Developed Countries;

Whereas the European Parliament has requested, in several Resolutions, the
establishment of a global Community programme to combat drug trafficking,
including provisions on prevention of money laundering;

Whereas for the purposes of this Directive the definition of money laundering is
taken from that adopted in the Vienna Convention; whereas, however, since money
laundering occurs not only in relation to the proceeds of drug-related offences
but also in relation to the proceeds of other criminal activities (such as
organized crime and terrorism), the Member States should, within the meaning of
their legislation, extend the effects of the Directive to include the proceeds of
such activities, to the extent that they are likely to result in laundering
operations justifying sanctions on that basis;

Whereas prohibition of money laundering in Member States' legislation backed by
appropriate measures and penalties is a necessary condition for combating this
phenomenon;

Whereas ensuring that credit and financial institutions require identification of
their customers when entering into business relations or conducting transactions,
exceeding certain thresholds, are necessary to avoid launderers' taking advantage
of anonymity to carry out their criminal activities; whereas such provisions must
also be extended, as far as possible, to any beneficial owners;

Whereas credit and financial institutions must keep for at least five years copies or references of the identification documents required as well as supporting evidence and records consisting of documents relating to transactions or copies thereof similarly admissible in court proceedings under the applicable national legislation for use as evidence in any investigation into money laundering;

Whereas ensuring that credit and financial institutions examine with special attention any transaction which they regard as particularly likely, by its nature, to be related to money laundering is necessary in order to preserve the soundness and integrity of the financial system as well as to contribute to combating this phenomenon; whereas to this end they should pay special attention to transactions with third countries which do not apply comparable standards against money laundering to those established by the Community or to other equivalent standards set out by international fora and endorsed by the Community;

Whereas, for those purposes, Member States may ask credit and financial institutions to record in writing the results of the examination they are required to carry out and to ensure that those results are available to the authorities responsible for efforts to eliminate money laundering;

Whereas preventing the financial system from being used for money laundering is a task which cannot be carried out by the authorities responsible for combating this phenomenon without the co-operation of credit and financial institutions and their supervisory authorities; whereas banking secrecy must be lifted in such cases; whereas a mandatory system of reporting suspicious transactions which ensures that information is transmitted to the abovementioned authorities without alerting the customers concerned, is the most effective way to accomplish such co-operation; whereas a special protection clause is necessary to exempt credit and financial institutions, their employees and their directors from responsibility for breaching restrictions on disclosure of information;

Whereas the information received by the authorities pursuant to this Directive may be used only in connection with combating money laundering; whereas Member States may nevertheless provide that this information may be used for other purposes;

Whereas establishment by credit and financial institutions of procedures of internal control and training programmes in this field are complementary provisions without which the other measures contained in this Directive could become ineffective;

Whereas, since money laundering can be carried out not only through credit and financial institutions but also through other types of professions and categories of undertakings, Member States must extend the provisions of this Directive in whole or in part, to include those professions and undertakings whose activities are particularly likely to be used for money laundering purposes;

Whereas it is important that the Member States should take particular care to ensure that co-ordinated action is taken in the Community where there are strong grounds for believing that professions or activities the conditions governing the purusit of which have been harmonized at Community level are being used for laundering money;

Whereas the effectiveness of efforts to eliminate money laundering is particularly dependent on the close co-ordination and harmonization of national implementing measures; whereas such co-ordination and harmonization which is being carried out in various international bodies requires, in the Community context, co-operation between Member States and the Commission in the framework of a Contact Committee;

Whereas it is for each Member State to adopt appropriate measures and to penalize infringement of such measures in an appropriate manner to ensure full application of this Directive,

HAS ADOPTED THIS DIRECTIVE:

Article 1

For the purpose of this Directive:

- "credit institution" means a credit institution, as defined as in the first indent of Article 1 of Directive 77/780/EEC [1], as last amended by Directive 89/646/EEC [2] and includes branches within the meaning of the third indent of that Article and located in the Community, of credit institutions having their head offices outside the Community;

- "financial institution" means an undertaking other than a credit institution whose principal activity is to carry out one or more of the operations included

---

(1) OJ No L 322, 17.12.1977, p. 30
[Directive 77/780/EEC provides:

Article 1

For the purposes of this Directive:
– 'credit institution' means an undertaking whose business is to receive deposits or other repayable funds from the public and to grant credits for its own account, ...]

(2) OJ No L 386, 30.12.1989, p. 1.
[This directive adopts without change the definition in Directive 77/780. However, the directive contains a number of substantive provisions relating to credit institutions generally. These are not reproduced here.]

in numbers 2 to 12 and number 14 of the list annexed to Directive 89/646/EEC,[*]

or an insurance company duly authorized in accordance with

Directive 79/267/EEC [1] as last amended by Directive 90/619/EEC [2], insofar

---

[* Directive 89/646/EEC provides:

ANNEX
LIST OF ACTIVITIES SUBJECT TO MUTUAL RECOGNITION

1. Acceptance of deposits and other repayable funds from the public.   2. Lending([1]).
3. Financial leasing.   4. Money transmission services.
5. Issuing and administering means of payment (e.g. credit cards, travellers' cheques and bankers' drafts).
6. Guarantees and commitments.
7. Trading for own account or for account of customers in:
   (a) money market instruments (cheques, bills, CDs, etc.);   (b) foreign exchange;
   (c) financial futures and options;   (d) exchange and interest rate instruments;   (e) transferable securities.
8. Participation in share issues and the provision of services related to such issues.
9. Advice to undertakings on capital structure, industrial strategy and related questions and advice and services relating to mergers and the purchase of undertakings.
10. Money broking.   11. Portfolio management and advice.
12. Safekeeping and administration of securities.   13. Credit reference services.
14. Safe custody services.

([1]) Including *inter alia:*
   – consumer credit,
   – mortgage credit,
   – factoring, with or without recourse,
   – financing of commercial transactions (including forfaiting).

(1)OJ No L 63, 13.3.1979, p. 1.
   [Directive 79/267/EEC provides:

Article 6

1. Each Member State shall make the taking up of the activities referred to in this Directive in its territory subject to an official authorization.

2. Such authorization shall be sought from the competent authority of the Member State in question by:
   (a) any undertaking which establishes its head office in the territory of such State;
   (b) any undertaking whose head office is situated in another Member State and which opens an agency or branch in the territory of the Member State in question;
   (c) any undertaking which, having received the authorization required under (a) or (b) above, extends its business in the territory of such State to other classes;
   (d) any undertaking which, having obtained, in accordance with Article 7 (1), an authorization for a part of the national territory, extends its activity beyond such part.

3. Member States shall not make authorization subject to the lodging of a deposit or the provision of security.

Article 7

1. An authorization shall be valid for the entire national territory unless, and in so far as national laws permit, the applicant seeks permission to carry on his business only in a part of the national territory.

2. Authorization shall be given for a particular class of insurance. The classification by class appears in the Annex. Authorization shall cover the entire class unless the applicant wishes to cover only part of the risks pertaining to such class.

The supervisory authorities may restrict an authorization requested for one of the classes to the operations set out in the scheme of operations referred to in Articles 9 and 11.

3. Each Member State may grant an authorization for two or more of the classes, where its national laws permit such classes to be carried on simultaneously.

(2) OJ No L 330, 29.11.1990, p. 50.
   [This directive contains no provision affecting the provisions on authorization in Directive 79/267.]

as it carries out activities covered by that Directive; this definition
includes branches located in the Community of financial institutions whose head
offices are outside the Community;

- "money laundering" means the following conduct when committed intentionally:

  . the conversion or transfer of property, knowing that such property is derived
    from criminal activity or from an act of participation in such activity, for
    the purpose of concealing or disguising the illicit origin of the property or
    of assisting any person who is involved in the commission of such activity to
    evade the legal consequences of his action;

  . the concealment or disguise of the true nature, source, location,
    disposition, movement, rights with respect to, or ownership of property,
    knowing that such property is derived from criminal activity or from an act
    of participation in such activity;

  . the acquisition, possession or use of property, knowing, at the time of
    receipt, that such property was derived from criminal activity or from an act
    of participation in such activity;

  . participation in, association to commit, attempts to commit and aiding,
    abetting, facilitating and counselling the commission of any of the actions
    mentioned in the foregoing paragraphs.

Knowledge, intent or purpose required as an element of the abovementioned
activities, may be inferred from objective factual circumstances.

Money laundering shall be regarded as such even where the activities which
generated the property to be laundered were perpetrated in the territory of
another Member State or in that of a third country.

- "property" means assets of every kind, whether corporeal or incorporeal, movable or immovable, tangible or intangible, and legal documents or instruments evidencing title to or interests in such assets;

- "criminal activity" means a crime specified in Article 3(1)(a) of the Vienna Convention and any other criminal activity designated as such for the purposes of this Directive by each Member State;

- "competent authorities" means the national authorities empowered by law or regulation to supervise credit or financial institutions.

<u>Article 2</u>

Member States shall ensure that money laundering as defined in this Directive is prohibited.

<u>Article 3</u>

1.   Member States shall ensure that credit and financial institutions require identification of their customers by means of supporting evidence when entering into business relations, particularly when opening an account or savings accounts, or when offering safe custody facilities.

2.   The identification requirement shall also apply for any transaction with customers other than those referred to in paragraph 1, involving a sum amounting to ECU 15 000 or more, whether the transaction is carried out in a single operation or in several operations which seem to be linked. Where the sum is not known at the time when the transaction is undertaken, the institution concerned shall proceed with identification as soon as it is apprised of the sum and establishes that the threshold has been reached.

3. By way of derogation from paragraphs 1 and 2, the identification requirements with regard to insurance policies written by insurance undertakings within the meaning of Directive 79/267/EEC, where they perform activities which fall within the scope of that Directive shall not be required where the periodic premium amount or amounts to be paid in any given year does or do not exceed ECU 1 000 or where a single premium is paid amounting to ECU 2 500 or less. If the periodic premium amount or amounts to be paid in any given year is or are increased so as to exceed the ECU 1 000 threshold, identification shall be required.

4. Member States may provide that the identification requirement is not compulsory for insurance policies in respect of pension schemes taken out by virtue of a contract of employment or the insured's occupation, provided that such policies contain no surrender clause and may not be used as collateral for a loan.

5. In the event of doubt as to whether the customers referred to in the above paragraphs are acting on their own behalf, or where it is certain that they are not acting on their own behalf, the credit and financial institutions shall take reasonable measures to obtain information as to the real identity of the persons on whose behalf those customers are acting.

6. Credit and financial institutions shall carry out such identification, even where the amount of the transaction is lower than the thresholds laid down, wherever there is suspicion of money laundering.

7. Credit and financial institutions shall not be subject to the identification requirements provided for in this Article where the customer is also a credit or financial institution covered by this Directive.

8. Member States may provide that the identification requirements regarding transactions referred to in paragraphs 3 and 4 are fulfilled when it is established that the payment of the transaction is to be debited to an account opened in the customer's name with a credit institution subject to this Directive according to the requirements of paragraph 1.

Article 4

Member States shall ensure that credit and financial institutions keep the following for use as evidence in any investigation into money laundering:

- in the case of identification, a copy or the references of the evidence required, for a period of at least five years after the relationship with their customer has ended;

- in the case of transactions, the supporting evidence and records, consisting of the original documents or copies admissible in court proceedings under the applicable national legislation for a period of at least five years following execution of the transactions.

Article 5

Member States shall ensure that credit and financial institutions examine with special attention any transaction which they regard as particularly likely, by its nature, to be related to money laundering.

Article 6

Member States shall ensure that credit and financial institutions and their directors and employees co-operate fully with the authorities responsible for combating money laundering:

- by informing those authorities, on their own initiative, of any fact which might be an indication of money laundering;

- by furnishing those authorities, at their request, with all necessary information, in accordance with the procedures established by the applicable legislation.

The information referred to in the first paragraph shall be forwarded to the authorities responsible for combating money laundering of the Member State in whose territory the institution forwarding the information is situated. The person or persons designated by the credit and financial institutions in accordance with the procedures provided for in Article 11(1) shall normally forward the information.

Information supplied to the authorities in accordance with the first paragraph may be used only in connection with the combating of money laundering. However, Member States may provide that such information may also be used for other purposes.

Article 7

Member States shall ensure that credit and financial institutions refrain from carrying out transactions which they know or suspect to be related to money laundering until they have apprised the authorities referred to in Article 6. Those authorities may, under conditions determined by their national legislation, give instructions not to execute the operation. Where such a transaction is suspected of giving rise to money laundering and where to refrain in such manner is impossible or is likely to frustrate efforts to pursue the beneficiaries of a suspected money-laundering operation, the institutions concerned shall apprise the authorities immediately afterwards.

Article 8

Credit and financial institutions and their directors and employees shall not disclose to the customer concerned nor to other third persons that information has been transmitted to the authorities in accordance with Article 6 and 7 or that a money laundering investigation is being carried out.

Article 9

The disclosure in good faith to the authorities responsible for combating money laundering by an employee or director of a credit or financial institution of the information referred to in Article 6 and 7 shall not constitute a breach of any restriction on disclosure of information imposed by contract or by any legislative, regulatory or administrative provision, and shall not involve the credit or financial institution, its directors or employees in liability of any kind.

Article 10

Member States shall ensure that if, in the course of inspections carried out in credit or financial institutions by the competent authorities, or in any other way, those authorities discover facts that could constitute evidence of money laundering, they inform the authorities responsible for combating money laundering.

Article 11

Member States shall ensure that credit and financial institutions:

1) establish adequate procedures of internal control and communication in order to forestall and prevent operations related to money laundering;

2) take appropriate measures so that their employees are aware of the provisions contained in this Directive. These measures shall include participation of their relevant employees in special training programmes to help them recognize operations which may be related to money laundering as well as to instruct them as to how to proceed in such cases.

Article 12

Member States shall ensure that the provisions of this Directive are extended in whole or in part to professions and to categories of undertakings, other than the credit and financial institutions referred to in Article 1, which engage in activities which are particularly likely to be used for money-laundering purposes.

Article 13

1. A Contact Committee (hereinafter referred to as "the Committee") shall be set up under the aegis of the Commission. Its function shall be:

(a) without prejudice to Articles 169 and 170 of the Treaty, to facilitate harmonized implementation of this Directive through regular consultation on any practical problems arising from its application and on which exchanges of view are deemed useful;

(b) to facilitate consultation between the Member States on the more stringent or additional conditions and obligations which they may lay down at national level;

(c) to advise the Commission, if necessary, on any supplements or amendments to be made to this Directive or on any adjustments deemed necessary, in particular to harmonize the effects of Article 12.

(d) to examine whether a profession or a category of undertaking should be included in the scope of Article 12 where it has been established that such profession or category of undertaking has been used in a Member State for money-laundering.

2. It shall not be the function of the Committee to appraise the merits of decisions taken by the competent authorities in individual cases.

3. The Committee shall be composed of persons appointed by the Member States and of representatives of the Commission. The secretariat shall be provided by the Commission. The Chairman shall be a representative of the Commission. It shall be convened by its Chairman, either on his own initiative or at the request of the delegation of a Member State.

Article 14

Each Member State shall take appropriate measures to ensure full application of all the provisions of this Directive and shall in particular determine the penalties to be applied for infringement of the measures adopted pursuant to this Directive.

Article 15

The Member States may adopt or retain in force stricter provisions in the field covered by this Directive to prevent money laundering.

Article 16

1.   Member States shall bring into force the laws, regulations and administrative decisions necessary to comply with this Directive before 1 January 1993 at the latest.

2.   Where Member States adopt these measures, they shall contain a reference to this Directive or shall be accompanied by such reference on the occasion of their official publication.   The methods of making such a reference shall be laid down by the Member States.

3.   Member States shall communicate to the Commission the text of the main provisions of national law which they adopt in the field governed by this Directive.

Article 17

One year after 1 January 1993, whenever necessary and at least at three yearly intervals thereafter, the Commission shall draw up a report on the implementation of this Directive and submit it to the European Parliament and the Council.

Article 18

This Directive is addressed to the Member States.

Done at Luxembourg, **10. VI. 1991**

For the Council
The President

(s.) **J.-C. JUNCKER**

Certified true copy
For the Secretary-General

Director-General

EUROPEAN COMMUNITIES
THE COUNCIL

Brussels, 7 June 1991

6467/91
COR 1 (en)

RESTREINT

EF   39
ECOFIN   46
CELAD   55

CORRIGENDUM

Subject: Council Directive on prevention of the use of the financial system for the purpose of money laundering

Page 12, Article 3(8), line 3

For : "that the payment of the transaction is to be debited to an account..."

Read: "that the payment for the transaction is to be debited from an account .."

DOCUMENT G

Statement by the Representatives of the Governments of the Member States of the European Communities Meeting within the Council Concerning the Council Directive of 10 June 1991

Source: Official Journal of the European Communities, No L 166/83

The representatives of the Governments of the Member States, meeting within the Council,

Recalling that the Member States signed the United Nations Convention against illicit traffic in narcotic drugs and psychotropic substances, adopted on 19 December 1988 in Vienna ;

Recalling also that most Member States have already signed the Council of Europe Convention on laundering, tracing, seizure and confiscation of proceeds of crime on 8 November 1990 in Strasbourg ;

Conscious of the fact that the description of money laundering contained in Article 1 of Council Directive 91/308/EEC   derives its wording from the relevant provisions of the aforementioned Conventions ;

Hereby undertake to take all necessary steps by 31 December 1992 at the latest to enact criminal legislation enabling them to comply with their obligations under the aforementioned instruments.

CHAPTER V

OTHER INITIATIVES AND DEVELOPMENTS

DOCUMENT A

Inter-American Program of Action of Rio de Janeiro
Against the Illicit Use and Production of Narcotic Drugs
and Psychotropic Substances and Traffic Therein
April 1986 (extracts)
Source: Organization of American States, Washington, D.C.

CHAPTER II

The Conference also recommends to the OAS member states the following actions to combat the unlawful production and supplying of narcotic drugs and psychotropic substances:

1. The development and expansion of mechanisms for an exchange of information on the structures of illegal marketing and any other aspects of unlawful trafficking in drugs among affected nations;

2. The study - and possible approval - of draft legislation designed:

   i) to strengthen the ability of appropriate agencies to investigate and prosecute unlawful drug trafficking, including their ability to trace the origin of monies deposited in or transferred among financial and other business institutions by drug traffickers;

   ii) to forfeit assets derived from or used to facilitate drug trafficking, irrespective of where such trafficking occurred; and

   iii) to treat as a punishable offense the acquisition, possession, use, or so-called laundering of assets that are known to be directly or indirectly the proceeds of unlawful drug trafficking, irrespective of where such trafficking occurred, and to enable such assets to be forfeited.

CHAPTER IV

To help the member states implement the actions and institute the measures set forth in Chapters I, II, and III through regional cooperation, the Conference recommends:

1. To the General Assembly of the OAS
    a) That it establish an Inter-American Drug Control Commission (CICAD) composed of representatives of member states. That Commission would be responsible for developing, coordinating, evaluating, and monitoring the measures prescribed in this Program of Action and for submitting proposals for increasing the effectiveness of drug abuse prevention and of the campaign against trafficking in narcotic drugs and psychotropic substances in the region; and

2. To the Inter-American Juridical Committee

That it conduct juridical research to help the member states explore the advisability of:
    a) Adopting specific bilateral or multilateral instruments on particular aspects of drug abuse and unlawful trafficking in drugs, including mechanisms for extradition and for cooperation among judicial, police, and customs authorities of the member states, leading to more effective action against all drug traffickers;

    b) Seeking to harmonize national laws on trafficking;

    c) Coordinating at the national level judicial, police, and customs procedures with respect to unlawful trafficking; and

    d) Promoting regional cooperation in the judicial, police, and customs areas with respect to unlawful trafficking.

DOCUMENT B

Basle Committee on Banking Regulations and Supervisory Practices
December 1988 Statement on Prevention of Criminal Use of the Banking System for the Purpose of Money-Laundering
Source: Commonwealth Secretariat, London

Preamble

1.   Banks and other financial institutions may be unwittingly used as intermediaries for the transfer or deposit of funds derived from criminal activity.   Criminals and their associates use the financial system to make payments and transfers of funds from one account to another; to hide the source and beneficial ownership of money; and to provide storage for bank-notes through a safe-deposit facility.   These activities are commonly referred to as money-laundering.

2.   Efforts undertaken hitherto with the objective of preventing the banking system from being used in this way have largely been undertaken by judicial and regulatory agencies at national level. However, the increasing international dimension of organised criminal activity, notably in relation to the narcotics trade, has prompted collaborative initiatives at the international level.   One of the earliest such initiatives was undertaken by the Committee of Ministers of the Council of Europe in June 1980. In its report[1] the Committee of Ministers concluded that "... the banking system can play a highly effective preventive role while the co-operation of the banks also assists in the repression of such criminal acts by the judicial authorities and the police". In recent years the issue of how to prevent criminals laundering the proceeds of crime through the financial system has attracted increasing attention from legislative authorities, law enforcement agencies and banking supervisors in a number of countries.

----

1.   Measures against the transfer and safeguarding of funds of criminal origin.   Recommendation No. R(80)10 adopted by the Committee of Ministers of the Council of Europe on 27th June 1980.

3.   The various national banking supervisory authorities represented on the Basle Committee on Banking Regulations and Supervisory Practices[1] do not have the same roles and responsibilities
in relation to the suppression of money-laundering. In some
countries supervisors have a specific responsibility in this
field; in others they may have no direct responsibility. This
reflects the role of banking supervision, the primary function of
which is to maintain the overall financial stability and soundness of banks rather than to ensure that individual transactions
conducted by bank customers are legitimate. Nevertheless, despite the limits in some countries on their specific responsibility, all members of the Committee firmly believe that supervisors
cannot be indifferent to the use made of banks by criminals.

4.   Public confidence in banks, and hence their stability, can
be undermined by adverse publicity as a result of inadvertent
association by banks with criminals. In addition, banks may lay
themselves open to direct losses from fraud, either through
negligence in screening undesirable customers or where the integrity of their own officers has been undermined through association with criminals. For these reasons the members of the Basle
Committee consider that banking supervisors have a general role
to encourage ethical standards of professional conduct among
banks and other financial institutions.

5.   The Committee believes that one way to promote this objective, consistent with differences in national supervisory practice, is to obtain international agreement to a Statement of
Principles to which financial institutions should be expected to
adhere.

----

1.   The Committee comprises representatives of the central banks
      and supervisory authorities of the Group of Ten countries
      (Belgium, Canada, France, Germany, Italy, Japan, Nether-
      lands, Sweden, Switzerland, United Kingdom, United States)
      and Luxembourg.

6.   The attached Statement is a general statement of ethical principles which encourages banks' management to put in place effective procedures to ensure that all persons conducting business with their institutions are properly identified; that transactions that do not appear legitimate are discouraged; and that co-operation with law enforcement agencies is achieved.   The Statement is not a legal document and its implementation will depend on national practice and law.   In particular, it should be noted that in some countries banks may be subject to additional more stringent legal regulations in this field and the Statement is not intended to replace or diminish those requirements. Whatever the legal position in different countries, the Committee considers that the **first** and most important safeguard against money-laundering is the integrity of banks' own managements and their vigilant determination to prevent their institutions becoming associated with criminals or being used as a channel for money-laundering.   The Statement is intended to reinforce those standards of conduct.

7.   The supervisory authorities represented on the Committee support the principles set out in the Statement.   To the extent that these matters fall within the competence of supervisory authorities in different member countries, the authorities will recommend and encourage all banks to adopt policies and practices consistent with the Statement.   With a view to its acceptance worldwide, the Committee would also commend the Statement to supervisory authorities in other countries.

Basle, December 1988

Statement of Principles

I.   Purpose

Banks and other financial institutions may unwittingly be used as intermediaries for the transfer or deposit of money derived from criminal activity.   The intention behind such transactions is often to hide the beneficial ownership of funds.   The use of the financial system in this way is of direct concern to police and other law enforcement agencies; it is also a matter of concern to banking supervisors and banks' managements, since public confidence in banks may be undermined through their association with criminals.

This Statement of Principles is intended to outline some basic policies and procedures that banks' managements should ensure are in place within their institutions with a view to assisting in the suppression of money-laundering through the banking system, national and international. The Statement thus sets out to reinforce existing best practices among banks and, specifically, to encourage vigilance against criminal use of the payments system, implementation by banks of effective preventive safeguards, and co-operation with law enforcement agencies.

II. Customer identification

With a view to ensuring that the financial system is not used as a channel for criminal funds, banks should make reasonable efforts to determine the true identity of all customers requesting the institution's services. Particular care should be taken to identify the ownership of all accounts and those using safe-custody facilities. All banks should institute effective procedures for obtaining identification from new customers. It should be an explicit policy that significant business transactions will not be conducted with customers who fail to provide evidence of their identity.

III. Compliance with laws

Banks' management should ensure that business is conducted in conformity with high ethical standards and that laws and regulations pertaining to financial transactions are adhered to. As regards transactions executed on behalf of customers, it is accepted that banks may have no means of knowing whether the transaction stems from or forms part of criminal activity. Similarly, in an international context it may be difficult to ensure that cross-border transactions on behalf of customers are in compliance with the regulations of another country. Nevertheless, banks should not set out to offer services or provide active assistance in transactions which they have good reason to suppose are associated with money-laundering activities.

IV. Co-operation with law enforcement authorities

Banks should co-operate fully with national law enforcement authorities to the extent permitted by specific local regulations relating to customer confidentiality. Care should be taken to avoid providing support or assistance to customers seeking to deceive law enforcement agencies through the provision of altered, incomplete or misleading information. Where banks become aware of facts which lead to the reasonable presumption that money held on deposit derives from criminal activity or that transactions entered into are themselves criminal in purpose, appropriate measures, consistent with the law, should be taken, for example, to deny assistance, sever relations with the customer and close or freeze accounts.

V.   Adherence to the Statement

All banks should formally adopt policies consistent with the principles set out in this Statement and should ensure that all members of their staff concerned, wherever located, are informed of the bank's policy in this regard. Attention should be given to staff training in matters covered by the Statement. To promote adherence to these principles, banks should implement specific procedures for customer identification and for retaining internal records of transactions. Arrangements for internal audit may need to be extended in order to establish an effective means of testing for general compliance with the Statement.

DOCUMENT C

ICPO - Interpol General Assembly Resolution on Money Laundering and Related Matters, November 1989

Source: ICPO - Interpol, Lyon

AGN/58/RES/4

RESOLUTION

Subject: FOPAC* Working Group

WHEREAS the ICPO—Interpol General Assembly, meeting in Bangkok from 17th to 23rd November 1988, recognized that the ICPO—Interpol must continue to support law enforcement efforts and intensify co-operation between countries and their respective law enforcement authorities to combat narcotics traffickers and other criminals and their money-laundering activities, decided to transform the FOPAC Working Group into a world—wide group to:

A. STUDY existing, and develop new, mechanisms for the gathering of financial information connected with, arising from, related to or resulting from narcotics transactions and other crimes,

B. DEVELOP proposals for the sharing of the above-described information between countries for the use by, among others, their respective law enforcement authorities, and,

C. DEVELOP a proposal and implementation plan for creating, within an appropriate international body, a clearing—house for the receipt, co-ordination and execution of requests for the above—described information,

RECOGNIZING the utility of financial information to the successful prosecution of money launderers and traffickers in illicit narcotic drugs and psychotropic substances and other criminals and the forfeiture of assets acquired directly or indirectly through the use of proceeds from such trafficking and other crimes,

The ICPO—Interpol General Assembly, meeting in Lyons from 27th November to 1st December 1989 at its 58th session:

RECOMMENDS that national administrations:

A. Take measures to record and, where appropriate, report financial information connected with, arising from, related to or resulting from narcotics transactions and other crimes, including suspicious and large currency transactions and large currency exchanges involving domestic and/or foreign currency;

---

* FOPAC (Fonds Provenant d'Activités Criminelles): Interpol working groups formed to develop programs and to monitor investigations involving the movement of funds associated with international criminal activity.

B. Contribute the above-described financial information to an
    Interpol data base and/or create their own data base for
    the above-described financial information and provide such
    information as permitted by the member country's laws;

C. Agree that these data bases may include information iden-
    tifying:

    (1) persons conducting large currency transactions and
         exchanges,

    (2) the individuals or organizations for whom such tran-
         sactions and exchanges are conducted,

    (3) the account(s) affected by such transactions and
         exchanges, and,

    (4) when appropriate, the amount seized and confiscated;

D. Agree that countries that have their own data bases may
    share information from the data bases directly with other
    countries or through the Interpol General Secretariat.
    Countries that elect to participate shall so advise the
    Interpol General Secretariat and specify the contents and
    form of any request for information from their data bases.
    Upon receipt of a request for information, the Interpol
    General Secretariat will forward the request to such par-
    ticipating countries which may either respond directly to
    the requesting country or respond through the Interpol
    General Secretariat;

E. Agree that information contained in the Interpol General
    Secretariat data base shall be protected in accordance
    with established guidelines which shall provide for three
    different levels (Tiers One, Two and Three) of controlled
    dissemination. Countries contributing information to the
    Interpol General Secretariat data base shall specify which
    guidelines are to be applied in releasing such information
    as they may have contributed. Countries contributing
    information to the Interpol General Secretariat data base
    may specify any one or more of the following tiers of
    controlled dissemination:

    Tier One: Tier One shall contain information from coun-
    tries which provide the Interpol General Secretariat data
    base with all or some of the recorded details from their
    financial records and which impose no restrictions on the
    dissemination of this information to requesting countries.
    The Interpol General Secretariat will disseminate Tier One
    information directly to requesting countries;

    Tier Two: Tier Two shall contain information identifying
    individuals for whom contributing countries hold financial
    records. Upon receipt of a request for information, the
    Interpol General Secretariat will alert the requesting
    country as to which member countries hold information
    relevant to the request. The member country holding re-
    cords will be notified of the request, by the Interpol
    General Secretariat, and will be expected to respond di-
    rectly to the requesting country;

Tier Three: Tier Three shall contain information contri-
buted by those countries requiring the greatest degree of
controlled access to financial records. Information contained in Tier Three shall identify individuals for whom
contributing countries hold financial records.   Upon receipt of a request for information, the Interpol General
Secretariat will alert the country holding relevant records of the request and of the identity of the requesting
country. The country holding records may transmit records
directly to the requesting country, provide no response,
or transmit a notice of "records not available" through
Interpol General Secretariat if records are not available
or may not be released for reasons of law and/or policy;

F.   Agree that the above-described financial information may
     be made available for law enforcement purposes when pro-
     perly requested by another member country through estab-
     lished Interpol or diplomatic channels;

G.   Agree that requests for financial information contained in
     the Interpol General Secretariat's data base shall: iden-
     tify the requesting authority; specify the charges or
     violations of law being prosecuted or under investigation;
     briefly summarize the facts of the case under investiga-
     tion or prosecution; state the specific purpose for and
     intended use of the requested information; and provide
     data identifying the individual and institutions about
     whom information is requested;

H.   Agree that implementation of the above-described measures
     shall not abrogate any of the responsibilities assumed by
     parties to the United Nations Convention Against Illicit
     Traffic in Narcotic Drugs and Psychotropic Substances
     adopted on 19th December 1988, in Vienna, Austria;

I.   Agree that Tiers One and Two can be in operation as soon
     as the mechanism is put into place to store and transmit
     such information. It is noted that Tier One and Tier Two
     information guidelines conform to Article 7 of the Rules
     on International Police Co-operation. As Tier Three may
     not conform to these guidelines, the General Secretariat
     will explore ways to remedy this and will determine how
     Tier Three can be implemented.

                         Adopted with 92 votes in favour,
                         none against and 6 abstentions.

DOCUMENT D

Declaration of Cartagena
15 February, 1990 (extracts)
Source: Foreign and Commonwealth Office, London

The Presidents of Bolivia, Colombia, the United States of America and Peru, met in Cartagena de Indias, Colombia on the fifteenth day of February one thousand nine hundred and ninety and issued the following

DECLARATION OF CARTAGENA

The Parties consider that a strategy which commits the Parties to implement or strengthen a comprehensive, intensified anti-narcotics program must address the issues of demand reduction, consumption and supply. Such a strategy also must include understandings regarding economic cooperation, alternative development, encouragement of trade and investment, as well as understandings on attacking the traffic in illicit drugs, and on diplomatic and public diplomacy initiatives.

The Parties recognize that these areas are inter-connected and self-reinforcing. Progress in one area will help achieve progress in others. Failure in any of them will jeopardize progress in the others. The order in which they are addressed in the document is not meant to assign to them any particular priority.

Economic cooperation and international initiatives cannot be effective unless there are concomitant, dynamic programs attaching the production of, trafficking in and demand for illicit drugs. It is clear that to be fully effective, supply reduction efforts must be accompanied by significant reduction in demand. The Parties recognize that the exchange of information on demand control programs will benefit their countries.

The Parties recognize that the nature and impact of the traffic in and interdiction of illicit drugs varies in each of the three Andean countries and cannot be addressed fully in this document. The Parties will negotiate bilateral and multilateral agreements, consistent with their anti-narcotics efforts, specifying their responsibilities and commitments with regard to economic cooperation and intensified enforcement actions.

CONTROL OF FINANCIAL ASSETS

The Parties agree to identify, trace, freeze, seize, and apply other legal procedures for the disposition of drug crime proceeds in their respective countries, and to attack financial aspects of the illicit drug trade. In accordance with their respective laws, each of the Parties will seek to adopt measures to define, categorize, and criminalize money laundering, as well as to increase efforts to implement current legislation. The Parties agree to establish formulas providing exceptions to banking secrecy.

FORFEITURE AND SHARING OF ILLEGAL DRUG PROCEEDS

The Parties pledge to implement a system for forfeiture and sharing of illegal drug profits and assets, and to establish effective programs in this area.

In United States cases related to forfeiture of property of illegal drug traffickers where Bolivia, Colombia, and Peru provide assistance to the United States Government, the Government of the United States pledges to transfer to the assisting government such forfeited property, to the extent consistent with United States' laws and regulations. The Parties will also seek asset sharing agreements for Bolivia, Colombia, and Peru, with other countries.

10. LEGAL COOPERATION

The Parties pledge to cooperate in the sharing of instrumental evidence in forms admissible by their judicial proceedings.

The Parties also agree to seek mechanisms that permit the exchange of information on legislation and judicial

decisions in order to optimize legal proceedings against the traffic in illicit drugs.

The Parties recognize the value of international cooperation in strengthening the administration of justice, including the protection of judges, judicial personnel, and other individuals who take part in these proceedings.

ECONOMIC SUMMIT

The 1989 Economic Summit in Paris established a Financial Action Task Force to determine how governments could promote cooperation and effective action against the laundering of money gained through illegal drug trafficking.

The United States will host the next Economic Summit on July 9-11, 1990, in Houston. The United States will use this opportunity to seek full attention on a priority basis to the fight against illegal drug trafficking.

The Parties call upon the Economic Summit member countries, and on the other participants in the Financial Action Task Force, to give greater emphasis to the study of economic measures which may help to reduce drug trafficking. In particular, the Parties call upon the Economic Summit countries to take the steps necessary to ensure that assets seized from illicit drug trafficking in Bolivia, Colombia and Peru are used to finance programs or interdiction, alternative development and prevention in our countries.

REPORT TO THE OAS MEETING OF MINISTERS AND CICAD

The Organization of American States has called an Inter-American meeting of Ministers responsible for national narcotics programs, to be held on April 17-20, 1990 in Ixtapa, Mexico. The Parties urge that the meeting of Ministers and the Inter-American

Drug Abuse Control Commission (CICAD) give priority to the understandings set forth in this document and lend support to their
early implementation within the context of regional cooperation
against drugs.

DOCUMENT E

Declaration of the World Ministerial Summit to
Reduce Demand for Drugs and to Combat the Cocaine Threat
London, 9-11 April, 1990
Source: Foreign and Commonwealth Office, London

INTRODUCTION

We, the States*[1] participating in the World Ministerial Summit to Reduce Demand for Drugs and to Combat the Cocaine Threat,

Deeply concerned by the magnitude of the rising trend in the illicit demand for narcotic drugs and psychotropic substances in countries throughout the world, which is a grave and persistent threat to the health and well-being of mankind and to the lives and dignity of millions of human beings, most especially young people,

Conscious that the problem of illicit demand is not confined to developed, industrialised countries which provide the main economic market for illicitly produced narcotic drugs and psychotropic substances and that it now increasingly affects developing countries as well,

Believing that national and international action to combat drug abuse and illicit trafficking requires not only continuing enhancement of the efforts to reduce the illicit production, supply, trafficking and distribution of narcotic drugs and psychotropic substances, but also calls for urgent measures at the national and international level, to reduce the illicit demand for drugs,

----

Footnote:* References to States in the present Declaration should be understood to refer also to regional economic integration organisations within the limits of their competence.

Believing also that action to tackle the problem of drug abuse often requires a partnership between international organisations, national authorities and non-governmental organisations at the regional, national and community levels and acknowledging that non-governmental organisations have been major contributors to the provision of demand reduction programmes,

Convinced that, in order to deal with this plague affecting society, a balanced approach is needed and that the prevention of drug abuse and treatment and rehabilitation of drugs abusers should therefore be accorded the same importance in policy and in action as the reduction of illicit supply and illicit trafficking,

Alarmed by the devastating damage to individual health and community life which cocaine in all its forms, particularly including crack, has wrought in some countries and by the massive outbreak of crime and violence which has sometimes accompanied it,

Noting, with grave concern, the sharply rising trend in seizures of cocaine by law enforcement authorities, not only in Western European countries but in many other countries also, which suggests that determined efforts are being made by ruthless criminal organisations to develop new markets for cocaine to add to the continuing problem of heroin and other drugs,

Recognising the illicit traffic in drugs as a part of the much wider world of crime undermining human life and society,

Noting also that the large financial profits derived from illicit drug trafficking and related criminal activities enable transnational criminal organisations to penetrate, contaminate and corrupt the structure of governments, legitimate commercial activities and society at all levels, thereby vitiating economic development, distorting the process of law and undermining the foundations of States,

Mindful of the results already achieved by the United Nations and its specialised agencies in the field of drug abuse control, including the Declaration and the Comprehensive Multidisciplinary Outline of Future Activities in Drug Abuse Control, adopted at the International Conference on Drug Abuse and Illicit Trafficking in 1987, the United Nations Convention against Illicit Trafficking in Narcotic Drugs and Psychotropic Substances as well as the positive action undertaken by the Division of Narcotic Drugs of the Secretariat, the International Narcotics Control Board and its secretariat, and the United Nations Fund for Drug Abuse Control,

Welcoming and endorsing, in its entirety, the Declaration and the Global Programme of Action adopted by the 17th Special Session of the United Nations General Assembly in New York in February 1990,

Rejecting the legalisation of unauthorised or uncontrolled production, traffic, supply and possession of narcotic drugs and psychotropic substances and reaffirming our treaty-based commitments to, and belief in, the control of such substances under the 1961 United Nations Single Convention on Narcotic Drugs, or that Convention as amended by the 1972 Protocol, the 1971 United Nations Convention of Psychotropic Substances and the 1988 United Nations Convention against the Illicit Traffic in Narcotic Drugs and Psychotropic Substances,

Believing that the said Global Programme of Action constitutes a viable and realistic basis for action to tackle the problem of drug abuse and illicit trafficking over the next decade and that priority should now be given by national authorities and interested organisations to translating it into action, at the national, regional and international level and to ensuring that the United Nations has sufficient resources and the necessary structure to enable it to undertake an enhanced role in accordance with the expectations of the international community,

Agree on the following:

COMBATING THE COCAINE THREAT

Need <u>for</u> <u>Global</u> <u>Strategy</u>

20. We are convinced that, if we are to combat the cocaine threat now facing many parts of the world, in addition to the threat from heroin and other drugs, we must pursue strategies that are comprehensive and multidisciplinary in scope and which comprise measures to reduce illicit demand for cocaine and other drugs, to eliminate the cultivation of illicit crops and illicit drug trafficking, to prevent the use of the financial and banking systems for laundering funds derived from drug trafficking and to promote effective treatment, rehabilitation and social reintegration. We commit ourselves to do so.

<u>UN</u> <u>Convention</u> <u>against</u> <u>Illicit</u> <u>Drug</u> <u>Trafficking</u> <u>1988</u>

31. We regard the United Nations Convention against Illicit Traffic in Narcotic Drugs and Psychotropic Substances 1988 as a vital weapon against those who ply the drug trafficker's evil trade. We attach particular importance in this context to those provisions dealing with the criminalisation of money laundering, confiscation of assets, extradition, mutual legal assistance, co-operation between operational services, controlled delivery, substances frequently used in the illicit manufacture of narcotic drugs and psychotropic substances and illicit traffic by sea. We commit ourselves to make all necessary arrangements to ratify or accede to the Convention as soon as possible and meanwhile to apply its terms provisionally, to the extent we are able to do so.

<u>Identification</u> <u>and</u> <u>Confiscation</u> <u>of</u> <u>proceeds</u> <u>of</u> <u>drug</u> <u>trafficking</u>

34. Much progress has already been made in concluding bilateral and multilateral agreements for the identification and confiscation of the proceeds of drug trafficking, and we commit ourselves to accelerate our efforts in this regard, so that there should be no safe havens for the proceeds of drug trafficking. We commit ourselves likewise to intensified action to conclude agreements

whereby the tainted proceeds of drug trafficking may be tracked down and those who seek to launder them brought to justice and put out of business.

35. We welcome the forthcoming publication of the report of the Financial Action Task Force established following the Paris Summit of the Group of Seven in July 1989. We call for worldwide distribution and careful study of the Task Force's conclusions and recommendations.

DOCUMENT F

Declaration and Program of Action of Ixtapa
adopted by a Meeting of Ministers of the Organization of American States
Ixtapa, Mexico, 17-20 April, 1990 (extracts)
Source: Organization of American States, Doc. OEA/ser.K/XXVII.2.1.RM/NARCO/doc. 29/90

The high-level representatives of the member states of the Organization of American States, responsible for the control of illicit drug trafficking and abuse, meeting in Ixtapa, Mexico, April 17-20, 1990, at the Meeting of Ministers on the Illicit Use and Production of Narcotic Drugs and Psychotropic Substances and Traffic Therein - Alliance of the Americas Against Drug Traffic;

Based on the principles, rights and duties of the states embodied in the Charter of the OAS, and on the principles, goals and general objectives of the Program of Action of Rio de Janeiro Against the Illicit Use and Production of Narcotic Drugs and Psychotropic Substances and Traffic Therein (Program of Action of Rio de Janeiro), and on the solidarity in the fight against drug trafficking, proclaimed in the Declaration of Guatemala "Alliance of the Americas against Drug Trafficking";

Based on the resolutions adopted by the General Assembly of the Organization that emphasize the urgent need to safeguard their peoples, their democratic institutions and their economies from the dangers of drug trafficking;

Inspired by the Declaration and the agreements recently signed in Cartagena de Indias by Bolivia, Colombia, Peru and the United States, by the Political Declaration and Global Programme of Action adopted by the United Nations General Assembly at its Seventeenth Special Session, and by the Declaration of the World Ministerial Summit held in London in April 1990;

Deeply concerned by the increase in the Americas of the illicit demand for and cultivation, production, supply, transit, distribution and use of narcotic drugs and psychotropic substances, as well as of substances frequently used in their manufacture, and the laundering of money derived from these illegal operations - activities that breed corruption and violence increasingly tied to clandestine arms trafficking, terrorism and subversion and that constitute a grave and persistent threat to the fabric of society, to the political stability of countries, to the growth and consolidation of democracy, to the rule of law, to balanced socioeconomic development, to the environment, to public health and to the welfare of their peoples, especially the younger generations;

Noting that the large financial profits and wealth derived from illicit drug trafficking and related criminal activities enable transnational criminal organizations to penetrate, contaminate and corrupt the structures of governments, legitimate commercial activities and society at all levels, thereby compromising economic and social development, distorting the process of law and undermining the foundation of states;

Recognizing that a growing number of member states are affected by drug trafficking, which forces them to divert resources away from pressing national needs;

Condemning once again the crime of illicit drug trafficking, which transcends the borders of member states, and convinced that its elimination demands a common front involving uninterrupted, priority activities as part of each government's respective programs, based on the principles of international solidarity and collective responsibility, with absolute respect for the sovereignty of each state and in accordance with its own situation;

Recognizing the links between the illicit demand for and cultivation, production, supply and distribution of narcotic drugs and psychotropic substances and traffic therein, and the economic, social and cultural conditions in the countries thus affected;

Emphasizing the imperative need for an objective and in-depth knowledge of the factors that lead to, cause or foster drug trafficking, and underscoring the fact that to be more effective, this battle must be waged on all fronts; and

Supporting fully the Inter-American Drug Abuse Control Commission (CICAD) in its efforts to put into effect the measures in the Programme of Action of Rio de Janeiro to promote cooperation and coordination between the member states and with the pertinent organs of the United Nations, for the purpose of promoting an ever more effective response to the scourge of drugs in the Americas.

RESOLVE:

1.   To condemn once again illicit drug trafficking in all its forms and to recognize that it is a criminal activity that affects all mankind.

2.   To assign top priority, based on the principle of collective responsibility, to the fight against drug trafficking and to redouble national and international efforts in this field in strict accordance with the principles of the Charter of the Organization, in particular national sovereignty, territorial integrity and nonintervention.

3.   To support the agreements contained in the Declaration of Cartagena and in the Political Declaration and Global Programme of Action of the aforementioned Seventeenth Special Session of the United Nations General Assembly, and particularly recognize the close linkage that exists between the global struggle to eliminate the illicit consumption and production of narcotic drugs and psychotropic substances and traffic therein, and the capacity of our nations to address this situation, which forces the diversion of scarce resources and thereby affects urgent development needs, making international coordination and cooperation a priority.

4. To reiterate their decision to broaden and increase the scope of inter-American cooperation and coordination through CICAD.

THE HIGH-LEVEL REPRESENTATIVES FURTHER AGREE TO ADOPT THE FOLLOW-ING PROGRAM OF ACTION:

1. To promote in their respective countries the actions neces-sary to ratify or accede to, as the case may be, the United Nations Convention against Illicit Traffic in Narcotic Drugs and Psychotropic Substances, signed in Vienna, December 20, 1988, so that it may enter into force in 1990.

2. To approve the actions taken by CICAD to facilitate the harmonious application by the member states of the provi-sions of the aforementioned Convention, in order to effect its full implementation in the Americas through the broadest possible intergovernmental cooperation.

3. To recommend to the General Assembly that it instruct CICAD to identify, in consultation with the Inter-American Judical Committee, areas in which the member states might consider more strict or severe regional measures than those provided by the 1988 Vienna Convention, in accordance with Article 24 of that Convention, to prevent or suppress illicit traffic in narcotic drugs and psychotropic substances.

4. To recommend that national laws and the means and instru-ments to enforce them be updated or modernized so as to establish stricter, surer, more expeditious and more effec-tive penalties and means to combat drug trafficking.

6. To emphasize the need for legislation that defines as a crime all activities related to the laundering of property and proceeds related to illicit drug trafficking and which makes it possible to identify, trace, seize and forfeit such property and proceeds.

To recommend to the member states that they encourage banks
and financial institutions to cooperate with the competent
authorities to prevent the laundering of property and proceeds related to illicit drug trafficking and to facilitate
the identification, tracing, seizure and forfeiture of such
property and proceeds.

To recommend to the member states that, within the framework
of their respective legal systems, they consider developing
mechanisms and procedures for bilateral and multilateral
cooperation to prevent the laundering of property and proceeds related to illicit drug trafficking and to facilitate
the identification, tracing, seizure and forfeiture of such
property and proceeds.

To recommend to the General Assembly that it direct CICAD to
convene an inter-American group of experts to draft model
regulations in conformity with the U.N. Convention Against
Illicit Traffic in Narcotic Drugs and Psychotropic Substances of 1988, to:

-     criminalize the laundering of property and proceeds
related to illicit drug trafficking;

-     prevent the use of financial systems for the laundering, conversion or transfer of property related to illicit
drug trafficking;

-     enable authorities to identify, trace, seize and forfeit property and proceeds related to illicit drug trafficking;

-     change legal and regulatory systems to ensure that bank
secrecy laws do not impede effective law enforcement and
mutual legal assistance; and,

-     study the feasibility of reporting large currency
transactions to national governments and permit the sharing
between governments of such information.

To recommend to the General Assembly that it forward the model regulations to the United Nations General Assembly for consideration by its Expert Group on Money Laundering created under United Nations General Assembly Resolution No. 44/142.

DOCUMENT G

United Kingdom Model Agreement Concerning Mutual Assistance in Relation to Drug Trafficking, May 1990

Source: Home Office, London

The Government of the United Kingdom of Great Britain and Northern Ireland and the Government of [   ];

Desiring to intensify their collaboration in the fight against drug trafficking;

Have agreed as follows:

ARTICLE 1

SCOPE OF APPLICATION

(1) The Parties shall, in accordance with this Agreement, grant to each other assistance in investigations and proceedings in respect of drug trafficking including the tracing, restraining and confiscation of the proceeds and instruments of drug trafficking.

(2)   This Agreement shall be without prejudice to other obligations between the Parties pursuant to other treaties or arrangements or otherwise, and shall not prevent the Parties or their law enforcement agencies from providing assistance to each other pursuant to other treaties or arrangements.

ARTICLE 2

DEFINITIONS

For the purposes of this Agreement:

(a)   "confiscation" means any measure resulting in the deprivation of property;

(b)   "instruments of drug trafficking" means any property which is or is intended to be used in connection with drug trafficking;

(c)   proceedings are instituted:

    (i)   in the United Kingdom, when an information has been laid before a justice of the peace, or when a person is charged with an offence or when a bill of indictment is preferred, or when a petition warrant is granted;

    (ii) in [   ], when
    ....
    ....

(d)   "proceeds" means any property that is derived or realised, directly or indirectly, by any person from drug trafficking, or the value of any such property;

(e)   property includes money and all kinds of moveable or immoveable and tangible or intangible property;

(f)   "drug trafficking" means any drug trafficking activity referred to in:

        (i)   Article 3.1 of the Convention Against Illicit Traffic in Narcotic Drugs and Psychotropic Substances opened for signature at Vienna on

20 December 1988; or

(ii)   any international agreement binding upon
both Parties, when such activity is treated as an
offence pursuant to that agreement;

(f)   "the restraint of property" means any measure
for the prevention of dealing in or transfer or
disposal of property.

ARTICLE 3

CENTRAL AUTHORITIES

(1) Requests for assistance under this Agreement shall be made
through the central authorities of the Parties.

(2) In the United Kingdom the central authority is the
Home Office. In [   ] the central authority is
[   ].

ARTICLE 4

CONTENTS OF REQUESTS

(1) Requests shall be made in writing. In urgent circumstances,
or where otherwise permitted by the Requested Party, requests may
be made orally but shall be confirmed in writing thereafter.

(2)   Requests for assistance shall include a statement of:

(a)   the name of the competent authority conducting the investigation or proceedings to which the request relates;

(b)   the matters, including the relevant facts and laws, to which the investigation or proceedings relates;

(c)   the purpose for which the request is made and the nature of the assistance sought;

(d)   details of any particular procedure or requirement that the Requesting Party wishes to be followed;

(e)   any time limit within which compliance with the request is desired;

(f)   the identity, nationality and location of the person or persons who are the subject of the investigation or proceedings;

(3)   If the Requested Party considers that the information contained in a request is not sufficient to enable the request to be dealt with, that Party may request that additional information be furnished.

ARTICLE 5

EXECUTION OF REQUESTS

(1)   A request shall be executed as permitted by and in accordance with the domestic law of the Requested Party and, to the extent not incompatible with such law, in accordance with any

requirements specified in the request.

(2)   The Requested Party shall promptly inform the Requesting Party of any circumstances which are likely to cause a significant delay in responding to the request.

(3)   The Requested Party shall promptly inform the Requesting Party of a decision of the Requested Party not to comply in whole or in part with a request for assistance and the reason for that decision.

(4)   The Requesting Party shall promptly inform the Requested Party of any circumstances which may affect the request or its execution or which may make it inappropriate to proceed with giving effect to it.

ARTICLE 6

REFUSAL OF ASSISTANCE

(1)   Assistance may be refused if:

(a)   the Requested Party is of the opinion that the request, if granted, would seriously impair its sovereignty, security, national interest or other essential interest; or

(b)   provision of the assistance sought could prejudice an investigation or proceedings in the territory of the Requested Party, prejudice the safety of any person or impose an excessive burden on the resources of that Party; or

(c)   the action sought is contrary to principles of the law of the Requested Party; or

(d)   the request relates to an offence in respect of which the person had been finally acquitted or pardoned, or has served any sentence imposed and any order made as a result of the conviction has been satisfied.

(2)   Before refusing to grant a request for assistance, the Requested Party shall consider whether assistance may be granted subject to such conditions as it deems necessary.   If the Requesting Party accepts assistance subject to conditions, it shall comply with them.

ARTICLE 7

CONFIDENTIALITY AND RESTRICTING USE
OF EVIDENCE AND INFORMATION

(1)   The Requested Party shall, to any extent requested, keep confidential a request for assistance, its contents and any supporting documents, and the fact of granting such assistance except to the extent that disclosure is necessary to execute the request.   If the request cannot be executed without breaching confidentiality, the Requested Party shall so inform the Requesting Party which shall then determine the extent to which it wishes the request to be executed.

(2)   The Requesting Party shall, if so requested, keep confidential any evidence and information provided by the Requested Party, except to the extent that its disclosure is necessary for the investigation or proceeding described in the request.

(3) The Requesting Party shall not use for purposes other than those stated in a request evidence or information obtained as a result of it, without the prior consent of the Requested Party.

ARTICLE 8

INFORMATION AND EVIDENCE

(1)   The Parties may make requests for information and evidence for the purpose of an investigation or proceedings.

(2) Assistance which may be given under this Article includes but is not limited to:

(a) providing information and documents or copies thereof for the purpose of an investigation or proceedings in the territory of the Requesting Party;

(b) taking evidence or statements of witnesses or other persons and producing documents, records or other material for transmission to the Requesting Party;

(c) searching for, seizing and delivering to the Requesting Party any relevant material, and providing such information as may be required by the Requesting Party concerning the place of seizure, the circumstances of seizure and the subsequent custody of the material seized prior to delivery.

(3) The Requesting Party may postpone the delivery of material requested if such material is required for proceedings in respect of criminal or civil matters in its territory. The Requested Party shall, upon request, provide certified copies of documents.

(4) Where required by the Requested Party, the Requesting Party shall return material provided under this Article when no longer needed for the purpose for which it was supplied.

ARTICLE 9

RESTRAINT

(1) In accordance with the provisions of this Article, a Party may request the restraint of property in order to ensure that it is available for the purpose of enforcement of a confiscation order which has been or may be made.

(2) A request made under this Article shall include:

(a)   information establishing that proceedings have been or are to be instituted as a result of which a confiscation order has been or may be made;

(b)   where applicable, a statement of when proceedings are to be instituted;

(c)   either:

> (i)   a summary of the facts of the case including a description of the offence, the time and place of its commission, a reference to the relevant legal provisions, the grounds on which the suspicion is based and a copy of any relevant restraint order; or

> (ii) where a confiscation order has been made, a copy of that order;

(d)   to the extent possible, a description of the property in
       respect of which restraint is sought or which is believed
       to be available for restraint, and its connection with the
       person against whom the proceedings have been or are to be
       instituted;

(e)   where appropriate, a statement of the amount which it is
       desired to restrain and the grounds on which this
       amount is estimated;

(f)   where applicable, a statement of the estimated time
       expected to elapse before the case is committed for trial
       and before a final judgement may be given.

(3)   The Requesting Party shall advise the Requested Party of any
alteration in an estimate of time referred to in paragraph (2)(f)
above and in doing so shall also give information about the stage
of proceedings reached.   Each Party shall advise the other
promptly of any appeal or variation made in respect of restraint
action requested or taken.

(4)   The Requested Party may impose a condition limiting the
duration of the restraint. The Requested Party shall notify the
Requesting Party promptly of any such condition, and the reason
for it.

ARTICLE 10

ENFORCEMENT OF CONFISCATION ORDERS

(1)   This Article applies to an order, made by a court of the
Requesting Party, for the purpose of confiscating the proceeds
or instruments of drug trafficking.

(2)   A request for assistance in enforcing such an order shall be accompanied by a copy of the order, certified by an officer of the court that made the order or by the central authority, and shall contain information indicating:

(a)   that neither the order nor any conviction to which it relates is subject to appeal;

(b)   that the order is enforceable in the territory of the Requesting Party;

(c)   where appropriate, property available for enforcement or the property in respect of which assistance is sought, stating the relationship between that property and the person against whom the order has been made;

(d)   where appropriate, and where known, the interests in the property of any person other than the person against whom the order has been made; and

(e)   where appropriate, the amount which it is desired to realise as a result of such assistance.

(3)   Where the law of the Requested Party does not permit effect to be given to a request in full, the Requested Party shall give effect to it insofar as it is able to do so.

(4)   If a request under this Article relates to an amount of money, that amount shall be converted into the currency of the Requested Party in accordance with its domestic law and procedures.

(5)   Property obtained by the Requested Party in the enforcement of an order to which this Article applies shall remain with that Party, unless otherwise agreed upon between the Parties.

ARTICLE 11

COSTS

The Requested Party shall bear any costs arising within its territory as a result of action taken upon request' of the Requesting Party. Extraordinary costs may be subject to special agreement between the Parties.

ARTICLE 12

LANGUAGE

Except where otherwise agreed between the Parties in a particular case, requests in accordance with Articles 8, 9 and 10 and supporting documents shall be drawn up in the language of the Requesting Party and shall be accompanied by a translation into the language of the Requested Party.

ARTICLE 13

AUTHENTICATION

Unless otherwise required under national law, and without prejudice to Article 10(2), documents certified by a central authority shall not require further certification, authentication or legalisation for the purposes of this Agreement.

ARTICLE 14

TERRITORIAL APPLICATION

This Agreement shall apply:

(a)   in respect of requests from [   ]

        (i)   to England and Wales and Scotland;

        (ii)   upon notification by the United Kingdom to [   ] through the diplomatic channel, to Northern Ireland, the Channel Islands and the Isle of Man;

        (iii)   to any territory for the international relations of which the United Kingdom is responsible and to which this Agreement shall have been extended by agreement between the Parties, subject to either Party being able to terminate such extension by giving six months' written notice to the other through the diplomatic channel; and

(b)   in respect of requests from the United Kingdom, to [   ].

ARTICLE 15
FINAL PROVISIONS

(1)   Each of the Parties shall notify the other Party as soon as possible in writing through the diplomatic channel of the completion of their respective requirements for entry into force

of this Agreement. The Agreement shall enter into force on the first day of the month following the expiration of one calendar month after the date of the later of these notifications.

(2) It may be terminated by either Party by giving notice to the other Party through the diplomatic channel.

The Agreement shall cease to be effective six months after the date of receipt of such notice.

In witness whereof the undersigned being duly authorised thereto by their respective Governments, have signed this Agreement.

Done in duplicate at [   ] this [   ] day of [   ] in the English and [   ] languages, both texts being equally authoritative.

For the Government of
the United Kingdom of
Great Britain and
Northern Ireland:

For the Government
of [   ]:

DOCUMENT H

Agreement Between the United States of America and the Republic of Venezuela Regarding Co-operation in the Prevention and Control of Money Laundering Arising from Illicit Trafficking in Narcotic Drugs and Psychotropic Substances

5 November 1990

Source: U.S. Department of State, Washington, D.C., U.S.A.

The Government of the United States and the Government of the Republic of Venezuela,

Recognizing the need for bilateral cooperation in matters related to the administration and enforcement of the laws against illicit trafficking in narcotic drugs and psychotropic substances and other related activities, and

Mindful of the fact that mutual cooperation is needed in order to combat increased activity in international money laundering of funds related to the illicit traffic in narcotic drugs and psychotropic substances,

Have reached the following Agreement the intent of which is to define the relationship that exists between the Parties in the terms set forth below and to establish a mechanism for cooperation and mutual assistance in the prevention and control of the laundering of money derived from the illicit trafficking in narcotic drugs and psychotropic substances and from other related unlawful activities.

ARTICLE I

DEFINITIONS

(1)   "Currency" means any coin and paper money that is
designated as legal tender and that circulates and is
customarily used and accepted as a medium of exchange in
the country of issuance.   Currency includes U.S. silver
certificates, U.S. notes, and Federal Reserve notes as
well as official foreign bank notes that are customarily
used and accepted as a medium of exchange in the country
of issuance.

(2)   "Currency transaction information" means information
or records retained by a financial institution, or
reports prepared by a financial institution concerning
transactions in currency in excess of 10,000 USD or its
foreign currency equivalent.   Such information shall
include, at a minimum:

> (a)   the identity of the person(s) conducting the
> transaction(s), including name(s), which is (are)
> verified by requiring the production of reliable
> identification, the address, business and/or
> occupation, and any other identifying data;
>
> (b)   if the person conducting the transaction(s) is
> not acting on his own behalf, reasonable measures
> taken to obtain and record the identity of the
> person(s) on whose behalf the transaction(s) is
> (are) being conducted, including the name and
> address, the business and/or occupation and any
> other identifying data;

(c)   the amount(s), date(s), and type(s) of the transaction(s);

(d)   the account(s), if any, affected by the transaction(s); and,

(e)   the name, address, identification number (if applicable), and type of financial institution where the transaction(s) has (have) taken place.

(3)   (a)   In the United States, the term "Financial Institution" means all persons included in the Currency and Foreign Transactions Reporting Act, 31 U.S.C. Section 5312, as implemented by regulations, 31 C.F.R. Part 103.11.

(b)   In Venezuela, the term "Financial Institution" means the commercial banks as well as the currency exchange houses, governed by the General Law of Banks and Other Credit Institutions and Special Laws.

(4)   "Person(s)" means an individual, a corporation, a partnership, a trust or estate, a joint stock company, joint venture, or other unincorporated organizations or groups, and all entities cognizable as legal personalities.

(5)   "Transaction in currency" means any transaction involving the transfer of currency in excess of 10,000 USD or its foreign currency equivalent, except to the extent that the transaction is conducted exclusively in Venezuelan Bolivars within the national territory of Venezuela.

ARTICLE II

PARTIES AND EXECUTING AGENCIES

The Parties to this Agreement are the Government of
the United States of America and the Government of the
Republic of Venezuela. The executing agencies for this
Agreement are: (1) for the United States of America,
the Department of the Treasury; (2) for the Republic of
Venezuela, the Ministry of Finance and the Central Bank
of Venezuela.

ARTICLE III

MATTERS WITHIN THE SCOPE OF THIS AGREEMENT

(1) The Parties shall ensure that financial institutions
under their jurisdiction and financial institutions
subject to their domestic laws maintain currency
transaction information for a period of no less than five
(5) years.

(2) In accordance with the terms of this Agreement, the
Parties or their designees shall provide each other the
fullest measure of mutual assistance with regard to the
sharing of currency transaction information for use in
their governmental investigations, proceedings or
prosecutions of a criminal, civil, or administrative
nature, regarding money laundering arising from the
illicit trafficking in narcotic drugs and psychotropic
substances and from related unlawful activities, as well
as from violations of currency transaction reporting and
recordkeeping laws and administrative regulations.

(3)   In sharing records of currency transaction information the Parties shall ensure that the records and any documentary information other than official records will be authenticated by the attestation of a person competent to do so in a manner indicated in Form I attached hereto.

(4) Consistent with their domestic law, the Parties shall use all reasonable measures, and shall employ the full scope of the authority vested in them by applicable law, in order to provide the assistance described in this Agreement.

ARTICLE IV
REQUESTS FOR ASSISTANCE

(1)   Requests for assistance must be in writing, and in a language acceptable to the requested Party.   The response too should be in writing and accompanied by a translation, or prepared in a language acceptable to the requesting Party.

   (a)   for the United States the acceptable language is English;

   (b)   for Venezuela the acceptable language is Spanish.

(2)   A request for assistance shall:

   (a)   provide a brief summary of the matter under review, investigation or prosecution, or the criminal, civil, or administrative proceeding that has been initiated by one of the Parties or other Government authority, for which the requested information is being sought;

(b) state the specific purpose for, and intended use(s) of, the requested information, including the identity of the government authority(ies) which will have access to the requested information;

(c) be signed, for the United States, by the Assistant Secretary for Enforcement, U.S. Department of the Treasury, or for Venezuela by the representative designated by the Ministry of Finance or the Central Bank of Venezuela, or their designees;

(d) where appropriate, identify and provide a summary of the text of the laws alleged to have been violated by the person(s) under investigation, being prosecuted or against whom a criminal, civil, or administrative proceeding has been initiated;

(e) state the name(s) of, and provide all available identifying information or data about, the person(s) regarding whom information is requested; and,

(f) provide all available information relating to the transactions which are the subject of the request for assistance, including: account(s) number(s); name(s) of account holder(s); name(s) of financial institutions involved in the transaction(s); location(s) of financial institution(s) involved in the transaction(s); and, date(s) of the transaction(s).

(3)   A request for assistance pursuant to this Agreement shall be directed to:

   (a)   in the United States:

         The Assistant Secretary (Enforcement)

         U.S. Department of the Treasury

   and, where appropriate, may be filed with

         The Embassy of the United States

         Caracas, Venezuela

   for transmittal to the Assistant Secretary

   (b)   in Venezuela:

         The Ministry of Finance or

         The Central Bank of Venezuela.

(4)   Requests for Assistance in Urgent Circumstances: In urgent circumstances, requests for assistance may be made by telephone which shall be immediately confirmed by fax. The request made by telephone shall also be confirmed by a written request, which shall be transmitted no later than 14 business days after the telephonic request.   A request made by telephone shall be directed to:

   (a)   for the United States:

         The Embassy of the United States

         Caracas, Venezuela

   (b)   for Venezuela:

         The Ministry of Finance or

         The Central Bank of Venezuela.

ARTICLE V

TERMS OF ASSISTANCE

(1)   All information obtained pursuant to this Agreement will be used only in accordance with the purpose stated in the request for assistance.

(2)   Information provided under the provisions of this Agreement will not be disseminated, disclosed, or transmitted in a manner not set forth in the original request for assistance without the prior and express written approval of the requested Party or his designee.

(3)   A request for assistance under this Agreement may be denied on the grounds that execution of the request is likely to prejudice the security, public policy, or other essential interests of the requested Party. Notice of, and reason for, such a denial shall be provided in a timely manner. A request denied for the above reasons shall not be considered a breach of this Agreement.

(4)   A Party may postpone execution of a request for assistance on the grounds that such execution is likely to interfere with an ongoing investigation, prosecution or other criminal, civil, or administrative proceeding initiated by one of the Parties, or other Government authority. Notice of such postponement shall be given in a timely manner.

(5)   The ordinary costs of executing a request shall be borne by the requested Party, unless otherwise agreed by the Parties.

ARTICLE VI

LIMITATIONS

This Agreement does not create nor confer any new rights, privileges, or benefits on any person, third party or other entity other than the Parties to the Agreement.

ARTICLE VII

AMENDMENTS

This Agreement may only be amended by mutual written consent of the Parties. Amendments shall enter into force upon exchange of diplomatic notes confirming that all domestic requirements for entry into force have been fulfilled.

ARTICLE VIII

RESOLUTION OF DISPUTES

Any doubts or disputes arising from the interpretation or implementation of this Agreement shall be resolved by negotiations conducted by the executing agencies and arranged through diplomatic channels.

ARTICLE IX

TERMINATION

Either Party may terminate the Agreement at any time after it enters into force, provided that notice of termination is given to the other Party at least three months prior to the date on which the Agreement is to be terminated.

ARTICLE X

ENTRY INTO FORCE

This Agreement shall enter into force on the first day of January, 1991.

Done at the City of Washington, D.C. on the fifth day of the month of November, 1990, in duplicate, in the English and Spanish languages, both texts being equally authentic.

FOR THE GOVERNMENT OF THE   FOR THE GOVERNMENT OF

UNITED STATES OF AMERICA: THE REPUBLIC OF VENEZUELA:

                                     FOR THE CENTRAL BANK OF

                                     VENEZUELA IN ITS CAPACITY

                                     AS EXECUTING AGENCY:

FORM I

AFFIDAVIT WITH RESPECT TO DOCUMENTS
OF A REGULARLY CONDUCTED BUSINESS ACTIVITY

NOTE: AFFIDAVIT MUST BE EXECUTED BY CUSTODIAN OF
              RECORDS OR SUCH OTHER PERSON WHO CAN EXPLAIN
              THE RECORDKEEPING PROCEDURE.

I _____ state as follows:

(1) I am employed by _____
                           (Financial institution from which

_____.
records are sought.)

(2) _____
        (Financial institution from which records are

_____ engages in the regular business of _____
sought.)   (Describe

_____.
business activity.)

(3) My position is _____.

(4) My duties and responsibilities in that position

include: _____
             (Describe duties and responsibilities relating

_____
to books and records, e.g., "custodian of books and

_____
records, or supervision over books and records.")

(5) As a result of my duties and responsibilities I have

knowledge of the manner in which the books and records

are kept.

(6)   The information contained in the attached documents agrees with that of the original records (or they are true copies thereof) records which I obtained in the performance of the aforementioned duties and responsibilities at: _____
                        (Financial institution providing
_____.
records.)

(7)   The records containing the information appearing in the attached documents are _____
                        (Describe records: e.g.,

_____
"records of currency transactions in the checking account

_____.
of John Doe for the month of July, 1989.")

(8)   It is a regular practice of this business to make and keep _____
            (Describe records: e.g., "currency transaction

_____ in the following manner _____
records.")   (Describe how records

_____.
are made and kept.)

(9)   It is the regular practice of the business to base its records upon information transmitted by a person with knowledge of the matters recorded, who was acting in the course of the regularly conducted business activity.

(10)   It is the regular practice of the business to check the correctness of the information of the kind contained in the documents attached hereto.

(11)   It is the regular practice of the business to rely on information of the kind contained in the documents attached hereto.

(12)   The entries on the records containing the information appearing in the attached documents were made by persons with knowledge of the matters recorded, or are based on information transmitted by persons with such knowledge.

(13)   The persons making the entries on the records or transmitting the information for purposes of recording it were acting in the course of a regularly conducted business activity.

(14)   The entries on the records containing the information appearing in the attached documents were made at or near the time of the matters recorded, pursuant to systematic and routine procedures for the conduct of the business.

(15) The records containing the information appearing in the attached documents were kept in the course of the regular activity of this business.

_____
(Signature)

_____
(Date)

NOTE: Supplying false information herein shall be punishable by appropriate legal penalties.

DOCUMENT I

Initiative by the Organization of American States to Prepare Model Regulations on the Laundering of Property and Proceeds Related to Drug Trafficking: Articles Considered by the Inter-American Group of Experts, 9-13 December, 1991

Source: Organization of American States, Doc. OEA/Ser.L/XIV.4.4, CICAD/GT. LAVEX/doc. 20/91

I. BACKGROUND

The Meeting of Ministers on the Illicit Use and Production of Narcotic Drugs and Psychotropic Substances and Traffic Therein -- Alliance of the Americas Against Drug Traffic, held in Ixtapa, Mexico, April 7-20, 1990 -- approved the "Declaration and Program of Action of Ixtapa."

The "Declaration and the Program of Action of Ixtapa" repeats the principles and goals of the Inter-American Program of Action of Rio de Janeiro, the Declaration of Guatemala, "Alliance of the Americas against Drug Traffic," and the priorities established in resolution AG/RES.935 (XVIII-0/88), as well as the decision to back the agreements set forth in the Declaration and Agreements of Cartagena and in the Political Declaration and Global Program of Action on international cooperation against illicit production, supply, demand, trafficking and distribution of narcotic drugs and phychotropic substances adopted by the XVII Special Session of the United Nations General Assembly and by the World Ministerial Summit to Reduce Demand for Drugs and to Combat the Cocaine Threat;

The General Assembly of the Organization of American States, at its twentieth regular session held in Asunción, Paraguay, on June 4-9, 1990, decided "to endorse and incorporate into this resolution the "Declaration and Program of Action of Ixtapa," approved by acclamation by the Meeting of Ministers on the Illicit Use and Production of Narcotic Drugs and Psychotropic Substances and Traffic Therein --Alliance of the Americas against Drug Traffic.

Also the General Assembly decided "To recommend to the governments of the member states that they adopt the measures indicated in the Program of Action of Ixtapa, and among these, especially, ratification of the United Nations Convention against Illicit Traffic in Narcotic Drugs and Psychotropic Substances signed in Vienna on December 20, 1988, or accession thereto, as the case may be, so that it may enter into force during 1990."

The "Declaration and Program of Action of Ixtapa" establishes the following mandates in point 6:

6. To emphasize the need for legislation that defines as a crime all activities related to the laundering of property and proceeds related to illicit drug trafficking and which makes it possible to identify, trace, seize and forfeit such property and proceeds.

To recommend to the member states that they encourage banks and financial institutions to cooperate with the competent authorities to prevent the laundering of property and proceeds related to illicit drug trafficking and to facilitate the identification, tracing, seizure and forfeiture of such property and proceeds.

To recommend to the member states that, within the framework of their respective legal systems, they consider developing mechanisms and procedures for bilateral and multilateral cooperation to prevent the laundering of property and proceeds related to illicit drug trafficking and to facilitate the identification, tracing, seizure and forfeiture of such property and proceeds.

To recommend to the General Assembly that it direct CICAD to convene an inter-American group of experts to draft model regulations in conformity with the U.N. Convention Against Illicit Traffic in Narcotic Drugs and Psychotropic Substances of 1988, to:

-- criminalize the laundering of property and proceeds related to illicit drug trafficking;

-- prevent the use of financial systems for the laundering, conversion or transfer of property related to illicit drug trafficking;

-- enable authorities to identify, trace, seize and forfeit property and proceeds related to illicit drug trafficking;

-- change legal and regulatory systems to ensure that bank secrecy laws do not impede effective law enforcement and mutual legal assistance; and,

-- study the feasibility of reporting large currency transactions to national governments and permit the sharing between governments of such information.

To recommend to the General Assembly that it forward the model regulations to the United Nations General Assembly for consideration by its Expert Group on Money Laundering created under United Nations General Assembly Resolution No. 44/142.

Regarding point 6 of the "Declaration and Program of Action of Ixtapa," the Inter-American Drug Abuse Control Commission decided as follows at its eighth regular session, held at OAS General Secretariat headquarters on October 23-26, 1990:

- Pursuant to the mandate in point 6 of the "Declaration and Program of Action of Ixtapa," CICAD decided that the Chairman, in cooperation with the Secretariat, should set up the Inter-American Group of Experts to draft Model Regulations on Laundering Property and Proceeds Connected with Illicit Drug Traffic (CICAD/doc.248/90 and add. 1), taking into consideration the situation in each country regarding this problem.

- It was also decided to recommend that the Executive Secretariat make the necessary administrative arrangements to fund and publish the documentation on this subject.

In view of the decision made by CICAD, the Chairman of CICAD, with the assistance of the Executive Secretariat, proceeded to select on October 26, 1990, the following experts proposed by the member state governments (CICAD/doc.248/90 add.6 corr.1):

1.	Argentina	Dr. Julio Alberto Chirón
2.	Bahamas	Miss Marion Bethel
3.	Brazil	Mr. Paulo Gustavo Magalhaes Pinto
4.	Canada	Mr. Paul Saint-Denis
5.	Chile	Mr. Ignacio González
6.	Colombia	Dr. Ricardo H. Monroy Church
7.	Costa Rica	Lic. Eduardo Araya
8.	Jamaica	Mr. Canute Miller
9.	Mexico	Lic. José Elías Romero Apis
10.	Peru	Dr. Miguel Angel Barba Mitrani
11.	United States	Mr. Michael A. Defeo
12.	Uruguay	Dr. Alvaro Eguren
13.	Venezuela	Dr. Elba Torres Graterol

On October 31, 1990, the Executive Secretariat of CICAD, on instructions from the Chairman of CICAD, transmitted, through the Permanent Missions of the OAS, the Convocation of the First Meeting of the Inter-American Group of Experts to Prepare Model Regulations on the Laundering of Property and Proceeds Related to Drug Trafficking (OEA/SGE/CAD-62/90), which met at General Secretariat headquarters on November 26-30, 1990, to consider the agenda included as an appendix to this Final Report.

The Group of Experts held its First Meeting at the headquarters of the General Secretariat of the Organization of American States in Washington, D.C., November 26-30, 1990. In that meeting, the Group elected its officers, exchanged views about its working methods, and received the documents drafted by the Executive Secretariat. In addition, the Working Group drew up and approved a "Questionnaire on Money Laundering, Asset Forfeiture, Bank Secrecy Laws and Recordkeeping Requirements" (CICAD/GT.LAVEX/doc.8/90 rev.1), after deciding to distribute it to the governments of all member countries of the Organization so they could send in their answers by January 31, 1991.

As of September 27, 1991, the Executive Secretariat had received answers to the questionnaire from the governments of The Bahamas, Brazil, Canada, Chile, Colombia, Costa Rica, Ecuador, Mexico, Paraguay, Peru, Trinidad and Tobago, United States, and Venezuela.

At the First Meeting of the Group of Experts, a Drafting Subgroup was established to draw up a working document containing a draft Model Regulations. The Subgroup members were the delegations of Argentina, Chile, Mexico, and the United States.

The second meeting of the Group of Experts took place from the 20th to the 24th of March and the Third from the 30th of September to the 4th of October 1991, in Washington, D.C.

To comply with its mandate, the Subgroup met first on March 18-20, 1991; then again on May 13-17, 1991; the third time on September 23-27, 1991 and the fourth and final on December 2-6, 1991, at which time it decided to submit to the Fourth Meeting of the Group of Experts all the articles that it had reviewed (CICAD.GT/LAVEX/doc.3/91 rev. 3) at this last meeting.

The Subgroup had available to it for its work the document drawn up by the Executive Secretariat, "Model Legislation for the Group of Experts Responsible for Preparing Model Regulations on the Laundering of Property and Proceeds Related to Drug Trafficking (CICAD/GT/LAVEX/doc.20/91. add.1).

II.   OPENING, WORKING, AND CLOSING SESSIONS

Pursuant to the activities schedule approved for this Fourth Meeting of the Group of Experts (CICAD/GT.LAVEX/doc.17/91), the opening session was held in the morning of December 9, 1991, in the Padilha Vidal room of the OAS General Secretariat headquarters.

At this Fourth Meeting of the Group of Experts, eight working sessions were held, pursuant to the schedule of activities, at which articles for the Model Regulations were revised and approved, and suggestions and comments were made by the experts.

The closing session was held at noon on December 13, 1991. The meeting was addressed by Mr. Irving G. Tragen, Executive Secretary of CICAD, speaking for CICAD, and Dr. Eduardo Anaya Vega, expert of the Costa Rican Government and Chairman of the Group of Experts, who thanked the experts for their valuable contributions and participation. He then thanked Dr. Irving G. Tragen, the Executive Secretary, and Dr. Samuel A. Echalar, Assistant Executive Secretary as well as the General Secretariat officials and staff, for their efficient services provided at this Third Meeting.

III.   OFFICERS AND PARTICIPANTS

The first working session, held on November 26, 1990, elected by acclamation Mr. Eduardo Araya Vega, expert of Costa Rica, as Chairman of the Meeting of the Group of Experts, and Mr. Ignacio González, expert of Chile, as Rapporteur.

Also, Mr. Ignacio González, Delegate of Chile, was appointed President of the Drafting Subgroup, in this regard it is noted that the fourth and last meeting was chaired by Dr. Manuel Domper, Representative of Argentina.

The list of attending experts and names of the advisors are contained in the List of Participants (CICAD/GT.LAVEX/doc.19/91), which is appended to this Final Report.

IV. DOCUMENTATION

The documents submitted by the various experts and the information and working documents prepared by the CICAD Executive Secretariat are indicated in the List of Documents (CICAD/GT.LAVEX/doc.1/91) appended to this Final Report.

V. DECISIONS TAKEN

As a result of the sensitive work of the Group of Experts to Prepare Model Regulations on the Laundering of Property and Proceeds Related to Drug Trafficking, at this Fourth Meeting articles were reviewed and approved as they appear in the appendix to this Final Report. (CICAD/doc.3/91 rev. 4).

VI. DATE AND PLACE OF THE FIFTH AND SIXTH MEETINGS OF THE GROUP OF EXPERTS

Lastly, the Expert Group reiterated its decision to convene its Fifth Meeting, January 20-24, 1992 in San José, Costa Rica and set its Sixth Meeting, March 2-6, 1992 in Uruguay.

MODEL LEGISLATION FOR THE GROUP OF EXPERTS RESPONSIBLE
FOR PREPARING MODEL REGULATIONS ON THE LAUNDERING
OF PROPERTY AND PROCEEDS RELATED TO DRUG TRAFFICKING

(Articles considered by the Group of Experts
December 9 to 13, 1991)

Article 1 *

DEFINITIONS 1/

1.   "Convention" means the United Nations Convention Against Illicit Traffic in Narcotic Drugs and Psychotropic Substances, signed in Vienna, Austria, on December 20, 1988.

2.   "Confiscation", which includes forfeiture where applicable, means the permanent d_privation of property by order of a court or other competent authority;

3.   "Illicit traffic" means the offenses set forth in article 3, paragraphs 1 and 2, of this Convention;

4.   "Instrumentality" means something that is used in or intended for use in any manner for the commission of an illicit traffic offense or related offenses.

5.   "Proceeds" means any property derived from or obtained, directly or indirectly through the commission of an offense established in accordance with article 3, paragraph 1 of the Convention.

6.   "Property" means assets of every kind, whether corporeal or incorporeal, movable or immovable, tangible or intangible, and legal documents or instruments evidencing title to, or interest in, such assets;

7.   "Freezing" or "seizure" means temporarily prohibiting the transfer, conversion, disposition or movement of property or temporarily assuming custody or control of property on the basis of an order issued by a court or a competent authority;

8.   A "person" shall mean all entities capable of acquiring rights or entering into obligations, whether they be natural or juridical entities, including, among others, a corporation, a partnership, a trust or estate, a joint stock company, an association, a syndicate, a joint venture, or other unincorporated organization or group.

---

1.   For that which is not foreseen herein, the 1988 United Nations Convention shall apply.

*   the Group decided to postpone review of this Article until the second reading of the Draft.

Article 2

ASSETS LAUNDERING OFFENSES

1.   A criminal offense is committed by any person who converts or transfers property knowing (including willfully blind) or should have known that such property is proceeds from an illicit traffic offense, or any offense related to, connected to, or arising from such an offense.

2.   A criminal offense is committed by any person who acquires, possesses (has), or uses property knowing /at the time of receipt/ (including willfully blind) or should have known that such property is proceeds from an illicit traffic offense, or any offense related to, connected to, or arising from such an offense.

3.   A criminal offense is committed by any person who conceals, disguises or impedes the establishment of the true nature, source, location, disposition, movement, rights with respect to, or ownership of property, knowing (including willfully blind) or should have known that such property is proceeds from an illicit traffic offense, or any offense related to, connected to, or arising from such an offense.

4.   A criminal offense is committed by any person who participates in, associates with, conspires to commit, attempts to commit, aids and abets, facilitates and counsels, incites publicly or privately the commission of any of the offenses established in accordance with this Article, or who assists any person participating in such an offense or offenses to evade the legal consequences of his actions.

5.   Knowledge, intent or purpose resulted as an element of an offense set forth in this Article may be inferred from objective, factual circumstances.

6.   The assets laundering offenses defined in this article shall be investigated, tried and judged by the competent authorities as an offense distinct from the illicit traffic offenses.

Article 3

JURISDICTION

The assets laundering offenses define in Article 2 shall be investigated, tried and judged by the competent authorities regardless of whether or not the illicit traffic offense or related offenses occurred in another territorial jurisdiction.

Article 4

PREVENTIVE MEASURES RELATING TO PROPERTY, PROCEEDS OR INSTRUMENTALITIES

According to law, the competent authority or tribunal shall issue, at any time, without prior notification or hearing, a seizure or freezing order, or any other preventive or provisional measure intended to preserve the availability of property, proceeds derived from or instrumentalities used or intended to be used in any offense of illicit traffic or offenses connected thereto, for its eventual forfeiture.

Article 5

FORFEITURE OF PROPERTY, PROCEEDS OR INSTRUMENTALITIES

1. When a person is convicted of an offence of illicit traffic or offenses connected thereto, the tribunal shall order that the property or proceeds derived from or instrumentalities used or intended to be used, in connection with such offenses, be forfeited and disposed of in accordance with the law.

2. When any of the property and proceeds (or instrumentalities) described in the previous paragraph, as a result of any act or omission of the person convicted, cannot be forfeited, the tribunal shall order the forfeiture of any other property of the person convicted, for an equivalent value or shall order the person convicted to pay a fine of said value

Article 6

BONA FIDE THIRD PARTIES

1. The measures and sanctions referred to in articles 3 and 4 shall apply without prejudice to the rights of bona fide third parties.

2. In accordance with the law, proper notification shall be made so that all those claiming a legitimate legal interest in property, proceeds or instrumentalities may appear in support of their claims.

3. A third-party's lack of good faith may be inferred, at the discretion of the court or competent authority, from the objective circumstances of the case.

4. The court or competent authority shall (may) return the property, proceeds or instrumentalities to the claimant, when it has been demonstrated to the satisfaction of the court or competent authority that:

   a. the claimant has a legitimate legal interest in the property, proceeds or instrumentalities;

b.   no participation, collusion or involvement with respect to the
      illicit traffic offense or offenses connected thereto which are
      the object of the process can be imputed to the claimant;

c.   the claimant lacked knowledge (and was not wilfully blind) of
      the illegal use of the property. proceeds or instrumentalities,
      or if he had knowledge. did not freely consent to its illegal
      use;

d.   the claimant did not acquire any right in the property proceeds
      or instrumentalities from a person tried under circumstances
      that give rise to a reasonable inference that any right was
      transferred for the purpose of avoiding the eventual subsequent
      forfeiture of the property. proceeds or instrumentalities, and:

e.   the claimant did all that could reasonably be expected to
      prevent the illegal use of the property. proceeds or
      instrumentalities.

Article 7

DISPOSITION OF FORFEITED PROPERTY. PROCEEDS OR INSTRUMENTALITIES

Whenever property proceeds or instrumentalities are forfeited under
Article 4. the competent authority or court may. according to its domestic
law:

a)   retain them for official use or transfer them to any government
      agency that participated directly or indirectly in their seizure
      or forfeiture;

b)   sell those that are not required to be destroyed and that are
      not harmful to the public and transfer the proceeds from such
      sale to any government agency that participated directly or
      indirectly in their seizure or forfeiture. It may also deposit
      the proceeds from the sale in the Special Fund provided for in
      the Inter-American Program of Action of Rio de Janeiro, or in
      other funds to be used by the competent authorities in their
      fight against illicit traffic. prevention of the unlawful use of
      drugs, the treatment. rehabilitation and re-entry into society
      of those affected by their use;

c)   transfer the property. proceeds or instrumentalities or the
      proceeds from their sale to any private entity dedicated to the
      prevention of the unlawful use of drugs, the treatment.
      rehabilitation and re-entry into society of those affected by
      their use.

d)   transfer the object of the forfeiture or the proceeds from their
      sale to any other country which participated directly or
      indirectly in the seizure or forfeiture of the property. if such
      a transfer is authorized by an international agreement; or

e) transfer the object of the forfeiture or the proceeds from their sale to intergovernmental bodies specializing in the fight against illicit traffic, prevention of the unlawful use of drugs, the treatment rehabilitation, and re-entry into society of those affected by its use.

Article 8

PROPERTY, PROCEEDS OR INSTRUMENTALITIES OF FOREIGN OFFENSES

The court or other competent authority may order, according with the law, the seizure or forfeiture of any property, proceeds or instrumentalities within its territorial jurisdiction that is derived or was used in or intended to be used in an illicit traffic offense or a related offense against the laws of another country, so long as that offense would have been an offense if committed within its jurisdiction.

Article 9

FINANCIAL INSTITUTIONS AND ACTIVITIES

For the purpose of these Regulations financial institutions are those persons who engage in the following activities, among others:

a. A commercial bank, trust company, savings and loan association, building and loan association, savings bank, industrial bank, credit union, or other thrift institution or establishment authorized to do business under the domestic banking laws, whether these be publically or privately owned, or mixed;

b. A broker or dealer in securities;

c. A currency dealer or exchanger;

d. A systematic or substantial cashing of checks;

e. A systematic or substantial issuance, sale or redemption of traveler's checks or money orders;

f. A systematic or substantial transmitting of funds;

g. Any other activity subject to supervision by government bank or other financial institution authorities.

Article 10

IDENTIFICATION OF CLIENTS AND
MAINTENANCE OF RECORDS

1.   Financial institutions shall maintain accounts in the name of the accountholder. They shall not keep anonymous accounts or accounts which are in fictious or incorrect names.

2.   Financial institutions shall record and verify by authentic means, the identity, representative capacity, domicile, legal capacity, occupation or business purpose of persons, as well as other identifying information on those persons, whether they be occasional or usual clients, through the use of documents such as passports, birth certificates, drivers license, partnership contracts and incorporation papers, or any other official or private documents, when establishing business relations or conducting any transaction or operation, such as opening new accounts or passbooks, entering into fiduciary transactions, renting of safe deposit boxes or performing cash transactions over a certain amount as provided by domestic law.

3.   Financial institutions shall take reasonable measures to obtain and record information about the true identity of the person on whose behalf an account is opened or a transaction is conducted if there are any doubts that a client is acting on his/her own behalf, particularly in the case of a juridical person who is not conducting any commercial, financial, or industrial operations in the country where it has its headquarters or domicile.

4.   Financial institutions shall maintain during the period in which the operation is in effect, and for at least five (5) years after the conclusion of the transaction, the records of the information and documentation required in this Article, including at a minimu:

    a.   identification of accountholders; and

    b.   information on the identity of customers who are not accountholders and who establish business relations or conduct financial transactions, particularly substantial cash transactions and fund transfers.

5.   Financial institutions shall maintain records on customer identification, account files, and business correspondence as determined by the competent authority, for at least five (5) years after the account has been closed.

6.   Financial institutions shall also maintain records, as determined by the competent authority to enable the reconstruction of financial transactions in excess of a certain amount as stipulated by domestic law, for at least five (5) years after the conclusion of the transaction.

Article 11

AVAILABILITY OF RECORDS

1. Financial institutions shall be able to comply promply, and within the period of time established by the competent authority, with information requests from the competent authorities concerning the records of information and documentation referred to in the previous article, for use in criminal, civil, or administrative investigation, prosecutions, or proceedings regarding an illicit traffic offense or related offenses or violations of the provisions of these Regulations.

2. The competent authorities shall be able to share with other national competent authorities said information, in accordance with domestic law, and when it regards an illicit traffic offense or related offense or violations of the provisions of these Regulations.

The competent authorities shall treat as confidential the information referred to in this article, except insofar as such information is necessary for use in criminal, civil, or administrative investigations, prosecutions, or proceedings regarding an illicit traffic offense or related offenses or violations of the provisions of these Regulations.

3. The competent authorities of a State shall be able to share such information with the competent authorities of other States in accordance with its domestic law and international agreements in force between them.

4. The legal provisions referring to bank secrecy or reserve, shall not be an impediment to compliance with this article.

Article 12

RECORDING AND REPORTING OF CASH TRANSACTIONS

A)   Recording of cash transactions

1.   Each financial institution shall record, on a form designed by the competent authority each cash transaction involving a domestic or foreign currency transaction exceeding a fixed amount.

2.   The form referred to in the previous paragraph shall include the following data at a minimum for each transaction:

a.   The identity signature and address of the person who conducts physically the transaction:

b.   The identity and address of the person in whose name the transaction is conducted;

c.   The identity and address of the beneficiary or the person on whose behalf the transaction is conducted, as applicable;

d.   The identity of the account(s) affected by the transaction, if any;

e.   The type of transaction involved (deposit, withdrawal, exchange of currency, check cashed, purchase of certified or cashier's check or money order or other payment or transfer by, through, or to such financial institution):

3.   This record shall be recorded, accurately and complete, by the financial institution on the day the transaction has occurred and shall be maintained for a period of five (5) years from the date of the transaction.

4.   Multiple cash transactions in domestic or foreign currency which, altogether, exceed a certain amount shall be treated as a single transaction if they are undertaken by or on behalf of any one person during any one day or any other period established by the competent authority.   In such a case, when a financial institution, its employees, officers or agents have knowledge of these transactions, they shall record these transactions on the form determined by the competent authority.

5.   For transactions conducted on their own account between the financial institutions that are subject to supervision by the domestic banking and financial authorities defined in Article 9 (a), neither the record nor the form referred in these Regulations shall be required.

6.   These records shall be available to the competent authorities, in accordance with domestic legislation, for use in criminal, civil or administrative investigations, proceedings or prosecutions relating to illicit traffic or related offenses, or violations of the provisions of these Regulations.

B)   Reporting of cash transaction

When it deems advisable, the competent authority may establish that financial institutions file with it, within such time as the competent authorities may establish, the form designed in this Article pursuant to the provisions of paragraph A (2) and A (3). This form shall serve as a piece of evidence or as an official report, and shall be used for the same purposes designated in paragraph A-6.

Financial institutions, shall not notify persons about whom the competent authorities request information that such information has been requested or furnished and must also maintain the confidentiality of the information request until the competent authority authorizes notification to the client.